THE LOOKOUT *After* THE CLIMB

The Lookout After the Climb
by Anita Martin

Library of Congress Number: 2018933609
International Standard Book Number: 978-1601265753

Printed by:

Masthof Press
219 Mill Road | Morgantown, PA 19543-9516
www.Masthof.com

THE LOOKOUT AFTER THE CLIMB

Holding forth hope
in the struggle with mental illness . . .
questions and answers,
personal 'windows',
and helpful input from the community.

Dedication:

To those who are suffering silently.

With a love for God,

Who is ALWAYS good!

TABLE OF CONTENTS

ACKNOWLEDGEMENTS

Heart-felt thanks to . . .

. . . my dedicated husband, Frank, for the many times you conveyed this message, "We're in this together." Truly, you are an amazing man!

. . . each one of our five children, who have been through thick and thin as well. You have been courageous these many years. I love each one of you!

. . . Dr. Holmes Morton, for your warm wit and patient personality. I appreciate your words taken from the article 'Letter to a Student'—*"Write carefully, write thoughtfully about important problems, make enduring friendships . . . actively search for meaningful work."*

. . . Dr. Tony Byler, for having the "hallmarks" of a good doctor.

. . . Twila Sensenig, a dear childhood friend. You have patiently encouraged me onward with your unfailing inspiration and editing skills. Without you, this book would have remained in shambles.

. . . Ruthie, Lucy, Christine, Crystal, Lorraine, and Keturah, especially for your prayers, but also for being a part of many serious, humorous, and animated conversations that helped form this book.

. . . our parents and siblings for being supportive and helpful.

. . . many who took time to proofread and give helpful advice, you know who you are!

We also want to thank those who were vulnerable enough to give us a peek into your lives. We appreciate the hard work put into wording things that are very hard to word. Our greatest desire, along with you, is that 'our voice' of hope and courage would be heard . . . that others would receive our message:

"You are not alone!"

PREFACE

by D. Holmes Morton M.D.

I came to know Frank and Anita and their children because of Cynthia. She was born in Guatemala, July 17, 2008, and was soon found to have maple syrup urine disease. As an ill newborn, Cynthia brought her family from their home in Guatemala to the Clinic for Special Children in Lancaster County. Anita has written this book in part because of Cynthia. Cynthia's illness forced them to come back to their Lancaster County roots, back into the Mennonite Community to find care for her disorder. But this return also forced them to face the illnesses written about in this book.

Depressive and Manic Disorders are common in all people, in all families, not just those from the Plain Communities. The disorders seem common, in part, because mania and depression represent the extremes of a continuum of moods familiar to everyone – feelings of sadness and happiness, of being fatigued and energetic, disinterested and enthusiastic, of inactivity and creativity. The cycles of these emotions are familiar too. It is the extremes of these moods, linked to "real-trouble", that often leads to a medical diagnosis of depression or mania – By "*Real Trouble*", I mean the farm or business or household that falls into ruin because of an inability to overcome sadness, get-out-of-bed, go-to-work, or experience even the most basic pleasures or achieve basic tasks of daily life. Or, "*Real Trouble*" arises from periods of grandiose ideas, days without sleep, incessant talking, hallucinations, fabrications, or delusions witnessed in the troubled teenager found sleeping in a car, heavily armed with guns and knives, equally afraid of imagined demons and people who offer help. Mixed within the fall and rise of cycles of moods and fearfulness are lost jobs, lost money, lost trust, broken friendships, fragmented families, problems at school, problems with Church, with laws, debts, drugs and alcohol – which collectively represent the *Real-Troubles* caused by bi-polar illnesses that burden lives in ways that are not corrected only by medicines. Fortunate is the person in whom crisis leads to a hospital or another place that cares for people with such illnesses, instead of a jail or a grave. Whatever may be the medical or genetic basis of bipolar or depressive illnesses, the day-to-day troubles are *of-the-real-world* and can be deadly.

Recurrent stories of mood cycles and "real troubles" fill Anita Martin's book. The book will help others in her extended Mennonite family recognize manic depressive disorders. The collected stories in *The Lookout* tell us that these illnesses often affect several people in a family and across generations – great grandparents, grandparents, then a parent, several children and grandchildren – such family stories have long suggested that the manic depressive disorders are inherited – are influenced by a *genetic predisposition to disorders of mood.* However, family members also share life-long social and religious histories, environmental exposures, nutritional risks, and genes that affect general health in ways that undermine a sense of well-being. Just as it is obvious that genetics contribute to risk of mental illness, it is obvious that difficult personal experiences within an extended family and in Communities directly affect health and mind.

Anita's story as a mother suffering with post-partum depression and the emergence of bipolar illness connected to my life and another story-- that of Mary Stansbury Morton, my mother. She died at age 88 in Quarryville in the Presbyterian Retirement Community on July 9, 2008, just 8-days before Cynthia was born. The last Morton son, Frank, was born in 1954. He was healthy, but his birth was followed for Mary by a long, severe depressive illness. A deep paranoid depression developed. She was resistant to treatment and ultimately was committed to a psychiatric hospital near Columbus, Ohio, where she began to make a slow recovery when forced to take lithium and electroconvulsive therapy.

This illness haunted her, and her family, for the remainder of her life. Depressive illness, intermixed with periods of mania or paranoia, was a problem she shared with her mother's father Taylor George and his son William. Mary's troubled brother Bill Stansbury was also likely an unrecognized young victim of the disease. Bill was killed by a pistol shot to the chest at age 14, on May 8, 1940, Mary's 20th birthday. His death was officially ruled accidental, but Mary always believed his death was suicide, to end a troubled and unhappy life. Mary's youngest brother Sam was manic-depressive too.

Mary Morton's recovery from her first depressive illness was made possible by electroconvulsive therapy, lithium, a supportive husband and family, and by many understanding, helpful friends. Relief from the isolation of deafness was also no-doubt important. In the late 1950s she underwent a remarkably simple and successful surgery called a stapendectomy - an ossicle of left ear was replaced by a small metal post. The repair reversed deafness caused by inflammatory otosclerosis from measles and provided remarkable clear hearing for the remainder of her life. She also recovered by becoming immersed in art-work, writing, by using her natural athletic abilities to teach her young sons to play the game of golf, and by returning to competitive amateur golf.

In winter, and in the later years of her life, Mary Morton was known for writing long letters, keeping scrap-books of family records, for fine needle-point work and paintings. She had an unusual, natural sense for the use of color and design in needlework and painting. Her finest paintings are watercolors of mountain landscapes, birds and flowers in the style of ancient Chinese masters. Her letters to her children and friends were clearly written, precise, thoughtful, and she wrote often. After her husband Paul's death in October 1999, her letters, paintings and needlework gradually stopped, and the old paranoid depression, the illness we all feared, returned. So began her long slow decline.

Her last years were difficult, for her and for all of us who tried to help. Most of the time, I did not feel she was angry with *me*, rather, she was angry about being old, ill, depressed, fearful, and, finally, about living on and on well beyond her desire to be alive. In 2002, she fell and broke her hip. After that, weakness, and fear of falling, required a walker. Whether loss of will or loss of strength came first, the end was the same. Being confined to a wheel chair was the kind of dependence she wouldn't have imagined that she could accept.

Sadly, her waking hours were filled with unimaginable fear and despair, which is the nature of the illness called *paranoid depression*. Repeated treatments with ECT and medicines provided some relief, but memories failed, Parkinsonism, cerebral vascular disease progressed, and other problems came. By the end, I believed she had lost all awareness. In the evening of July 9, 2008, the life of Mary Stansbury Morton passed.

Because Mary Morton's brother Sam, an Air Force Veteran, had many severe problems associated with bipolar illness, and because of the remarkable history of the extended Stansbury & George families, many members of the Stansbury family became involved in the *National Institute of Mental Health* (NIMH) research on bipolar illness in the 1970s. My first interest in the genetics of these illnesses developed in association with these studies. NIMH also supported much of the basic research on these illnesses in the Plain Communities that started in the 1970s through the efforts of Victor McKusick, Janice Egleland, Abe Hostetler, and coworkers. Research continues today and involves many of the original families now working with Alan Shuldiner's group from the *University of Maryland*, and with colleagues from the *University of Pennsylvania*, as well as the staff of the *Clinic for Special Children.*

Genetic methods used to search for and find the single-gene recessive causes of inherited disorders like maple syrup urine disease, glutaric aciduria, and hundreds of other inherited disorders in the Amish & Mennonite communities had repeatedly over a 50-year-period failed to identify disease causing single-gene variants for bipolar and depressive illnesses. The use of increasingly powerful whole genome methods to search for the genetic basis of these illnesses in the Plain Communities and in older, larger inbred populations like those of Iceland and Israel as well as in the out-bred populations of Western and Northern Europe have the conclusions. *Collectively, studies of populations do provide important insights into bipolar and depressive illnesses, but studies convincingly show that our assumptions both about the nature of bipolar and depressive illnesses and the influence of genetics upon illnesses were too simplistic.*

Scientists & doctors were misled by assumptions about the nature of single gene disorders. We used MSUD (maple syrup urine disease) as an example of a single gene disorder and assumed for 50 years that the same methods that were used to find the genetic cause of MSUD could be used to find a single cause of bipolar illness. This assumption has been repeatedly proven to be wrong, but, we have also been misled by the belief that single gene disorders are biologically simple. Complexity of the relationship between gene & phenotype become more apparent when the functional consequences of a single gene mutation are studied during the treatment of MSUD and other biochemical disorders over a long interval of time.

MSUD, GA1, PCCB and the population-specific mutations that give rise to these familiar disorders are not in reality simple disorders. The biochemical disturbances in mitochondrial function within brain and muscle are poorly understood, and are complex. Successful treatment of these biochemical disorders is based upon crude biochemical models that do not reflect an understanding of the up-regulation and down-regulation of hundreds of interacting genes. Genes are involved in diverse functions such as mitochondrial energetics, mitochondrial replication, amino acid and organic acid transporters, regulators of protein synthesis and catabolism, and detoxifying pathways in liver, kidney, muscle, & brain that help prevent the accumulation of biochemicals that mediate toxicity in many different ways. Toxicity causes many different medical problems including muscle weakness, malnutrition and immune dysfunction, poor brain growth & development, and disturbances of brain energetics and biochemistry that can result in mental retardation, panic disorders, depression, coma, cerebral edema with strokes and death, and yes, in behaviors that could be classified as *bipolar disorder*.

The genetic basis of bipolar and depressive illnesses is complex, as are many other familiar disorders of the brain that also "run-in-families" – autism, seizures, mental retardation, cerebral palsy, and a distinctive manner of walking called a Charcot-Marie-Tooth gait. *Gene-Dx*, a Genomics Laboratory in Baltimore, offers sequencing of a panel of genes to look for genetic-autism & seizures that in 2018 includes more than 2,300 genes. In some families a single gene mutation may be found to underlie autism-spectrum disorder. For example, mutations in the gene CNTNAP2 cause a common recessive form of autism and seizures in the Amish community but more often the cause of an individual case of "Autism" will arise from a new "de-novo" mutation in a single gene or from deletion or duplication of a large cluster of genes. One particularly memorable example of the significance of a *denovo and dominant* cause of autistic behavior and extreme anxiety was in an identical twin whose brother was normal. How could this be? Identical twins share more-than-99% of their genome but one of these boys was severely disabled and the other normal. The difference was found by whole exome sequencing in a single copy of a gene called SYNGAP1. This disease-causing variant in SYNGAP1 was found only in the one boy, no other family member, and was a de-novo mutation, an error, in one copy of that gene.

Strong statistical associations have been found between bipolar I & II and medical problems like hypercholesterolemia (APO-B p.Arg3527Gln), sitosterolemia (ABCG8 p.Gly574Arg), and HFE p.Gly282Tyr, all common variants in the Kish Valley Amish Community. Bipolar illness was also strongly associated with thyroid disease – deficiency & excess - and especially with the presence of anti-thyroid antibodies. In one Amish family with multigenerational bipolar illness, a specific genetic variant in a potassium channel gene KCNH7 c.1181G>A; p.Arg394His was found to have a strong association with BP I & II, but, despite statistics, the majority of family members who carry this variant do not have bipolar illness. Within another family, a risk factor for bipolar disorder is fragile-X syndrome. Men who have fully expanded FMR1 CGG regions > 200 have a characteristic appearance, have mental retardation, are at risk for seizures, and some will have bipolar illnesses and depression. Women and men who carry premutations with 55-200 CGG-repeats are at risk for emotional problems – depression, anxiety, autism-spectrum disorder, and having a diagnosis of bipolar disorder is not uncommon.

In 79 patients with undiagnosed medical problems seen at the *Clinic for Special Children*, 51 (64%) had disorders of the brain. Seven of the 51 (14%) cases were diagnosed by chromosome analysis. Of the remaining cases with neurological disorders, over 50% were not inherited disorders, instead the condition arose from new de-novo errors in genes, the majority of which caused complex brain disorders including autism, seizures, mental retardation, and deafness. Ultimately, hundreds of genes and thousands of genetic variants will be found to give rise to bipolar and recurrent depressive illnesses.

FOR CYNTHIA AND HER FAMILY

I have been told that special children are gifts from God.

I have been told that special children are punishments from God.

I have heard scientists and doctors refer to these children only in terms of their genetic defects, aloof and with no human insight, as though the life of a child can be reduced to such terms.

My experiences have made me think in a different way about these children and their short, often difficult, lives.

I cannot say why these children come and go upon the Earth but I do know that they change the lives of those who know them.

Such children have been my most important teachers. I have learned more from them than I did from many instructors in Harvard Medical School, who were by reputation great teachers. These children have reshaped time and again the way I practice medicine, both the science and the art of it.

I have heard sermons by ministers about compassion, I have heard fine lectures about ethics and medicine, but no sermon or lecture has taught me as much as a single special child. These little children can change whole Communities of people in ways that last far beyond their brief lives.

They are not merely the focus of compassion but often are compassion's very source. Special children enrich the world in ways that many who are blessed with longer lives do not. They have much to give us, to teach us, about themselves and about ourselves.

-D. Holmes Morton, 1996

From the lecture, *Best of All Colors*, a story called "Croquet"

INTRODUCTION

This book was written in the soil of tears and tribulations. It expresses the inner turmoil of my battle with manic depression (Bipolar disorder). My illness has genetic roots and developed at a young age. However, as is typical, it did not catch a doctor's attention until life brought a string of stresses. My husband and I will never forget the slow, lonely learning process as I struggled back to my feet. What we learned comes from my own experience, doing research, asking my doctors questions, and watching others struggle. We do not offer simple solutions or concrete answers, only a glimpse into what we have learned.

Facing the reality of a fragile mental health condition left me feeling frightened, confused, and shamed. My brave confessions either met a wall of silence and consternation, or a flood of 'helpful' advice—anywhere from spiritualized quick-fix answers to sophisticated medical books with scary, technical terms. I found thin pamphlets that condemned and fat books that focused on terms and treatments. Sorting through secular manuals, I envisioned something written from a Christian perspective. How do I get help in safe ways and places? How can I stay healthy? How does this type of struggle affect my soul?

I began to write, pulling from a team of women who also were familiar with mental illness. Their input and feedback rounded things out and kept my dream alive. I could not have done this without their continual, loving support, immersed in an amazing sense of humor. I have also received input from a large circle of people across the States including Oregon, Iowa, West Virginia, Missouri, Arkansas, New York, Pennsylvania, Florida, and even Ontario and British Colombia. I have used pen-names freely. If an identity is hidden, please try to honor that for the sake of all involved.

Mental illness leaves us grappling with many questions: questions of our own, questions from the loved ones who journey with us, and questions from puzzled onlookers. It strikes anywhere, without respect for age, culture, or religion. The ability to weather the storm relies heavily on a basic understanding of what's happening and a personal support system. Some of us silently succeed under excellent care and family support. We slowly slide back into a functional norm and resume life. But our silence reinforces the belief that people with mental illness do not get well . . . people do not realize that there are teachers, preachers, successful business men, parents, and seasoned grandparents who have been treated successfully. The struggle with public stigma makes it very difficult to accept and be open about our realities.

Our perception of mental illness and its causes is influenced by the kind of 'window' we find ourselves looking through. Our experiences have shaped these windows. We tend to hang stubbornly on to our own perspective, not realizing how much we could learn from a panoramic view. We often act out of our determination to not to be a repeat of haunting examples in the past. Other people's windows feel unsafe because they expose our vulnerabilities or upset our conclusions. But it is liberating to stop and look through them. We learn a lot . . . why one person reacts to the word *depression* and another to the word *psychological* . . . why one person suspects sexual abuse and another focuses on diet . . . why one person thinks you have demons and another one thinks the way your head was shaped at birth affected your brains and emotions for life. The neurologist cites abnormal wiring in the brain, the psychiatrist sees a need for medication, the therapist finds wrong coping methods, the medical doctor blames genes or maybe an underlying disease, the minister sees a sick soul, the minister's wife thinks it's a lack of schedule, dad sees irresponsibility, mom sees a failure to protect like she should have, the nutritionist sees it as a lack of beans in the diet, the dentist sees TMJ, the artist sees an unpainted picture and the musician sees a harp hung upon a willow. They all look through their own windows; what each one sees represents truth to them. However, even though each one may only see a part of the picture, we can benefit from each other's viewpoint. Sharing what we know gives us the combined strength to find our way.

Genetic-based mental illnesses have unique challenges. Too often, the stressors that pull our weakness to the surface get the primary focus. Focusing solely on them, we go in exhausting circles for months while the illness continues wreaking havoc. Not understanding the root cause of this type of illness, we dismiss medication, viewing it as an effort to avoid the hard work of therapy. We cut off its power to make therapy doable, maybe even unnecessary! Two women were discussing a young girl's mental condition. One suggested the possibility of a genetic component to which the other replied with the sarcastic but typical response; "Well, she wishes that's what it would be." It may seem luxurious to blame a gene, but folks have no idea how we struggle to accept our reality. Shame and fear tempt us to live in denial of our genetic makeup. It is easier to accept or blame something we feel we can control!

When working with those who are experiencing trauma, including the effects of a mental illness, our most important job is to mirror God, the source of hope and healing. We can do this by making use of the various tools He offers to revive a faithful reflection of what Love truly is. However, they may come in unlikely forms we dislike, distrust, and despise. It is easy to be like the man who was trapped in a house surrounded by flood waters. This person prayed daily for deliverance, but out of a zealous desire to prove his faith, he turned down a man on foot, a boat, and a helicopter. He drowned. In heaven he asked God why his faith was disappointed. God replied that he had tried to save him three times!

We are complex beings, and sorting things out in a balanced way requires patience, humility, openness to other's input, and of course, PLENTY of TIME! As we learn from each other, we begin to realize we all have hard work to do . . .things no one else can do for us. We may conclude the quicker we get better, the more spiritual we are, and try to breeze over or deny our true condition. This makes it difficult to give ourselves the time and space we really need. Healing is a slow and difficult process. While gaining a clearer understanding is often possible, there are no quick and painless solutions or cut and dry answers. This inability to box things and give them a pat answer tends to intimidate us. We hate feeling powerless and vulnerable. We reconcile ourselves to the measly remains of our sanity, or we hound God and others with our 'whys'.

Shortly after my diagnosis I scribbled down three helpful guidelines:

1. *Learn all you can about your own illness.*
2. *Always be open to help.*
3. *Be honest about everything.*

I don't know where they came from, but these three simple keys steadied me many times. Accepting medical help and following the doctor's instructions are often the first two steps toward recovery. Refusing to do this may waste many precious years of our life. Our ability to move forward lies in the way we accept our struggle!

Some of you will devour this book. Others will find it deeply personal and difficult to read. As you read, strong emotions and maybe even painful memories may surface. Please don't close up and stop thinking. Give yourself space and share your questions with someone you trust. Too many of us zip the bag shut again because we simply don't have the strength to face things honestly. As a result, we stay stuck.

This book is not intended to be used as a medical manual. You will find explanations for common psychological terms and references to various medications that are sometimes used in treating mental illnesses, but do not try to diagnose yourself or others based on what you learn here. If you realize through reading this book that you or someone you love is dealing with a mental illness, please see a doctor. The therapy tips that are given are not intended to replace your medications, but to complement whatever treatment plan your doctor recommends. As you are reading, expect a certain amount of redundancy . . . each chapter was written as a unique section.

You can find most of my canvas paintings featured in this book scattered across the walls of our old country farmhouse. Painting and writing poetry were dots of light in the midst of confusion and uncertainty. They lit a pathway of hope and productivity. And so, as I enjoy the beautiful view of a lookout, I once again claim the precious verse of my youth—"*He makes everything beautiful in His time!*"

BEHIND THE MOUNTAIN . . .

Behind the Mountain
Is a Mountain.
For though we pause to rest,
And drink the beauty
Of a Lookout
We never span the crest;
Until we breach
The Final Summit
And pass the Final Test.

-Anita 2017

LOOKING THROUGH MY WINDOW . . .

It was an evening shortly before the birth of our fifth child. I rocked gently in the bedroom of our Guatemalan home, enjoying the beautiful full moon silhouetting a lovely palm tree right outside our window. It was one of those still moments. I called our oldest daughter to my side and said "See the moon? . . . the clouds keep moving over it! That is how life is. Sometimes our lives are so covered with clouds the 'light of the moon' can't shine through, but they always move on. The light always shines again!" She nodded. The rocking chair kept on rocking and the moon kept on shining, the roosters outside my window kept on crowing and the evening breezes sighed around the house. A strange sense of expectancy gripped me. Was I just a normal mom-to-be, or was it something more?

On July 17, 2008 Cynthia Anita was born in a hospital of the large town of Mazatenango. We were overjoyed with the perfection of our little dark-haired girl and called everyone with the good news. To my maid, Roxana, and our two little girls, it was too good to be true! Another girl! Nurses poked their heads through the door *cada rato* to see the new baby and exclaim over her. Since there was only one other patient in the hospital, we spent time chatting with the doctors and were released the following morning. Delighted shrieks and the enticing smell of dinner welcomed us home. Roxana had taken good care of things in our absence. However, the cold I had before Cynthia was born worsened, adding to the normal stresses of newborn days and nights. Frank and Roxana kept the house running smoothly, neighbors brought food, and friends sent *Dukal juices*, waiting to visit me till my strength returned.

When Cynthia was three days old, the whole family got food poisoning, which we suspect came from tainted milk. Only Marlena and I were spared; we attended to the others who were spread out through the house, some in bedrooms and some sprawled on the cool tile floor. That same day, Cynthia started refusing to nurse. This continued all night and we became concerned.

The fourth day after Cynthia was born, Frank's family came to see her. By times, she cried in a distressed way, arching her back slightly. His mom made a delicious stew while we anxiously hovered over her, trying to figure out what could be wrong. How I thought of Maple Syrup Disease and why we were prompted to smell her pamper for the telltale sweetness is a miracle I can't explain apart from God. The distinct smell of maple sugar filled us with shock, disbelief and fear. Even Roxana immediately said it smelled like sugar cane, having no clue what that meant! We quickly contacted family in the States, and in the hubbub and commotion that followed, tried to make decisions that would get help for Cynthia as soon as possible.

Dr. Holmes Morton, a doctor who works with genetic disorders, called us during this time, urging us to fly to the States immediately for help at his clinic in Strasburg, Pa. (Later on we found out that he was already making plans to fly down.) Somehow we made the decision; somehow we got through the next frantic hours. Through the blur of activity, I remember the shocked looks of our native friends, especially my dear maid, Roxana. She scurried around, packing clothing for the children and straightening up the house. I sat quietly in the Land Cruiser, cradling my baby, waiting for everyone to round things up. I cradled her, trying to grasp what was wrong, not sure if she would simply fade and disappear.

We left the remaining four children behind with their grandparents and drove into the city to purchase an emergency passport. We managed to do this early the next morning. We had a midday flight with a layover in Alabama, which was delayed two hours. Many fellow travelers asked about our baby and promised to pray for us. Friends in Pennsylvania started a prayer chain that lasted all night. We arrived at Harrisburg at

10:00 p.m. and more friends rushed us to Lancaster General Hospital where we were met by a competent and compassionate staff. We arrived in time . . . our daughter was spared the long term effects of brain damage that can happen when the luecine levels of maple syrup disease soar out of control.

For the next several weeks we swam around in a sea of questions and decisions. Reality slowly sank in. We would need to learn how to care for Cynthia's special needs. We would need to leave her behind with others, return to Guatemala to get our other children, and pack up. We would need to move to Pennsylvania. There would be monumental changes in our lives . . . new friends, new neighbors, new school, new church, new culture, new job, and plenty of bills. Life as we knew it was forever gone.

More than one cloud covered the moon! We scrambled to keep up with the constant pressure of our daughter's needs and all the changes in our pathway. One step at a time we numbly wove through the maze, trying to keep a sense of equilibrium, down to the smallest details. Merging from a small community into a large one was very intimidating; deciding which one was worse. Armed with a couple suitcases of clothing, we tried to settle into a lovely, modern house which happened to be available. It was loaded with food and a couple pieces of furniture. Since classes started a week after we arrived with the children, we needed to make a quick school decision. Because of a doctor appointment, we were unable to escort them the first day of school. Our children still talk about the awful fright of going to a strange school alone, without Dad and Mom.

The following years were full of learning. We had friends who brought food or washed clothing over Cynthia's crisis times. It was such a lift during the high-stress days when her amino acid levels needed to be adjusted. We never knew when we would be thrust into emergency mode:

> *It was one of those mornings—Cynthia drank her specially formulated formula poorly throughout the night and walked tipsily around the kitchen. Her eyes were not focusing. Our first thought was to check her levels. I set the DNPH supplies on the counter, the cotton balls, the tubes, and a timer. After getting a urine sample, I put it into the tube with the testing solution and waited 10 minutes to see the results. It turned cloudy instantly, which was alarming. I called the doctors and they asked me to come to the clinic immediately, which normally took us an hour and ten minutes.*

Continuing life was confusing and at times painfully lonely; relating to all the needs was exhausting! My husband spun like a top, from one need to the next. Cynthia's levels fluctuated alongside my own mood swings, making us all feel like we were losing our senses! Some days I sat in the recliner, buried under a blanket, feeling so poorly I wasn't able to focus. Other days I functioned at top speed, my mind boiling with inventive ideas and creative urges. I became bossy and aggressive, even indiscreet, and struggled to keep a perspective on life that was sane and safe. Then I slumped back into a period of painful depression, where I became dull and listless, loathing even the thought of life. I struggled to get out of bed in the mornings, resenting that my family needed me to keep going. In our search for answers, we stopped to investigate another genetic vulnerability in our family line . . . mental illness. If we thought a metabolic disorder like MSD boggled the mind, this was even worse!

The tussle with mental illness pulled and pushed at our levels of endurance and devotion. I felt like I was turning into a complete stranger and so did Frank. We both struggled to relate to that change in a redemptive way, but it was hard to do in the midst of all the other changes. Over this time I wrote in my diary: *"I am left to struggle alone, trying to understand God for who He is. He created me, knowing all these things . . . does He really care about us, or is this a punishment for who we happen to be?"* Does having a chemical imbalance—as the doctors call it—define *who* I am? I concluded it doesn't because neither does race, eye color, culture, nor handicap of any sort . . . but at the same time I realized how I relate to this will!

Thankfully, Dr. Holmes Morton not only did a wonderful job educating us about maple syrup disease and managing Cynthia's amino acid levels, he picked up on my struggle with bipolar illness, directing us to doctors who would be able to help. His caring attitude, ability to explain things in a comprehensible fashion, and sense of humor slowly helped us find solid ground. We regained the strength we needed to keep on going. One month after I started using medication to help control my mood swings, I wrote in my diary, "*There are a lot of things about life that I am grieving, but at least I feel like living!*"

We slowly adjusted to a new norm. I found solace in writing or painting, things I loved from childhood. Expressing myself in a productive way in spite of all the mental pain and confusion was soothing and healing. Our house started filling up with little glimpses of the life, country, and people we left behind.

Learning about and relating to my illness meant hard work for both of us. It meant asking questions and looking honestly at the answers. As we worked at untangling the 'ball', we found the strands of past and present finely intertwined. As we sifted through the years that brought us to this point, we began waking up to the way my illness had an impact on my whole life, even at a young age. As I shared these things with my family, I began to realize the way I perceived and experienced things as a child was unique, shaping struggles for me that my other siblings did not have.

As a young child, I had days when I basked in an overall sense of well- being. I was able to follow thru with my work, get good grades at school, and get along with my siblings. The little tinkley childhood song IT IS WELL hit each note with a poignant ding. But there also were days when I minded noise and quickly felt out of control. Sometimes I slept for hours in a dark corner or passed the time lying flat on my back in the orchard, picking out pictures in the endless mounds of clouds. It simply was the best place to be, away from the commotion of life. My skin felt crawly at night and I would lie awake, trying to think the bugs away. My thinking was foggy and erratic, making it hard to follow through with the simplest instructions. I had vivid dreams, so cunningly mixed with real life that it took me years to separate them. I remember puzzling over jumping rope . . . it really *FELT* like I was flying! I didn't share these things, maybe because I sensed they were strange. My mood fluctuations continued throughout my youth and on into adulthood. They intensified over times of stress such as heavy work schedules, change, and especially pregnancies. It was a puzzle to both of us.

Our move to the States and the resulting stress brought us nose to nose with the 'big black bear'! Slowly, we woke up to the broad impact of family genetics. While I spent some time looking at the past, I made more progress by looking at the present, reconnecting with family, and observing my own inherited weakness. We began to realize my mood swings did not come so much from unresolved psychological issues as from a physiological problem, a chemical imbalance in the brain. As I accepted medical help and got a fuller grasp on reality, I found acceptance of *what is* to be one of the most important keys. This included letting go of my desire to blame people or myself for my problems. Medication steadied my moods, producing healthy emotions and productive thought patterns.

I want to encourage others struggling with this type of illness to allow their perspectives to heal before they cement their conclusions. I found that in retrospect, things magnified, blocking my ability to trust or receive input from certain angles that could have been helpful. Feelings overruled facts. Time and medication took care of this, and as the years slowly moved by, my 'mental tunnel vision' slowly widened, broadening my perspective. I began to run my perspective through the perspectives of others and found it to be a stabilizing, balancing influence that encouraged healing. Throughout my illness, my siblings and parents were an invaluable source of help; cutting off their input by feeling *they* were the source of my problems would have been devastating! At the same time, it was a learning process for us all. Their ability to acknowledge their own failures without becoming defensive and reactive, when they could have, saved the situation. I felt heard. This built a bridge toward trust.

For a long time, I needed to give myself and others plenty of time and space, and I needed to find rest in parenting imperfectly and to the best of my ability. I also needed to let go of feeling too responsible for everything and everybody. Time is teaching me that my weakness brings out His strength, my limits are covered by His limitless resources, and my human frailties help me lean on Him. I looked to Him throughout the years, but I faced times when I wondered whether He was weak and uncaring or maybe even uninvolved. During my illness, I came nose to nose with these cries of pain. He is teaching me in His own gentle way—using many dear people along the way—Who He actually is.

I believe God is Master of the Universe—with wisdom and insight only He possesses, He looks down on each one of us, struggling along in the grip of trouble. I believe His Sovereign Hand reaches into each one of our lives. He is concerned about reaching us as we journey through the darkness of life on earth and the resulting pain and chaos. I also believe He will keep reaching down into the lives of each one of our dear children, infusing their lives with grace for whatever comes their way.

Look up, I see the moon!

SHADOWS & SHADES

What, you too?
I thought I was the only one.
C. S. LEWIS

1. What is mental illness?

"I believe you have a type of mental illness called bipolar disorder" the doctor said gruffly. I stared at him, my eyes large and frightened. "What does that mean?" I wondered. "I lost a couple of buttons, I'm short a couple of bricks, and I'm off my rocker . . . right?"

> *Sunlight is never more grateful than after a long watch in the midnight blackness.*
> CHARLES SPURGEON

The term "mental illness" is often feared, sat on, stood over, hidden, mocked, twisted, and wrung out like a mop. We get dubbed with evasive and odd phrases, some of them very descriptive and fitting. How many times have I wished I could find the 'bricks' I was missing!

"Why do you say that?" I asked the doctor, defensively.

"Well, the symptoms you are describing are classic hallmarks . . . excessive energy and elevated moods offset by low times where you are tired and immobile, living in a fog. The shifts in mood and function are very typical of someone struggling with this illness."

Mental Illness is a malfunction of the brain, causing changes in the way we relate to life. These changes may be obvious and bizarre, or subtle, but abnormal for us. Some may be rather harmless, while others are extremely dangerous. Here are some examples:

"My daughter began acting very strange. She started hallucinating and spent long times in her room. Sometimes she was very fearful. . . . Other times she was wildly enthusiastic, and did strange things like singing loudly in the parking lot of stores, or driving her car across the lawn. She spent a lot of money

on things she didn't need. She slept very little. We never knew what she would do next. We didn't know who would come down the steps in the morning- someone wildly enthusiastic or someone angry and violent. . . . ?" - *'Kayla'*

"My father had two major nervous breakdowns in his life. While his illness may have been a hereditary weakness, they both came at times of extreme stress. The first time, his mind snapped because he couldn't sleep. Fourteen years later he had a second breakdown. He went to visit an old friend; since it was Labor Day, bus connections were poor and he ended up hitch hiking a lot of the way. When he finally arrived, he got the shocking news that the friend he came to visit had just been killed. After he came home, he was quiet—too quiet. Then he went wild, running outside, and trying to climb a tree, etc."

-Anna P.

The "onset" (beginning) of mental illness can be sudden, or so gradual that we don't realize what is happening. Maybe our normal work load suddenly looks impossible, or we feel supercharged, driven toward unrealistic expectations. Maybe we no longer enjoy being with friends, or we are terrified to be alone. Maybe we can't stop washing our hands, or don't care at all how we look. When our minds and emotions have been affected to the point that we struggle to cope with daily life, we need to stop and seriously look at what is going on.

"It started years ago, when there was a flood at Harrisburg. My husband and I went to help with cleanup. At the time, I was on a diet of my own and I was eating less and working hard. I couldn't sleep and one night I woke up feeling like I couldn't breathe. I had several panic attacks in a row. Afterwards, I experienced deep depression."

-'Jana'

"I lost a baby in her 4th month and a year later had a miscarriage. I think this may be what set off my depressions, because I was not aware that I had it before. At first I thought it was 'the baby blues' because of the physical upheaval my body went through. But this continued long after I thought it should have. After that I thought I had a spiritual problem. After a number of years, and reading up on it, I came to the conclusion that I had 'clinical depression'—that there was something actually wrong with me other than a lack of faith."

-*'Kayla'*

"Mom sat motionless in her favorite chair; her cheeks flushed an unnatural red. She suddenly leaned forward. Reaching with one hand, she felt for her pulse. Glancing at the clock, she expertly counted the number of beats, and then settled back into her chair. The house was in disorder. Even mom's usual love of cooking was suffering greatly. Her long walks were the most she could do and that was also heart related. Her anxiety was directed mostly toward her health. Right now, she thought her heart was bad. When I was little, it was cancer lumps or gall stones. She avoided hospitals or doctors until her agony forced her to get checked. She lived in deep anxiety until test results came back, and then shouted hallelujah when they were clear."

-*'Tabitha'*

Mental Illness takes on all sorts of shapes and configurations. Some have consistent, predictable patterns, while others are known for their inconsistencies. Instead of defining all the variations, we will take a look at some common disorders that surface among us, mainly those with a biological component. The 'windows' give a glimpse into these, and as you can see, tailored doctoring is needed to address the specific needs of each person. At the back of the book, I have also included a list of reading material. Some of these books are secular and need to be 'sifted' accordingly; while I do not endorse everything they say, I have found them helpful.

Mental illness cripples life as we knew it. Just as arthritis sufferers know the slow, insidious crippling of bone and muscle structure that earmarks their disease, those of us suffering with a mind illness slowly but surely find ourselves losing control of our ability to think, reason, and behave. The pain is elusive and indescribable. Sometimes it changes our sleeping and eating habits, impacting our emotional and social responses. Its progress can be likened to subtle shades of gray creeping over us, along with an uncanny sense that something is not right. As the 'shades of gray darken', and the symptoms change from slight to moderate to severe, it can be very difficult to recognize the shifts in mood without the help of others. The following illustration shows the gradual changes that often take place during the onset of a major depression:

> *Not everything that is faced can be changed, but nothing can be changed until it is faced.*
> GEORGE BALDWIN

> ***Light gray stage***—"I am able to keep after normal duties, but no extras. I feel sad and draggy. I am so happy to tumble into bed at the end of the day. But I still enjoy my cup of hot chocolate."

> ***Moderate gray stage***—"Ironing looks hard and mending looks impossible; it takes deliberate concentration to follow a recipe. Menus are mind-boggling and exhausting. Going away looks big, especially if I realize I have to fill up with gas. I feel increasingly sad. Unrealistic thoughts play at the edges of my mind—"I think the neighbor lady hates me. I believe I married the wrong man. None of my children will amount to anything. My life is a waste." Doing dishes and sweeping the floor is the limit. I go to bed

an hour or so earlier than normal and get up an hour later. It takes too much effort to get a mug out to make hot chocolate."

Dark gray stage—"It takes heroic effort to get out of bed. Arms feel heavy, and I move slowly and methodically around the house. My thinking is very foggy, and I struggle to remember what day of the week it is or what month. Noise, touch, light and conversation hurt. Food is a necessary evil. An overwhelming sadness pervades everything. Hot chocolate doesn't even cross my mind."

Black stage—"My life revolves around bed and bed only. Going to the bathroom is exhausting and combing my hair looks impossible. Washing my hair is unthinkable. I feel immobilized . . . in a trance of supreme discomfort. My thinking and talking is irrational, and sometimes incoherent, full of lost phrases, floating fragments of thoughts. Someone brings me a steaming mug of my favorite hot chocolate, but hot chocolate stinks. Living hurts and death looks inviting. . . ."

Depression is not the only way a genetic- based illness expresses itself. Other common diseases are schizophrenia and manic depression, as well as agoraphobia and personality disorders. I will outline their symptoms below:

Schizophrenia includes impaired, mixed up thinking that affects all areas of life, making it hard for a person to interpret their surroundings in a realistic way. Behavior can change severely from a show of emotion to none at all and often includes sensory issues where unreal things are felt, heard, or seen. With the use of medication, these folks are able to regain stability and function well, even though their perceptions may always be somewhat affected. I have a dear friend with this type of illness who has become a writer, and blesses many people with her cards of support and encouragement.

Manic depression (bipolar illness) mainly consists of both deep depressions as pictured above and highs—simply meaning periods of intense energy and enthusiasm, sometimes to the point of losing control. The 'two-edged' component of this disease makes it more difficult to work with. Since this is my diagnosis, and thus, close to my heart, I have dedicated a chapter to it. If we are open to the help that is available, I believe we are also able to live balanced, useful lives.

Phobias and anxiety (such as Obsessive-Compulsive Disorder) are another kind of mental illness. This includes intense, irrational fears about specific things or certain surroundings. Some people with this illness live in seclusion for years, simply because their fears keep them home-bound. Both medication and therapy have been very helpful with relieving these symptoms.

Personality Disorders cover a wide spectrum of disorders. They generally tend to develop early in adulthood and persist for extended periods of time, sometimes coming alongside other psychiatric conditions. Medication may be helpful, but usually much time and effort needs to be put into therapy to unravel crippled ways of coping and thinking.

2. What factors impact our mental health?

Some people believe mental illness is strictly an organic problem such as a chemical imbalance in the brain, which can be cured with the use of medication. Others believe mental illness is caused by trauma, which in turn impacts the psychological makeup of a person (attitudes, beliefs, and thought patterns.) These folks see therapy or counseling of some sort as the answer. Still others maintain that its causes and cures are strictly spiritual.

Mental Health is *impacted* by at least three basic factors:

(1.) BIOLOGICAL FACTORS:

Primarily, malfunction of the brain's neurotransmitters, especially serotonin. . . . Many times this is a genetic problem, thus the problem is present from birth. Sometimes these tendencies will lie dormant for years, and only be triggered later in life by other physical or environmental changes. Sometimes prolonged emotional stress or a specific trauma can actually alter brain chemistry, such as decreased serotonin levels, causing depression.

Physical Illnesses, ongoing health problems in general, old age.

Side effects from certain medications.

(2.) ENVIRONMENT:

Trauma—accidents, moving, job changes, major changes of any sort . . .

The effects of trauma in utero (before birth), or during childhood to a developing brain. Scientists continue to research and document the evidence of the long-term impacts of childhood trauma to actual brain function.

Abuse—physical, sexual, verbal, or emotional

Financial Stress

Loss—death, offenses, broken relationships, deep hurt of any sort.

High stress—living with an unrealistic authority figure, anger, fear, extreme work load, or chaos.

(3.) OUR SPIRITUAL CONDITION:

Guilt, whether true or false

Distorted views of God.

These three aspects impact us to a greater or lesser degree. If a problem exists in one area, the other areas are often affected. Things can travel both directions, as diagrammed below. The spiritual thread of our natures winds itself around our physical makeup and life's experiences.

A stressful environment > can aggravate >
anything inherited or biological in nature.

Anything inherited or biological in nature >
can aggravate > a stressful environment.

The many factors that often enter in, complicate an answer. Every person is unique; solutions are not cut and dry. The cause in one situation may be the effect in another. While stress itself does not often cause mental illness, it is true if you are prone to mental health issues, you are probably more vulnerable to stress. While rebellion against God does cause mental and emotional turmoil, spiritual unrest is also an *effect* of being mentally ill. Identifying root issues takes discernment, time, and often a good bit of trial and error.

> *God, give us grace to accept with serenity the things that cannot be changed, courage to change the things that should be changed, and the wisdom to distinguish the one from the other.*
> REINHOLD NIEBUHR
> *(Reinhold has suffered many depressions.)*

Several of Calvin's family members struggle with anxiety and depression. Last fall, a fire destroyed his woodworking shop, leaving him with a large debt and little income. In the months since the fire, Calvin has had difficulty sleeping, and is losing an unhealthy amount of weight. Normally a calm, steady person, suddenly he seems constantly uptight, and frequently lashes out at his wife and children. His wife often finds him pacing the floor in his study, and she can hardly coax him to leave the house. Lately he confided to one of his friends that he finds it hard to trust God, and he feels like the fire was God's punishment for not being as close to God as he should have been.

What is the answer for Calvin? Where shall we start? Does he need medication to control his anxiety? Or does he need a counselor to help him work through the trauma of losing his business, and manage his finances? Or is it enough to simply encourage him to trust in God? Probably all three angles will need attention. Isolating one aspect or the other will usually result in a partial recovery. A holistic approach will be the most effective.

3. What does a diagnosis mean?

> *"I stood with the bottle of lithium pills in my hands, straining to read the attached paperwork. 'Used to treat manic depression' . . . in a panic, I dropped the bottle and closed my eyes. Manic. Maniac. So that's why I've been feeling so crazy. I'm a crazy person! I always knew something was wrong with me!"*

Naming our illness may make us feel better or worse. We may be thankful for the way it clarifies our problems or we may focus on the terms, feeling 'engraved in stone'—like someone who is helplessly doomed to be ill for the rest of our life.

> *We need people to not meet us as a disease or an illness, but as a person.*
> DR. ABRAHAM SCHMITT
> *Brilliant Idiot*

A diagnosis or a label is simply an orderly way to organize a cluster of symptoms. It gives our doctors a place to start in finding the right kind of treatment plan. Naming our illness can make us feel like a foreigner, but actually, bits and pieces of our symptoms are found within everyone. The *severity* of our problem is what earns it a name! Learn as much about your illness as you can, but always remember that you are still you. Don't shield yourself with your label and don't sit on it to hide it; just walk beside it and accept it. It is nothing to be ashamed of. And remember—One good way to end up with ten of them is waiting too long to accept one!

Understanding the terms that the medical world uses to classify illness helps avoid unnecessary fears and misunderstandings. Studying them dissolves the sinister shadows. In Plain circles, terms like *bipolar or depression* often get a different response than the term *cancer.* They tap into hushed stories of uncles that were a little loony, or aunts that locked themselves in their rooms. Shame lurks around things that are not understood, or wrongly understood. Sometimes more information helps, but usually it is wise to simply say less. It is okay to not always be understood.

What if people act like we're from Mars over a mental diagnosis? It is hard to relate positively to those who get icy, or handle us pityingly with gloved fingers. We need to overlook these types of reactions and not give in to self-pity. Self-pity excuses things that shouldn't be excused, keeps things impersonal, and strips us of our dignity—leaving us glossed over, smudged out, sugared up, trodden under, and reduced to a thin strip of paper with a couple words on it.

When we remember that we are all mad, the mysteries disappear and life stands explained.
MARK TWAIN

My first impulse to a diagnosis was protest. It couldn't be true. Bipolar Illness. . . . It sounded ominous . . . like the sound of a trap snapping on my foot. I stood in the hall of the clinic and felt myself slipping away into a terror too big for me. Our doctor put a hand on my shoulder. He said nothing at the time, but later told me about his own mom and her struggles with the same illness. He recognized the signs and knew the enormity of it. It felt like a death blow—I had prayed for years, that I would be spared such a dreadful thing. But now, my life turned upside down as I sorted through the monumental mound of questions that my diagnosis threw into the air.

Denial knocked on my door. It invited me to do just

that! Deny reality. Why not, if life is unreal anyway? But I knew from past experience that denial mocks. It laughs from behind doors and buries our pain, intensifying it at the same time. So I looked the truth in the face, and then despair took a turn. "You aren't a good mom. . . . How can you trust yourself if your mind is sick? Anyhow, you can't be a Christian. Christians don't get sick this way. Where is your faith? For your punishment, you'll probably be this way for the rest of your life."

I holed up. I didn't want to feel anymore. Part of this was the illness itself and part of it was the grief of my loss. In time, I let go. I let go of the right to mental health and looked around for something to replace it. My hand landed on paintbrushes, pen and paper, and prayer. Slowly, and in time, my faith in a kind and loving heavenly Father returned.

A correct diagnosis is very important. Many times a psychiatrist will need to work with a patient for a period of time, observing patterns and monitoring responses to medications before a diagnosis can be made. When in doubt, it may be helpful to get a second opinion. Progress is being made by scientists to identify the genes or medical problems that impact a person's mental makeup. The more they learn, the easier it will be to get an accurate diagnosis. The more accurate a diagnosis, the more successful treatment is bound to be, and the faster the recovery.

4. What are some common misconceptions?

During my illness, I picked up a pamphlet at a local book store. This is what I read:

> *"How many totally selfless people do you know with serious emotional problems? If you want to stay sane, you must forget yourself entirely and devote all your energies to helping others.*

If you found yourself hanging by your fingertips at the edge of a cliff, you would become pretty self-centered too!
CHRISTINE M.

Going to a minister or a caring friend will get you as good results as going to a psychiatrist. It will not be as dangerous and it is cheaper.

The cause of emotional problems is self-centeredness and lack of faith in God. Satan is the instigator of emotional problems. Therapy tries to justify our disobedience, comfort us in our rebellion, and provide the peace and joy that only God can give to those who trust and obey Him."

I scribbled my astonishment into the margins. In the following low when I couldn't begin to process what I read, much less trust what I read, I stuck it into a drawer and forgot about what I read. It depressed me even more. Was I rebellious, disobedient, self-centered, faithless, maybe even demon possessed?!

Being mentally weak is often seen as a result of spiritual weakness.

It is true that a spiritual need causes mental turmoil. Satan uses our minds as a battleground to accomplish his work. The Scriptures offer hope for times like this: confession, repentance, and accepting the forgiveness of God. (1 John 1:9) But our minds are physical and can get sick just like the rest of our body. It is ridiculous to assume that a person with cancer is spiritually weak; it is also cruel to assume that a person's mental struggles reveal spiritual weakness.

Many people with mental health struggles in Plain communities deal with a terrific amount of false guilt. Does your family or church community see weakness as unacceptable or humiliating, tainting the group's reputation? Does being out of control in anything, including emotions, trigger overwhelming fear? When this happens, it is a lot easier to criticize the struggler instead of accepting him and helping him come to grips with the reality of living in a fallen world. (Including our own!)

Mental illness is sometimes attributed to demon possession.

> *"Maybe you are being bothered by a demon—a genetic demon!?"*
> DR. HOLMES MORTON
> *Clinic for Special Children*

Those who feel this way see the devil as the instigator of the problem. I asked our doctor about this. He frowned and thought a little, then said with a crooked smile "Maybe you are being bothered by a demon—a *genetic* demon!? "The introduction of this idea that we are possessed by demons usually adds tremendous weight to our depression, or gives us a false 'explanation,' reinforcing our denial of the need for medical help. We may see black devils around every bush or vigorously deny our illness in order to prove that we are not demon possessed. Obviously, these responses don't get us anywhere.

Isn't demon possession a possibility? It is true that an existing biological or genetic problem can make a person vulnerable to Satan's attacks, especially if a person has also been abused or dabbled with the occult. However, we cannot start here. Casting out a devil will not take care of a biological problem and medication will not remove a demon. They are two separate problems.

Mental illness does leave us feeling more vulnerable to Satan's attacks. We tend to think—things will never get better, life is too painful to live, we are all alone, and what a complete failure I am, God hates me. It may be these thoughts are a part of deeper beliefs or strongholds. But if we believe that mental illness is of the devil, when illness strikes, the stage is set for much spiritual damage. We may deny that we are ill, or conclude we have blasphemed God and are headed to hell. Our illness may hopelessly lock us in these tormenting thought patterns; we may falsely conclude our destiny is sealed.

As a youth, I took it upon myself to rebuke a filthy-mouthed man at a laundromat for his words. He became enraged and I left with his menacing words ringing in my ears, "I'll be seeing you." During my depression, this incident came back clearly. I don't know if it was simply one of the many scenes the mind digs up in its frantic state, or if it was the devil, but it doesn't really matter. Feeling like the devil was right at my elbow and God was distant and uncaring left me powerless. I shared it with my husband and we prayed over that specific hold of fear. The terror of his words left me, even though my depression continued and it seemed like God was unavailable.

We can offer this type of protection to those who find themselves spellbound by beliefs that deepen their hurt and confusion. Satan has no mercy for strugglers and will try to use our weakness to destroy us spiritually. We need to hang onto the truth of God's Word, and reach out to others to help us fight off his lies. Satan is certainly able to add to the tortures of mental illness, but it will not help us to picture him around every corner. Our imaginations do not need this fuel. Medication often helps to lessen our vulnerability in this area by stabilizing our minds and emotions.

When someone is mentally ill, hallucinations, dreams, or memories can take on sinister and terrifying proportions. They cannot always separate reality from the concoctions of the mind. Your reassuring words and presence can help them stay connected with reality. Do not try to normalize their struggles, but help them realize it is a clear sign that they need help. Ignoring the problems in hopes they will just go away can be life threatening.

Beware of the ditches on either side of the road! When we spiritualize everything, down to which pair of socks we put on in the morning, we create a tense world of struggle. On the other hand, it is damaging to only acknowledge the physical part of our illness and avoid looking at what God wants us to learn. Our struggles do impact our spirits. The trial of mental illness can leave us caught up in patterns of denial and bitterness, just like facing a bout of cancer.

Don't these folks always come from abusive and/or dysfunctional families?

There are people, including therapists or counselors, who believe mental illness always rises out of abuse and dysfunction without considering a third factor . . . the impact of genetics. Viewing poor parenting as a root cause, they add to the frustration of the already traumatized parents! They also reinforce the black and white thinking already present in the one who is struggling, causing them to reject the input of their own parents and families. While a genetic source points back to the parents and the resulting 'parenting gaps', highlighting them instead of helping the individual understand the illness and how it affected their own life encourages the blame game they may be already be playing.

> *Helping children understand how mental illness affects their parents is a golden opportunity. It gives them the ability to see beyond the illness to the love that is there!*
> KERI

There are people who struggle with mental illness that come from families with caring relationships and a healthy environment. These families relate to their struggles openly and objectively, learning all they can as the challenges arise. Doing this may help curb the illness, but even so, it does not promise to annihilate it. It can surface at any time!

However, abuse or dysfunction does have the potential to leave indelible scars in any child's brain development. When those with a genetic vulnerability are born into homes that relate poorly to their struggles—either by ignoring, shaming, or hiding them—they will face the same emotional struggles as an abuse victim. A family atmosphere that is secretive and relationally empty or rigid and fearful also invites abuse and addictions. It pushes children toward relationships that are unrealistic and harmful. This mixture is devastating, and improvement almost impossible if only one segment of the problem is faced.

Doesn't everyone get depressed sometimes?

There is a distinct difference between simply feeling depressed and having a depressive illness. Depression is commonly understood to mean a feeling of gloom or sadness. Normal emotions tend to cycle along with hormone changes or immune system fluctuations. At high points, we are able to cope just fine and at low points we sink into depression. If we understand what is happening, we can cope with these minor depressions by not expecting as much out of ourselves. Sometimes people find that sugar or stimulants like coffee exaggerate the normal cycle of their emotional highs and lows.

Depression is often a natural response to life's difficulties. It can be triggered by losses such as the death of a loved one. When people make the accusation that "it's just in his head", they are literally quite right. Subtle chemical changes in our brain affect our physical functions, slowing us down and placing a 'cushion' around us while we heal. In this way, depression functions a bit like pain, sounding an alarm and the need to adjust. It is a natural part of God's design for our bodies.

This type of minor depression often corrects itself with a bit of time and care. Proper diet, exercise, vacations, no overwork, saving time to do things you enjoy, good relationships, and a healing faith alleviates it. But if we are vulnerable, the depression can linger, become worse, or turn into a chronic problem. We sink deeper into the shades of grey. All of our normal functions are affected. A simple job looks huge, and we may feel like we are looking on from a distance. Irrational fears, unpredictable frustration, and explosive anger often plague a chronically depressed person. Our emotions fall over each other, and kick up their heels. Medication can help to restore our balance; waiting too long to get help impairs our ability to bounce back, and leaves permanent scars.

Depressive illness is caused by ongoing chemical or hormonal imbalances in the body. While these imbalances are often tied into our genetic makeup and may appear unprovoked, they can also be brought on or aggravated by extensive trauma or physical causes that wreak havoc on the wiring in our brains. Depressive illness is more severe and requires something beyond lifestyle adjustments or improved thought patterns. Proper diet, exercise, vacations, no overwork, and saving time to do things you enjoy may alleviate, but usually medical help is needed.

What happens when we confuse different types of depression? Many times, a person who is depressed is accused of being selfish, self-centered, unthankful, and undisciplined. He is told that if he would change those unhealthy patterns of living and thinking, his illness will go away. And so, he goes on another guilt trip until he can once again see that it's not all that simple. But is there *any* truth in what the well-meaning minister is saying to depressed people?

Some people feel an ongoing struggle with this type of illness is proof of faithless living. But really, learning to live with and accept an illness like this takes a lot of faith! It takes inner strength to relate to our inner weakness.
'KERI'

"One Sunday at church the minister stressed that depression was caused by selfishness and lack of discipline. Afterwards, one sister told me it was just what she needed. She had been struggling with the fact that she wasn't getting anything extra done after the birth of a baby. Someone else told me she had been offended by something someone had told her the week before. She realized she must forgive the offense. I listened quietly to these women. But the fact was, it left me feeling drained, misunderstood, and discouraged."

-*'Keri'*

A Snapshot of Depression:

Scientists have long known that when depression sets in, a person suffers not only miserable emotions but also the inability to concentrate on even the simplest tasks.

Texas Health Science Center, using brain imagery techniques, reveal a lack of communication between regions of the brain where cognitive tasks like planning and paying attention are performed (the neocortex) and regions where emotions are processed (the limbic system). When one region revs up and requires more blood, the other region shuts down, using less. In normal brains, that feedback loop is flexible. In depressed individuals, the loop runs wild, so the cortex becomes stuck in a dysfunctional state and the limbic system in a hyperactive one.

Medication and psychoanalysis can restore the balance of a depressed brain within months . . . in other words, it doesn't take much to see that depression is rooted in the brain.

U.S. NEWS

Depressive illness, where the root problem is biological, is often overlooked. It is true that those of us living with the pain of depressive illness face the temptation to become unforgiving, self-centered, undisciplined, and unthankful, but these things are not the main fuel for our depression. Controlling ourselves is important, but taking medication can help to make this possible, just like a swinging bridge helps us cross a canyon. We need to remember this, or we can become extremely frustrated in our efforts to conquer our depression. While these things can be tools to help us fight our depression, they do not take away the cause like it may do for a reactive depression. While a victorious, disciplined life of gratefulness can be a powerful tool in fighting depression, it does not change the physical nature of our illness.

The suffering we experience is often so great we prefer to die. Proverbs 18:14 says "The human spirit can endure in sickness, *but a crushed spirit* (italics added) *who can bear?"* Since the two are so interwoven with this kind of illness, it can become unbearable. William Styron's book *Darkness Visible* says the old term for depression used to be melancholia. He feels this word is more fitting for 'such a dreadful and raging disease,' and goes on to describe it as a 'veritable howling tempest in the brain.'

Becky McGurrin voices her experience with depression:

> *It's lonely here;*
> *All strangers and language unknown*
> *I'm frightened here;*
> *Abandoned, I wander alone.*
> *So tired here;*
> *How weary my labor has grown.*
> *I want to go home.*

Depression increases our longing for the Healing One and yet veils our view of Him.
KATHRYN GREENE MCCREIGHT
Darkness is my only Companion

"I'm learning that I have to be content with whatever I'm suffering and not to complain about what God allows in my life. But in the long run I'd rather have physical pain—no matter how intense it is. At least people understand it better because it's 'physical' not 'mental'. Somehow it seems like no one can fully understand until they have suffered it themselves."

-'Angela'

"I feel trapped in a miserable existence. It's so frustrating! I just want to escape my problem but I can't go anywhere. I just get so sick of this empty nothingness in my brain. Life is a nightmare; like hell on earth."

-'Martha'

Just like a tornado sweeping the countryside, mental illness leaves a path of destruction behind. As we struggle to accept the losses, we not only suffer the depression of our illness, but the added depression of facing reality. We don't want to accept that we are ill—we don't want to see we are out of control—and we didn't ask to be born with this weakness. Our own attitudes or negative reactions from other people can cause additional depression. It takes courage, time, and persistence to face these challenges and move on with our lives.

Why is life So Vibrant?

Why is life so vibrant?
Softness, I can take—
Not the devastation
In the whirlwind's wake;
Not the lack of warning
Ere a dream takes flight,
Or the sudden heart- cry
In the silent night.
Give me life in dewdrops;
Do not crush with hail—
A teardrop, small and lonely,
But, Father, not a wail!
Why, when pounds are heavy,
Must I bear a ton?
Why Everest the mountain
Which my feet must run?
I pray tomorrow's sunset
Be a muted one . . .

-Sheila Petre

Winter Blues

Icy Winter
Barren Hours
Sobbing Sadness
Overpowers.

Icy Feelings
Empty Breast
Shuddering Sighs
Long for Rest.

Icy Work
Tired Time
Passes by
Right in Rhyme.

Icy Snow
Crushes Me.
Twinkling Stars
I cannot See.

Icy Joy
Frozen Stiff
Cannot Cross
The Highest Rift.

Icy Hope
Hovers By
Watching Me
As I cry.

-Anita 2012

CHARTING A COURSE

Every
path
has its
puddle.

1. *Where should I go for help?*

When you suspect that you or someone you love is struggling with their mental health, what should you do? Friends, family, and community can be helpful, but especially in the realm of mental illness, we often need to reach out for professional help. Ignorance of how damaging mental illness can be can cost someone their life. Even being surrounded by caring people doesn't help if they don't understand what is causing your problem or aren't unified on what kind of help you need; their efforts can actually prolong and intensify everything. Those of you who have gone through this know that this is no joke. 'Doubled over' in pain and out of control, you become a specimen who is scrutinized and poked at from all sides—not only you, but your family life, your marriage, your childhood, your parents, your grandparents, your spiritual status, your church relationship, your eating habits, and your housekeeping. Opinions are as numerous as the sands of the sea. At a time like this, even kind attempts at encouragement tend to feel like a slap in the face.

> *They always say that time changes things, but you actually have to change them yourself.*
> ANDY WARHOL

Many times the place to begin is with your family doctor. A good family doctor will be able to evaluate your symptoms and help to determine the level and kind of help needed. He may also order blood work to test for various physical conditions that can trigger emotional or mental difficulties, such as a thyroid imbalance. Don't miss this step! It is very basic and may avoid years of misguided wanderings.

If the problem you are dealing with is fairly straightforward, he may be able to prescribe a simple medication that may bring you relief, such as an antidepressant. However, no matter how well you know him, how much you like him, and how cheap he is, he has not been extensively trained to diagnose or treat mental health conditions. If he is a good doctor, he himself will quickly acknowledge that. Going to him with *your idea* of the problem and asking for medicine based on your own (or your aunt's) conclusions is a risky thing to do, and usually ends up being unfair to both of you.

Your family doctor will probably refer you to a **psychiatrist** or a **psychologist.** A psychiatrist is a medical doctor trained in the diagnosis of psychological problems and prescribing medication. A psychologist is not trained to prescribe medications; instead, he focuses on accurate diagnosis, mentoring, and helping us correct destructive thought patterns. He helps to solve day –to-day problems such as dealing with symptoms and accepting our illness and limitations. This field of diagnosing and treating mental health conditions in the medical world is known as **psychotherapy**. What can you expect from a visit like this?

Here is a nurse's description of the process:

> *While exploring the course of the disorder, a brief look will be taken at the following aspects: diagnosis, family background and health, progression of symptoms, danger of worsening symptoms, and importance of identifying episodes. It may take two or three visits to gather all the information. A psychiatrist will conduct a clinical interview inquiring about the patient's medical history, symptoms, and what has made the symptoms better or worse in the past. He will also discuss past family history of depression, suicide, or other mental illnesses. Generally, he will also order a physical examination and blood tests by the medical doctor before the final diagnosis to rule out any other existing medical conditions.*
>
> *Anyone in the patient's family history with bipolar disorder, depressive episodes, or other psychiatric problems like panic attacks and eating disorders will indicate genetic vulnerability is higher. Sometimes there is no family history, but there may be prolonged drug abuse, head injuries, neurological illnesses, complications during birth, or a virus during the mother's pregnancy.*

How can I find a good doctor? This is a 'million dollar' question! To find a good doctor we need a basic understanding of what makes one. There are some well-loved doctors among us; what makes them effective is their ability to see life as a whole. Good doctors are not only well studied, but need a basic comprehension of trauma and how it affects human beings. They need to be able to see the variables and explore them so no facet is missed. This means they are open to specific types of help you may need, including therapy or counseling. A good doctor is a real treasure! If you have one, thank him!

Good medicine treats an individual, not merely a disease.
HIPPOCRATES

2. *What about medication?*

"As someone who has been taking an antidepressant for seventeen years, I can't help but feel that fears about medication are just that—largely unrealistic and often blown far out of proportion. But perhaps the real fear is in facing and accepting that one's brain is indeed imbalanced to the point of needing extra help. At the back of one's mind may be the thought that, "as long as I can function without medication I don't really have a mental illness. I'm not that bad."

Also, for some people medication may almost seem like cheating or taking the easy way out. "If I just try a little harder, surely I can handle this. . . ." But really, what merit is there in struggling on in such misery when help is readily available? We are hardly being fair to ourselves and our loved ones by refusing to try this one avenue which may make a big difference.

It's not the years in your life that counts, it's the life in your years.
ABE LINCOLN

Accepting and understanding that my brain was not functioning quite normally was actually a turning point for me. It was a revelation to me that the depression itself was causing the dread, anxiety, and feelings of worthlessness and hopelessness that I was experiencing, not that my feelings were causing the depression. That is why I would be very hesitant to imply to anyone struggling with depression that he has brought it on himself with faulty thought patterns or by believing Satan's lies. My own experience has been that it can be the other way around. The negative and fearful thoughts are the result *of a depressed brain, not the cause of it.*

I have learned to accept that my brain needs the support of medication, and have decided that it is best to take a matter-of-fact point of view, neither perceiving myself as a victim nor carrying a load of false guilt. Everyone has his bundle to carry . . . this happens to be mine. I think this will always be a part of who I am. I still need to work with negative thoughts and feelings, and experience some down times. The big difference is that it is on a manageable level. I can cope with life, and for that I am deeply grateful.

Medication may not be needed in every case, but neither should it be considered as something to be avoided if at all possible, or as an absolute last resort. For myself I have to say that untreated depression and anxiety are far scarier and much harder to live with than anything I have experienced with medication. Thank God this type of help is available. I do not feel that my healing is any less from God because I take medication. All our help ultimately comes from him and to Him alone be the glory."

-Ellen O.

Most of us don't like the idea of medication, period, especially if it's for a 'brain problem'! Not understanding how it works makes us feel out of control, a feeling we hate. We may even suspect a sneaky sort of trick bent on sedating us into submission. Our ears quickly tune in to horror stories of overdoses and misdiagnoses. We fear the side effects along with the prescriptions, and become transfixed by the warnings that come in tiny print. They themselves are enough to start a headache or a methodical twitch in the leg! But we need to stop and realize that medication has been and can be a lifesaver!

One lady began enumerating the side effects of a medication but added with a sheepish smile, "I can't imagine living without it." We tend to focus on the negatives instead of thinking beyond our own discomfort to those who live with us. What does my ten year old daughter do day after day while I am trying to sleep off my depression? What about the confusing messes, discombobulated speech, and irrational outbursts that has everyone sitting on edge? In an ongoing illness, we may do things we never fathomed we would do! It is frightening to realize we are capable of disconnecting from reality to the point of abusive behavior. Always keep in mind—if the negatives of your illness outweigh the negatives of the medication, it is a wise decision to use it.

Medication is a tool that helps us control our illness instead of it controlling us.
J.W.

Mental Illness is no less physical than diabetes or maple syrup disease, yet we question the need for medication. Why? We are told the psyche, not the brain, is at the root of our problem, or that crediting pills is taking the credit away from God. We are told depression is learned and needs to be unlearned through willpower and the grace of God. It is not an illness, but a lifestyle. We are told we need to talk everything out; messed up thought patterns are always a sign of a sick soul. We are told that taking a pill is popular because it is a quick, effortless solution that puts a bandage over the real problem. Are these things true?

Most of these beliefs grow out of the fear that the use of medication avoids important spiritual or character issues. I have had some of these fears myself! My doctor explained that medication treats the physical part, leaving spiritual and character needs intact. And shouldn't we make it a priority to stabilize the mind?

Stable emotions and thought patterns help us see truth more clearly. An illness like this does affect our perceptions about life. It can drive us to harm those we love, believe things that aren't true, reject our faith, or take our own lives!

There are people that need medication to *maintain* a healthy state of mind. Repeated relapses weaken the brain, just like epilepsy seizures.

> *"I still don't think people understand this, and it is hard to convince them otherwise. I have tried explaining that we have something physically wrong with our brains, just as people with diabetes or heart trouble have something wrong with their bodies. I have read that a brain scan will actually look different. . . ."*
>
> *-'Kayla'*

We may find even doctors and therapists disagree on how and when to use medication. Some see medications as inferior and only use them as a last resort while others slap them on with little thought. We need to be alert to imbalanced approaches, and not be too intimidated to ask questions or get another opinion. Welcome the input of other people! They can help us understand our doctors or communicate how we are actually functioning (or not functioning.)

It is easy to become inconsistent with our medication doses; we disagree with the diagnosis, don't like the side effects, our doctor, or simply don't like having our blood drawn. Other times we just forget, because it isn't all that important to us. Renewing medications can be a pain and paying the bills drains our wallets. For some of us, fighting help is a part of the illness. We may miss the pleasure of our high; we tend to forget there was ever a low. We feel just fine, and think we always will be. We can't imagine why we need medication to straighten things out. What needs straightened out?

Another reason we may fight medication is that we don't want to be considered sick . . . we want to be well! We resent that little pill that keeps us connected to our sanity. We resist therapy, because it constantly reminds us of our illness. We want to forget it all and move on with our life. But medication tempers our strong emotions, stabilizes our perceptions, and keeps us from ruining our lives and relationships. It helps us to be able to help ourselves.

One woman testified of feeling completely helpless, locked inside her malfunctioning mind. Looking back on her manic condition she said, "I knew I needed help, but I couldn't say it!" Someone else likened it to being "mentally paralyzed." It is very difficult when someone fights our help, but do we consider they may be unable to help themselves? Why ignore their need when it has the potential to cost them their life? Anyone who has suffered mental illness echoes this cry! I believe God is merciful and sees our best efforts in spite of the results. And I believe His heart cries for the suffering of the helpless ones.

3. How will my doctor know what kind of medication I need?

Many of life's failures are people who did not realize how close they were to success when they gave up.
THOMAS EDISON

To determine if you need medication and what kind, the doctors will ask you a lot of questions:

Have there been major changes in your life lately—such as the death of a loved one, a major move or job loss, or the birth of a baby? Do you have persistent negative and hopeless feelings? Do you have trouble falling or staying asleep, or do you sleep too much? Are you tired or lacking energy most of the time? Do you have a poor appetite or find yourself overeating? Are you overly anxious? Do you have trouble concentrating on things, such as reading? Do you move or speak so slowly that it is noticeable to others, or are you extra fidgety or restless? Are you hurting yourself or others? Are you thinking a lot about death or wishing to die?

These things may be difficult to admit, but be honest with yourself and your doctor! It is critical in order for him to be able to help you. Your doctor is not being nosy; he is simply trying to understand the whole picture. If talking to a doctor makes you too nervous, or you can't think clearly at the time, it might help you to write everything down ahead of time.

If your doctor prescribes a medication, remember that it is only his best guess. Be sure you are communicating clearly with them about the effects of your medication. Some kinds work better than others; some may not work at all, or may actually aggravate your problems. For instance, an antidepressant may intensify mood swings. This is a very common mistake when bipolar is mistaken for mere depression. Be prepared! It is not as simple as 'putting a band aid on' because many of us try different medications before we find what works. The fact that most drugs take at least six weeks to really start working makes this a *long, discouraging process.*

Medication often has side effects, but most certainly not all the ones mentioned. Finding the right balance of positive results and negative side effects is a trial and error process. In my experience, one kind increased my appetite, another made my ears ring, and still another made me feel sluggish. When we finally found one that helped, I gained weight rapidly. In time, we hit upon one that kept my mood stable with no side effects. It was worth everything!

Bob Olson, the author of *Win the Battle,* tried all the medications available at the time and still suffered tremendously. After several unsuccessful shock treatments, his persistent doctor once again started over the list of medications. Amazingly, the third one on the list clicked. Bob's life changed with a second try at lithium. Never give up! The answer may be just around the corner.

MEDICINES

The introduction of medications to treat mental illnesses is a relatively recent development in the history of medicine and no doubt reflects the gradual acceptance by doctors and the public that mental illnesses are in fact illnesses that arise from the disorders within the brain. Most of the medications in use target chemical systems that are believed to be disturbed by the illness. Tricyclic antidepressants, MAO inhibitors, and SSRIs more or less increase norepinephrine, dopamine, or serotonin to stimulate people out of depression. Antipsychotics like Thorazine and sedatives like Valium or Ativan block the stimulatory effects of the dopamine & nor-epinephrine to help suppress acute mania. The observation that one class of medications, the antidepressants, could cause mania and a very different class of medications, catecholamine-blockers, could cause depression, long suggested that bipolar illness may represent abnormal cycling of activity in these chemical systems.

In about 1-2% of patients, treatment of a depressive illness – post-partum or post-traumatic - with Prozac or another serotonin re-uptake inhibitor (SSRI) induces mania or hypomania. Medication-induced mania is then treated with antipsychotic drugs or mood stabilizers. The side effects of these drugs range from somnolence and fatigue, to uncontrolled movements in some people. On the other hand, some people have little to no side effects.

By definition, Bipolar Disorder is first recognized because of mania - days without sleep, grandiose ideas, compulsive activities, uncontrollable behaviors, drug use, gambling, and risk-taking behaviors. Mania may also include obsessions with work or sex or art or religious ideas. When mania is the presenting problem, instead of depression, treatment starts with antipsychotics and/or mood stabilizers and/or Lithium.

Regardless of the historical success of these medications in treating the symptoms of bipolar illness and depression, no one should claim that they correct the underlying cause of the disease. Taking medication for Bipolar Disorder can make you more stable only for as long as you take them. If you stop them, you will eventually find out that the Bipolar Disorder is still there.

ECT – ELECTRO-CONVULSIVE THERAPY

For severely depressed, paranoid, suicidal, hospitalized patients, electroconvulsive therapy (ECT) remains a mainstay of treatment.

When my mother was admitted – against her will, (she was legally committed) to the Psychiatric Floor of the Community Hospital in Harrisonburg Virginia, and later to Johns Hopkins University Hospital in Baltimore, I was told by the attending psychiatrists at both hospitals - "Dr. Morton, we can try any medication your mother or you or other family members wish to suggest, but I will tell you that given the severity of her illness with paranoid depression and her history of prior, prolonged hospitalizations for the same illness that she is not likely to recover significantly or leave this hospital until she has had ECT therapy. This old and crude therapy remains the most effective therapy we have for her illness."

I simply could not believe in modern times that this could be true but so-it-was.

Rapid Transcranial magnetic stimulation is now sometimes used as an alternative. Deep brain stimulators, which are widely used in medication-resistant Parkinson disease, DYT-1 dystonia, and other movement disorders, may become the modern replacement for transcranial ECT for intractable illnesses.

-D. Holmes Morton, M.D.

4. What about therapy or counseling?

Genetic-based mental illnesses are often fraught with trauma. Learning to deal with them is traumatic enough, not to mention the stresses that brought them to the surface! Struggling alone for years with an illness without the proper kind of help usually rolls out a string of problems over and beyond the illness itself. Medication alone may do the job, but therapy and/or counseling is often needed to simply put the pieces back together again.

> *The **first** tool for persistence is to imagine how your future will be when you get better. The **second** is to focus on what is good in your life, rather than what is bad. The **third** is to develop your sense of humor.*
> BOB OLSON
> *Win the Battle*

Since few doctors do the work of both a psychiatrist and a therapist, it often takes a team. This makes us vulnerable, but is critical for recovery! Ask for recommendations from your ministry, a family doctor, people who work in the mental health field, or others who have struggled with mental illness. When trying a therapist, ask if they have *experience* with your specific condition and if so, to what extent. If they don't, find someone who has! A good therapist also has medical expertise and a conscientious way of relating; that is, careful to do no harm and not leaking information about his clients. We are able to benefit a lot more from someone we feel is competent and caring about our problems. If their manner or personality makes us feel threatened or uncomfortable, we probably won't benefit from their input. Their effectiveness hangs heavily on our ability to trust their advice. It is extremely important that you can trust your therapist. It may take some precious time to test this out!

Since this type of illness is so intertwined with our basic beliefs about life, it is important to find a therapist who respects and encourages our Christian beliefs. Having someone stay closely involved in therapy sessions can be a safeguard. If we are threatened in this area, it is important to change therapists, even if they have been helpful otherwise. However, deciding *not* to try therapy because of that risk robs us of a very powerful tool!

There are different kinds of therapy:

Cognitive therapy deals with day to day coping behavior rather than digging through the past. It teaches patients how to live with their illness: thinking right about a problem instead of letting it overwhelm them, establishing good sleep habits, dealing with strong emotions, painting 'word pictures' (put a continual worry on a 'leaf' and let it float down the stream), and getting back to the facts by talking about them or writing them down (I do have a good mind—I just need to learn to use it. This too shall pass.)

Family therapy is used when it seems like helping the family to relate differently would help the problem. Mental illness multiplies problems! When an existing illness is ignored or shoved under the carpet, it has a domino effect on the whole family. It is confusing if a parent is acting strangely and no one seems to see it or do anything about it. Ignoring the problem gives a signal of approval. As a result, children may conclude the behavior is normal even though their 'gut feeling' tells them otherwise. This is very crippling!

"Mom attacks anything that disturbs the routine she happens to be in, which right now consists of meticulously sweeping the carpet. Sometimes I sit behind the sofa until she forgets about her obsession. I just can't figure it out. Dad sticks his head in the door and stares wearily at her, and then disappears. When she gets me to sweep the beloved, old carpet for her, he nods his head and says, "Just do what she says, Mike." What hurts most is that she doesn't seem to see me. Neither

> *does Dad. It seems like I just don't matter anymore. I go to the neighbors to get away from it all, but I feel guilty there too, because I'm starting to like their videos pretty much. I know my parents would not approve. My friend tells me to just get over it. He says it's a good way to pass the time because no one really cares, anyhow."*
>
> *-'Mike'*

It is important to use a trained therapist, not a lay counselor, unless they are able to recognize the effects of an illness. They should refer you to a good doctor without wasting a lot of precious time, avoiding serious harm. Counseling is rarely beneficial until a certain measure of mental stability is gained. Bible studies and long, intense conversations only snowball the illness! When the one needing help is not able to process what is being said and apply it positively, it becomes not only unproductive, but harmful. Progress is full of little nudges in the *right* direction . . . more than a nudge, or a wrong nudge, overwhelms the weary mind.

> *It is what it is. It will become what you make of it.*
> ANON

Since the results of abuse and a genetic-based mental illness LOOK so similar, people tend to lump them together. It may be difficult to pinpoint the actual problem. However, it is interesting to note the effects of a biological illness are often so severe it would take something as traumatic as a 'concentration camp' experience to produce such a phenomenon through trauma only.

When relating to a troubled person who had past trauma such as abuse, beware if the effects seem exaggerated far beyond the degree of trauma, or they seem "stuck" in it. They are very likely also dealing with an ill mind.

Well-meaning mentors may address stressors without making an effort to stabilize the mind, the worst stressor of all! This approach only adds more stress, worsening the situation. Stabilizing the mind *first* through medication helps us be much more capable of receiving something beneficial from counseling or therapy.

What common issues do abuse and genetic-based mental illnesses cause?

- We both try to avoid truth.
- We both deal with shame, anger, confusion, and pain.
- Self- protection is a logical response for both of us.
- We both face slow and difficult healing processes.
- We both struggle to trust.
- We both tend to blame rather than embrace our pain.
- We both find it difficult to parent the next generation.
- We both face an attack to the core of our psyche, causing us to ask "Who am I?"

These are the similar faces of abuse and mental illness. However, there is a critical difference.

When someone has been abused, the key to ultimate healing is forgiveness. When someone is mentally ill, the key to ultimate healing is acceptance. How does this basic difference shape the type of help we need?

1. WHAT IS A LIE IN ONE CASE MAY BE THE TRUTH THE OTHER.

Abuse—I must not trust myself, my feelings, or my perceptions. Lie.
Mental illness—I must not trust myself, my feelings, or my perceptions. Truth.
Abuse—"I am powerless." Lie.
Mental illness—"I am powerless." Sometimes this is true!

Abuse—"I must not feel so strongly." Lie.
Mental illness—"I must not feel so strongly." Truth. We need to learn to downplay our strong feelings, maybe cut them in halves or quarters.

2. WE HAVE DIFFERENT STRUGGLES WITH CONTROL.

Abuse—I must stop habits of control and release my fears to God.

Mental illness—I must learn to differentiate between control that is helpful and control that is harmful. I need to watch for red flags; I also need to balance the need for consistent, predictable living on one hand, with letting go and learning to navigate the waters on the other.

3. A VICTIM OR NOT?

Abuse—I need to face the fact that I was a victim, and not responsible for the sin committed against me. Anything that distorts or silences God's voice is sinful.

Mental illness—I am not a victim! Mental illness is not a form of abuse, in which our Creator is the perpetrator. My illness is a part of the fall, just like any other disease. I am not sinful because I have it, even though I may do wrong things in the struggle of learning to relate to it. God wired every human being with the capacity for deep and satisfying relationships with Himself and others. This is possible for everyone, including those who are mentally ill, if they can accept their illness and the help of other people.

4. THE SIGNIFICANCE OF "MENTAL BLANKS".

Abuse—I may have large memory gaps, or respond to particular emotional triggers by "going away."

Mental illness—I may 'tune out' to be able to cope with the effects of the illness or memory blanks may be an effect of the illness. Don't read too much into these blanks!

5. THE IMPACT ON A PERSON'S PERCEPTIONS, PAST AND PRESENT, CAUSES DIFFICULTY IN DISCERNING REALITY.

Abuse—I must face the truth and establish the facts.

Mental illness—Establishing facts can be nearly impossible. To those who are helping: Help the person confront what is not real or true, but use gentleness and discretion. Your goal is to help them process the feelings they are dealing with at the time, not necessarily to establish facts beyond the shadow of a doubt. Be very careful with suggesting things you do not know; suggestions can quickly become realities for someone who is struggling with unrealistic perceptions or foggy realities. They are already grasping to sort what is real and what is not. Particularly when dealing with sexual issues, use extreme caution. Abnormal sexual awareness and sensitivity are often part of the illness, along with other heightened sensory issues. Do not immediately assume this awareness to be an indicator of abuse!

The journey to getting a complete picture is full of danger because of ignorance, loaded emotions, and sometimes incomplete memories. Stories vary greatly; applying conclusions from one story to the next can be very harmful. It is very important to allow our minds to heal before we cement our conclusions! During an illness, retrospect tends to magnify, blocking our ability to trust or receive input from other helpful angles. Feelings overrule facts. Time and medication work together to restore equilibrium. Once we are strong enough to run our perspective through the perspectives of others, we establish truth. This is a learning process for all involved! Their ability to help us feel heard, empathize with our distress, agree where they can (instead of becoming defensive and reactionary) and help us decide how to move forward, saves the situation. It builds a bridge toward trust.

5. How can the community and extended family help?

> *Healing is a matter of time, but it is also a matter of opportunity.*
> HIPPOCRATES

SPIRITUAL SUPPORT

- Since those who are struggling often lose complete sight of God in the smog, you need to hold out truth, fanning hope and believing that things will get better. Pray for them! Prayer is more than merely thinking of someone—it is knocking on God's door and asking Him to bless them with the strength they need to endure their illness and speed the healing. Pray with them! Many times they are too weak or confused to pray, but hearing someone else brings peace and comfort. Write out your prayer and leave it where they can read it.

- Please remember that just because they are struggling with a mental illness does not mean they are bad or evil. It does not mean they or their families did something wrong . . . many traumas are simply a result of life on earth. Very likely, in their search to figure things out, they are already consumed with self-reproach. Condemning them spiritually for this type of struggle will only add to their shame, giving them a downward shove. We all have areas that need growth, but there is a right time to address these things. This is not the time!

- Maintain a positive, hopeful attitude, even when it is difficult. Look for small signs of progress, and be quick to point them out. It keeps them from feeling that they are simply a hopeless case. Your enthusiasm and joy gives them something to rest on when they feel nothing under their feet.

- Try to protect them and be sensitive to their emotional needs. Also, remember their families. They are under strain and stress as well. Try to relieve stress, not add to it! 'Charles', who has supported his ill wife for many years, shares the following observation:

> *This may be shocking news to you. The most difficult thing in my life has not been the fact that my father died when I was seven years old, and my mother committed suicide a couple years later or the fact that my wife has schizophrenia. . . . By far the most difficult thing in my life has been the way some people have reacted to my wife's illness. . . .*

PRACTICAL SUPPORT

- One of the biggest supports is trying to understand what they are working with. Read about it! Educating yourself helps you to identify which symptoms are parts of the illness and which may be the result of other issues. This allows you to help them in a redemptive way, forming ways of coping that will be helpful, not hurtful. The need for education about mental health issues is a growing concern among professionals. They are realizing more and more that medical help alone is not enough and that a key help to success is having the support of the community. Check into the *Mental Health First Aid* classes that can be taken on the Phil Haven premises.

> *I sought my soul,*
> *but could not see;*
> *I sought my God,*
> *He eluded me.*
> *I sought my brother—*
> *And found all three!*
> UNKNOWN

'Charles' continues:

> *One of the main reasons we all have reacted in the wrong way to my wife's illness is ignorance. When we went to school, we were basically taught the three R's and perhaps some geography and health lessons. None of us took a course on schizophrenia . . . we have to admit that not one of us has even taken a ten minute course on it, let alone a ten week course.*

No wonder we were and perhaps still are ignorant. It would have been a real blessing if my wife's illness would have united us instead of dividing us; drawn us together, instead of causing us to drift apart. But because none of us knew anything about schizophrenia, it is only natural that we came up with different ideas on what causes it and how to deal with it. The more I read about it, the less frustrating it became. And the more I learned about it, the easier it was to not blame my wife for her actions. She really didn't realize or know what she was doing after she became sick.

- Helping with trips to the doctor, meals, babysitting, or paying bills is a big boost to a family or individual who is struggling. Don't be overbearing, just available. They may be too weak to brave the roads by themselves or even fill up with gas . . . (it takes grit to pick up the phone and ask a friend to take us somewhere.) Sometimes just someone stopping by with some flowers or hearing a voice on the phone- maybe even a message on their voicemail- can be a bright spot.

- Keep your visits short; socializing often takes a lot of effort. For some, evening is a good time and for others, morning is better. Politely 'bow out' of intense conversations that seem to be going nowhere. Delusional or obsessive thinking will become more and more engrained if you argue or try to redirect or correct their faulty reasoning.

- Remember that in their state of mind, their feelings are the only things they can grasp. In severe cases, one of the best things to do is gently inform them that you are not in a place to help and encourage them to share with their therapists or doctors. For the fighters, persistently and clearly encourage them to listen to their doctors and take their medication. Do not despair! You never know when there may be a lucid moment!

- Always be respectful, calm, and straightforward, offering frequent praise or specific criticism. Sometimes you will need space, especially when either of you are upset . . . little good is done in the heat of the moment. Suggest that the discussion continue when everyone is feeling better. When a person is going thru a psychotic episode, they do not always know or remember what they are feeling, doing, thinking, or saying. Your feelings may be hurt, and the ill person may feel guilty afterwards, whether or not they remember what they did or said. At times like this, remember to not take their words and actions personally. This is much easier said than done!

- A listening ear encourages honesty. But you will probably hear things you would rather not hear. Don't be shocked, don't interrupt, don't change the subject, and don't contradict—number one, simply listen and give affirmation. A simple "You'll be OK" can be very comforting. Repeating what was said back to them can help them be aware of what they just said. Was it what they really meant to say? Be present with your concern, but don't demand or expect much in return—sometimes they are silent for weeks simply because there are no words. If we desert them at this point, it deepens their sense of abandonment and loneliness. They desperately need a friend who will not leave, even in a crisis.

- Be patient while the medicines get sorted out. Give feedback about the changes you see while they go through the process of trying different things. Support what the doctors prescribe and don't make negative remarks, even if you personally would have chosen a different approach. Make sure that there is clear communication between the doctor involved and someone other than the one who is ill.

This cuts out unnecessary misunderstandings and provides missing puzzle pieces, both for the doctor and for the support people.

- Ask questions, but don't spread what is said all over the community. Try to discern what was *meant* to be said in spite of the strong language, garbled thoughts and incoherent phrases. And even then remember maybe nothing was meant by anything . . . they just *feel* so terrible. Respect them! Use the kind of respect that prompts police to put up barriers to deter curious onlookers at the scene of an accident. Don't stare or make fun of their helplessness or the stupid things they may say or do.

- Take what is said with a grain of salt and please be careful how you repeat these things. Shaming them secretly or in front of others will only encourage them to try to cover or deny their true condition. You may think you are hiding how you feel about them, but they are often more perceptive than they look. The way you relate to them feeds their beliefs about themselves! They are quick to perceive if you truly care or if you are simply out for a juicy story.

- Thoughts or talk of suicide always needs to be taken seriously. Too often we don't know how to relate, so we either ignore what they said or change the subject. The best thing a person struggling with suicidal thoughts can do is express it- it does not guarantee safety, but it may wake them up to the reality of what they are thinking of doing. Silencing them could push them into following thru with their plan. Help them contact their doctors and come up with a plan to help keep them safe. Your love and concern may remind them that while they don't see any worth in life, they need to stick with it for *your* sake!

- Remember to take a break yourself! Allow others to fill in for a time, even if you feel you are indispensable. It is crucial that you prevent your life from becoming as disorganized and chaotic as the life of the one who is ill. Figure out your own limits, keep active, and stay involved and interested in activities that do not include them. Make sure you are surrounded by people who are well.

- In his book *Holding out Hope,* Dr. Tony Byler talks about the helpfulness of a support team. This involves the formation of a small group of people from your community or specific church group that can give guidance and help with sensitive decisions, financial support, and encouragement in whatever form is needed. Because of the stickiness of family dynamics, it is best if these groups do not consist of family members. Meeting regularly with a group like this can prevent someone from falling through the cracks when they are too ill to reach out for help or to recognize their own needs. When groups like these have common goals and work together in a responsible way, they can be a great blessing.

It takes a lot of wisdom—how to help and when. What can you do when you see a parent who is ill and resisting outside help, with a partner who is either in denial or too afraid to reach out for help? It is heartrending to be on the outside looking in and feeling helpless to do anything for the little ones under their care. If you are caught *inside* of a situation like this, you need to face things honestly and go for help alone. It may even be necessary to involve someone with more authority such as the law if the need is greater than you have resources to meet. It is an act of love and service, even though the one you are trying to help will see it as hurtful, at least until they are well again. If possible, it is wise to discuss the problem with others before taking action and running the risk of making matters worse.

Special Support Groups (such as NAMI) for mental illness can also be helpful. Ask a doctor or a therapist if they are aware of any in your area, or hunt for a group within the surrounding church fellowships. These groups will consist of people who have this type of weakness or have a family member who does. I benefited greatly from a group like this, their sense of humor, cards, flowers, food, and prayer support was indispensable! Spending time with people who have similar experiences and difficulties can provide comfort and connections not found anywhere else. Expressing ourselves to others who understand what we are trying to say gives us validation, a sense of direction, and the ability to fight the hopeless loneliness that tends to encircle us. Tuning into the struggles of those around you reminds you of your own weak spots, and hearing the way they handle things gives you more 'tools'. We are often able to learn and accept things from each other that doctors and families have been trying, in vain, to tell us for years. The key lies in feeling understood.

I longed to talk to more women who went through anxiety and depression. I had many friends, but a lot were very busy or 'hadn't been there.' I called a close friend and wondered if she would like to go on a walk together. I can still feel the warmth and comfort over the phone. She said she'd love to! That fall and winter we walked every week. She invited another friend who had struggled with depression. Those two ladies, the walks and the friendships, were my LIFELINE! They were angels sent straight from God. I don't think they even realized it at the time because it was too discouraging to even admit or talk about. I felt so vulnerable and needy! I met others who struggled, and we talked about the need for a support group. We met at each other's homes once a month for several years. The journey, although not pain free, has been rich!

CRYSTAL A.

IMAGINE This Conversation . . .

Me: *I finally decided to go to a psychiatrist for my depression. It's really been getting bad.*
Solid, faithful good-hearted Mennonite: *Yeah, it probably was time. Did he prescribe anything?*
Me: *Yes. I'm on Prozac. I can tell a difference already.*
SFG-HM: *That's good.*

Now IMAGINE This:

Me: *I finally went to the doctor about my asthma. I've been coughing constantly.*
SFG-HM*:* *Oh. (Long pause) You did? (Another pause) Well . . . I hope that was wise. Who did you go to? Did someone you trust recommend her? Is she a Christian? Where did she go to school? Is she a naturopath, D.O. or M.D.? So many doctors today are schooled in humanistic philosophies that they can hardly tell truth from error even if they're Christians. I don't know. Why don't you ask the ministry to pray for you first? Did she put you on any medication?*
Me*:* *Yes, I'm on Advair. I can tell a difference already.*
SFG-HM: *Oh my, I don't know. Are you sure you need it? That stuff can really mess with you. I think you need to really seek the Lord about unconfessed sin in your life, first of all. I have a feeling you are jealous of Sadie Gingerich and how well she does with her blog compared to you. And there might be a root of bitterness because the girl you wanted for Matt went and married someone else. And you haven't been coming to sewing circle. You really need that fellowship, you know. And you've been so busy, I have a feeling you haven't spent much time in the Word. Maybe Emily can make*

breakfast for the family so you can read your Bible in the morning. You really have to get to the heart of what this asthma is all about.
Me: *Yes, well, I have been busy. And you're probably right about the Advair. But it IS nice to be able to sleep at night.*
SFG-HM: *I know people who have had a lot of success with ginger root and sphagnum moss for asthma. You make a tea and drink it in the evening. I'd be much more comfortable with that myself, rather than all these chemical things that you have no idea how they'll affect you in the long run and really, they just mask the issues. Asthma affects your breathing, and breathing affects every area of your life, you know. So please, just really be careful.*

Maybe there are times that we over-spiritualize our mental and emotional illnesses and under-spiritualize our physical disorders. We tend to treat physical ailments like they're on a different plane than mental or emotional issues. The truth is, you can make a good case for my asthma and Seasonal Affective Disorder being equally spiritual in origin, requiring an equally spiritual solution. On the other hand, maybe they are both entirely physical in nature. You could make a pretty good case either way. Either way, I should seek help from the Lord first, lest I be like Asa in 2 Chronicles 20.

In the thirty-ninth year of his reign Asa was afflicted with a disease in his feet. Though his disease was severe, even in his illness he did not seek help from the Lord, but only from the physicians.

-Dorcas Smucker

Vessels

God uses those we shove aside,
He sees beyond the surface side.
He takes His time—we run along
in search of men we think are strong.
He stops to touch the bowed-down head,
the muddy shoe, the broken bread . . .
He sets to work the feeble feet
the tattered coat, the simple sheep.
He uses those we shove aside
while blinded by our partial pride.

-Anita

Be Quiet and Listen

Be quiet and listen . . .
When pain is put into your hand,
do not rush to throw it away.
Hold it,
feel it,
ask for grace, and
listen . . .
If you hold it long enough,
Quietly,
you will notice
that you are changed;
you are stronger;
your heart will never go back
to its original size.

Look!
The hands that hold you
have nail holes in them.
You are sharing,
and through sharing
quietly,
you will be made perfect.
From strength to strength comes with
from pain to pain, not before.
You are changed more
from one hour of suffering than
from ten hours of instruction.
Be quiet and listen . . .
In quietness is your strength.

-Ivan R. Martin

TRANSFORMATION THROUGH PRAYER

A wilderness, such desert waste!
The barren place, oh, what disgrace!

Someone has seen with heart so keen;
And sent a faithful prayer unseen.

Desert transformed! Christ did the art,
His healing grace He did impart.

A fruitful field, a smiling face;
A rose to bloom and fill its place.

Keturah W.

WHAT GOES UP MUST COME DOWN . . .

I became insane,
with long intervals of
horrible sanity.

EDGAR ALLAN POE

1. What are the clinical features of manic depressive or bipolar illness?

Manic depressive illness, commonly known as bipolar disorder, is a type of mental illness characterized by drastic swings in mood and function. These swings often occur over weeks or months, and sometimes even years. A minority cycle rapidly, swinging from a low to a high several times a day. Rapid cycling is especially difficult because the issues are always shifting. By the time we recognize what is happening (if we do at all!) we are swung into the opposite set of problems. Just like some of my poems indicate, it keeps us reeling. Life flips from slow motion to fast motion without letting us catch our breath!

One step forward,
two steps back,
it seems that life
just has no lack,
Of trouble.

It hovers near like
morning fog
Or marshes full of
murky bog,
and rubble.

Or like the wind it
comes and goes
Bobs up and down
thru all its woes
Like bubbles.

One step forward
Two steps back
A dance that never
got the knack
Just wobbles.

ANITA

I did not develop the 'classic' kind, known as Bipolar I—I have been diagnosed with bipolar 2, a secondary and milder form of the illness. I suffered severely from lows, but experienced the highs as pleasant breaks, not as terrifying, uncontrollable surges of energy and emotion. My doctors call this *hypomania,* which is simply a low-grade mania. This condition brings surges of great creativity, brimming with physical and mental health without the excruciating edge of losing control. When hypomania escalates into a full-blown mania, people lose touch with reality and become *psychotic.* I will explain psychosis a little later in this chapter. I have experienced touches of this, but not the extreme, which is often present with bipolar 1. Also, in spite of my painful depressions and the resulting wish to cease existing, I was never suicidal.

By reading the autobiographies of other bipolar sufferers, I realize that I have been spared some of the more frightening and frustrating aspects of the illness. However, I can identify with many things. Some of their experiences coincide with mine and I have finally met a clan of people who not only know what's really painful, but what can be really humorous! I am not met by blank looks.

Mania, or hypomania, affects behavior in shocking ways. Because of our rapid thought processes, our 'normal stoppers' seem to shift or threaten to disappear completely! We try to do everything, including some of our wildest dreams, without stopping to think about the consequences. We become touchy and hard to live with. Life is lived excessively and impulsively . . . thinking and talking nonstop, being silly, planning big (including things that would normally intimidate or embarrass us), needing less sleep, and doing the unusual and difficult. We may astound you by walking out of a store with ten boxes of rubber bands, exceeding speed limits, filling our counters with baked goods, and rearranging furniture. In these highs, we feel bossy or elated, and discretion tends to go out the back door. Manias produce successful businesses, beautiful art, lovely flower gardens, and exquisite craft. But they also leave a trail of regrets in the shape of empty pocketbooks, broken relationships, and frustrated friends.

> *Manic Depression distorts moods and thoughts, incites dreadful behaviors, destroys the basis of rational thought, and too often erodes the desire and will to live. It is a quicksilver illness that can both kill and create. . . . It has been a fascinating, albeit deadly enemy and companion, seductively complicated, a distillation of what is finest in our natures and what is most dangerous.*
> KAY REDFIELD
> *An Unquiet Mind*

Lows bring foggy brains, buckets of tears, fears of being alone, suspicions, and the desire to sleep forever. They can be terrifying, giving the sensation of being drowned. While the euphoria of a mania infuses a heavenly feeling of being perched on the tippity-top of a wave, a low sinks us under the waves, pulling us along with the dangerous undercurrents. We wonder if and when we will ever see light again. We are dragged into the stagnant hold of a foreboding, eerie existence. It smells of sorrow and pain, the death of inspiration, and sounds like the pulsating efforts of a life struggling to live, or a train as it screeches to a halt.

Life is painfully empty and discouraging; it tempts us to tuck ourselves into a recliner for the day and sink into oblivion. But our minds fight on, vulnerable and alive. While crippling, immobilizing feelings take over our body, our minds are often deluged with images of death and decay, evil forebodings, and gore. In our turmoil, we feel like we look odd—grotesque—crippled. One young lady told me "I feel like I have wrinkles all over my body!" Is it any wonder we withdraw socially or hate to go out into public?

During my illness there were times I felt like I had green hair! I could identify with the zebra with red stripes, the giraffe with a short neck, and the baby calf that said "M-a-a" instead of "M-o-o". It may be debatable if this sense of social strangeness is a part of the illness, or if it is an emotional response to it, but it definitely adds to our feelings of being abnormal. It also contributes to the struggle for acceptance among our peers. Too often in Plain circles, 'different' is simply not acceptable; this way of thinking triggers a whole set of problems for us. We tend to react, becoming insecure and critical of others or holding everyone around us spellbound with our animated chatter. Our excited condition leaves us completely unaware of other people and how we may be affecting them. We deny we are ill and refuse help from others. To do this would be to admit (horrors!) that we are different.

I have been asked the question "Does Bipolar illness define who you are?" The sense of concern that often accompanies that question makes me stop and think. What do they mean—"*Who I am?*" Don't our specific types of struggles help to define us? Don't they—as the dictionary says- explain and clarify the meaning of things—at least in part? Doesn't my illness, in its own way determine what limits I have? Yes, in some ways my illness does define me. And I am quite sure that my struggles affect me as a whole. However, that does not have to threaten who I am in God. I can still be a 'broken vessel' for Him.

Oh, no, not this again. I shake my head, hoping to shake off the foggy feeling. Help me, what is wrong? Why are things going so slow? I try to comb my hair and my arm feels heavy, weighted. I struggle to lift it. I feel like I just moved a big stack of wood . . . like I'm walking through mud. My birthday? Rue the day! What year are we in? I can't think . . . can't remember. . . .

Please leave me alone, this is embarrassing. I may as well sleep; bury myself into my pillows, down under where no one can reach me. Down far enough and long enough to totally escape reality.

I don't want to BE.

Why are you making so much noise . . . silence, please! Don't talk so loud! Ouch, that hurts like crazy, please don't touch me! I wish I were in bed, sleeping.

Everything is so frustrating, I feel like hitting. Oh no, did my fist fly through the air? I didn't want to do that, but all this noise and hurt is pushing me over the edge. Out! I need to get out of here . . . go to bed where hopefully I can sleep this off. Maybe when I wake up things will be different.

I'm so tired, I could sleep for days. I don't feel like living either. Why am I still alive? Every breathe hurts, every thought smells of death, coffins, blood, and mangled, crippled bodies.

There is a bruise on my daughter's leg. Horrors, did I do that? Did some of the things flying through my mind actually happen? Maybe I am dangerous, out-of control like I feel.

Help! I need to go for help. Get me out of here! Get me to bed.

Must we go away? No thanks. My face feels contorted . . . my hair green. I feel crippled . . . like I should be in a wheelchair. I try to talk, but my mouth doesn't want to move. That lady is staring at me. Panic! What is she seeing? Can she read my face—does she see how completely out of sync I am?

In church I slowly followed the words of the song . . . the mournful words make me feel like crying. "When grief comes o'er me like a flood, my brightest day be turned to night, one thing remains . . .our God is good. . . ." Really? I look around. Everyone is singing heartily like they believe it. Why am I here? I should be at home sleeping where I won't do anything stupid. I feel like standing up in church and waving my arms . . . I have an urge to yell at all the hypocrites. Fake people. But then, I can't afford to be real with them, either. They would avoid me, criticize me, and condemn me. They are people with all their ducks in a row . . . people without any problems.

I really don't trust anyone . . . even God. Where is He? Does He even exist? These people are all out to get me . . . ruin me! I am being shot at from all sides. They are all sick of me, trying to figure out a way to get rid of me.

Home again. "You put that away, how many times do I have to tell you? No, wash the dishes first or next you'll forget. Didn't you make your bed yet? Oh no, well then go do that right now. That should have been done first thing way back there at the start of this awful day, no, just please leave the house so I can THINK." A huge sigh and I sink into a chair in a quiet room, trying to tolerate my own muddled, befuddled brain.

Wouldn't a cherry pie, some apple crisp, some cookies, and a chocolate cake be good? And I haven't made granola for ages. Come to think of it, that room looks awkward. I believe the sofa would look better in that corner, and I think I'll change those white curtains for that red flowered pair I have in the attic. Hey, those windows are dirty. When did I wash them last? Maybe I should run to Pinky's to see if they have a nice bookshelf and stop in at the greenhouse for a fern to hang in that one corner (while I am there I buy four other plants).

In the book store, I buy everything that I think might be helpful in my present condition—about eighteen booklets in all. Self-injury, OCD, becoming a Woman of Discretion, Asperger Syndrome, Sexual Sin, Bad Memories, Angry at God?, God's Love, It's all About Me, Self-Esteem, Depression, Just One More, A.D.D., Suicide, The Look, Man's Psychology . . . and even one on Marriage. I need them all. (In the following low I shove them into my bottom desk drawer, and forget about them.)

I always say shopping is cheaper than a psychiatrist.
TAMMY BAKKER

Rummaging thru my studio, I dig out my easel and set it up. I dig out my paints. Ideas flood my mind and I sort out the one that appeals the most. The painting flows onto the canvas, the picture expresses the sentiments I want to convey.

During the night, I wake up. I feel alert but calm. My mind hums and churns, like a concrete mixer working a message into the right consistency. It tosses phrases around until they become a poem. I get up, turn the light on and scribble down an eight stanza poem. Then I crawl back into the warmth and try to slow things down. Life scenes flit in and out and slowly fade into unconsciousness. When morning dawns, I excitedly face the busy day.

I am s-o-o happy! I didn't know life could get this heavenly! I really have gotten somewhere . . . see my silver wings and golden halos? God is so real. I just feel Him everywhere! He has blessed me with health and lovely children and a super husband and wonderful friends. I am the most blessed person in existence! Deck the halls with wreaths of holly- tra la la la la la la la la, tis the season to be jolly- tra la la la la la la la la . . . oh, that I'd be more like molly, tra la la la la la la la la, it would end all of this folly, tra la la la la la la la la. I feel silly and creative, full of spark and full of life.

Out of breath, I hurried into the doctor's office. "At least the police didn't get me that time", I remarked loudly. I was still uptight from the drive through a busy city. Eyebrows went up. A nurse showed us to a room and entered information into the computer. I eyed what she was doing, then jabbed a finger at her. "What did you enter? That's not right. You filled it in wrong. Here, let me do it. . . ." I bossed her, leaning towards her. She frowned and left the room.

Our faithful, old doctor entered the room. "How can I help *you*?" he asked with an amused twinkle. "It's not me, it's him. . . ." I replied indignantly, pointing at our son stretched out on a table. We talked things over and when the doctor gave me some information about a medication, I asked for his pen and scribbled the notes on my hand. When I was done, I gaily slipped the pen back into his pocket. He looked at me oddly.

> *There is a thin line between what is considered zany and what is thought to be – a ghastly but damning word- "inappropriate" and only a sliverish gap exists between being thought intense, or a bit violate or dismissively labeled "unstable."*
> KAY REDFIELD
> *An Unquiet Mind*

What does mania look like?

Ever since I was a child, I had a huge imagination. With my colorful way of living, symbolism was a real fascination to me. It was core to my way of thinking, and it really came out in time of mania. My mind worked overtime to make sense of my worlds, and symbolism was a real tool in attempting to make this happen. Things that could not be defined were as unclear as 'the water spots on the ceiling in the dark', when I was a child. I carried that formative thought processing into adulthood, and when things became unclear, my foggy mind "drew pictures" of the shadowy and shady things until I had them shaped and shaded as real. Any person I saw, book I read, conversations I overheard, were alive and real and apt to playing a part in my unreal world.

In my extremely high times, I thought I was already living in heaven. Life couldn't get better. I would sing at the top of my lungs. . . . I could handle life and all the lives of those around me. If I made one meal, why not make three or four while I was at it? Life was to be lived with no limits. God was good and the whole world should know it! No one could stop me. I heard the voice of God in ways no one else could interpret, and for them to challenge it, was to challenge the personal voice of God. I could go three days on five to six hours of sleep with short naps.

When I was in the hospital, a person in white was an angel, the temp in my room defined if I was in fiery hell or cold isolation, an announcement over the intercom gave some interpretation to what I was facing or direction as to what I would do next. One walk I took with my sister, the sun felt so warm and large I kept my eyes glued to it, perceiving that Christ was returning. Then I would act it out. Things were enlarged and out of proportion, but to me they were reality.

One of the ways to decipher if I was coming out or increasing in mania was to note the height and depths of the swings, also the width . . . how long until the mood would swing again. The faster and deeper the swing, the more we were headed into mania. When the swing lessened in speed and intensity, the more we were headed into reality. There was little warning to myself and others, and it didn't take me extremely long to "get ahold of things" and return to reality. But returning to reality meant a lot of things to sort through, pieces to pick up, relationships to mend, and trust to be rebuilt. But as I look back to the four major episodes since my one eighteen years ago, I am thankful and humbled that each time more reality was returned to me.

-by C. J. L.

Features of Bipolar Illness . . .
Centre for Clinical Interventions

MANIA is an extreme mood state of this disorder. It describes an abnormally elevated, euphoric, driven and/or irritable mood state. *Hypomania* is the term given to the more moderate form of elevated mood. It can be managed often without the need for hospitalization as the person remains in contact with reality. However, it is very easy to move rapidly from hypomania into a manic episode. Symptoms of mania include:

Irritability

Irritability as described in the Oxford dictionary means "*quick to anger, touchy.*" Many people, when in an elevated mood state, experience a rapid flow of ideas and thoughts. They often find that they are way ahead of other people in their thinking processes, already onto another idea before people around them have grasped the first concept. Because of this rapid thought process, they become easily angered when people don't seem to comprehend their ideas or enthusiasm for some new scheme.

Decreased need for sleep

One of the most common symptoms of mania and often an early warning sign is the increased experience of energy and lack of a need for sleep. This is often because the rapid flow of thoughts and ideas tend to keep people awake, exploring new schemes and plans.

Rapid flow of ideas

People who are becoming manic experience an increase in the speed at which they think. They move more quickly from one subject to another. Sometimes thoughts can become so rapid that they begin to make no sense, developing into a jumbled, incoherent message that the listener can no longer understand.

Grandiose ideas

It is common for people who are manic to think that they are more talented than others, or have unique gifts. As the person's mood becomes elevated, these beliefs can become delusional in nature, with people often believing they are famous people, or that they have been put on this planet for a special purpose (*often religious beliefs can become very intense, and take more significance than usual.)*

Uncharacteristically poor judgment

A person's ability to make rational decisions can become impaired and they may make inappropriate decisions or decisions that are out of character.

Increased sexual drive

People when they become manic often experience increased libido, and make less well-judged decisions about sexual partners

DEPRESSION is a mood state that is characterized by a significantly lowered mood. Its severity, persistence, duration, and the presence of characteristic symptoms can distinguish a major depressive episode, the other extreme mood state of bipolar disorder,, from a milder episode of (regular) depression. The most common symptoms of depression include:

Persistent sad, anxious, or empty mood

People often describe depression as an overwhelming feeling of sadness and hopelessness. They may lose the motivation to eat and experience a loss of enjoyment in the activities of everyday life that they used to take a lot of pleasure in.

Poor or disrupted sleep

A person when they are depressed often experience sleep disturbances, and this can be due to increased anxiety. They then find it difficult to fall asleep, or wake up frequently during the night worrying about day-to-day events or wake early in the morning and are unable to get back to sleep.

Feelings of worthlessness or hopelessness

Sometimes people become overwhelmed with a sense of their own inability to be of use to anyone, and can become convicted that they are useless and worthless. Thoughts may revolve around the hopelessness of the situation and the future.

Decreased interest in sex

As the person becomes more depressed, they gradually become less interested in social activities and sex.

Poor concentration

Thinking can become slowed and the person can have difficulty in making decisions. They find it difficult to concentrate on reading a book or on the day to day tasks such as shopping. This can often create anxiety or agitation in a person.

Thoughts of suicide, or suicide attempts

When a person becomes overwhelmed by their feelings of hopelessness and despair, they may have thoughts of ending their lives or make plans to commit suicide.

A **MIXED EPISODE** is characterized by the experience of both depressive and manic symptoms nearly every day for a period of time. The person experiences rapidly alternating moods, eg, irritability, euphoria, sadness, and there may be insomnia, agitation, hallucinations and delusions, suicidal thoughts, etc.

END OF QUOTE

Here is my experience with a mixed episode:

> *It was a rainy day and another bad day for me. My emotions changed like the tide of the ocean . . . in and out . . . I was left with a drained feeling mixed with restless spurts of energy. I lay down to rest, but my mind continued at such a speed that I got up again. Do something, I told myself. Anything! But I was too exhausted to think of what to do, much less do it. I walked from room to room, staring at all the projects beckoning at me, and yet, somehow, too tired to lift a finger. I felt like I was coming and going at the same time, swinging erratically from one side of the spectrum to the other.*
>
> *I sank back into a chair and my mind cascaded over a list of ideas for the next painting. There's the mama loon bending over her baby which is tucked under her wing, there's the moonlit night with the chilling breezes sweeping over the wild prairies, there's the chubby baby boy snuggled trustingly in the arms of his dad, there's the . . . I sighed and glanced toward my studio. Then I walked toward it and stared blankly at the motley assortment of paints on the table. I wished I could paint something today, but I was too tired, too discombobulated to do that. I wanted to eat . . . maybe it will boost my energy level.*
>
> *Once again I paced the house and sank into the sofa, hoping for blissful sleep, but my mind galloped on. I took a deep breath and buried myself deep under a furry blanket. I prayed "Lord, please slow me down and speed me up. . . ." Outside, the rain continued its consistent dripping.*

Unpredictable mood shifts pulled me hither and yon and dropped me into a different world in a matter of minutes, like the flipping of a light switch. They came and went as they pleased, without any rhyme or rhythm. Looking back, I remember specific days or events directly affected by these shifts of mood. Once for something special, Frank and I and our three little children went to a lovely lake a distance away from our coastal location. The trip was relaxing and beautiful, and we were excited because vacations were very rare. We got a hotel for the night . . . a lovely room situated on the side of the mountain, with an elegant courtyard surrounded with bougainvillea, my favorite flower. However, the next day I was overcome with a melancholy that would not loosen its grip for several days. I felt bad over everything, including the fact that we were on vacation. I felt fat and ugly, slow and boring. The blue sky, the exotic birds, the majestic mountains, the butterflies, the monkeys were all seen through a dark grey 'fog.' I scrambled to keep up with everyone's enthusiasm and felt bad for dampening their joy. I look back at the picture we took at the lake and see that I am smiling . . . somehow I did that. How is it? I look like a slim young girl, with three darling children and a wonderful husband.

For each ecstatic instant
We must an anguish pay
In keen and quivering ratio
To the ecstasy.

For each beloved hour
Sharp pittances of years
Bitter contested farthings
And coffers heaped with tears.

EMILY DICKINSON

2. What risk factors aggravate this disorder?

If there is no previous family history, there may be other triggers, such as drug or alcohol abuse, (even high amounts of caffeine can trigger an episode) injury to the head, neurological illness (encephalitis or multiple sclerosis) stress, change to sleep-wake cycle, conflict in ongoing relationships, overdose of antidepressants, and inconsistency with medication regimen. Stress can trigger the initial episode of bipolar disorder or increase the cycling. Types of stress include ***major positive life changes*** *(getting married, having a child, a promotion at work, buying a new home) and in contrast,* ***negative life changes*** *(death of a loved one, loss of a job or relationship, car accident, or development of a medical illness.)*

People with bipolar disorder are very sensitive to changes in the sleep-wake cycle. The time you go to bed, when you fall asleep, and when you wake up is critical. The lack of sleep (mania, or other causes) can trigger an episode and affect your mood. Sleep is so crucial that missing even a single night of sleep can upset a stable mood and trigger a manic episode. People with a disorder like this should find a job where they can work at the same time each day.

-A nurse

Within the bipolar diagnosis itself, there are variations in pattern and severity. While certain things contribute to the development of bipolar disorder, it is not caused by a person, event, or experience. Bipolar disorder tends to run in families, meaning first degree relatives of people with this disorder are at increased risk of developing it. Children of bipolar parents face an 8 percent risk, versus the 1 percent in the general population. Studies show that identical twins are more likely to develop it than fraternal twins. The sexes are equally affected by Bipolar I, whereas women are more prone to Bipolar II. However, symptoms in the general public often go undetected for years. It is common to have an eight year lag between the first depressive or manic episode and a correct diagnosis.

Many doctors feel it is strictly genetic—you won't get it if you don't have the gene for it. If the gene is powerful, it looms early in life, but when it is less powerful it may only be triggered by environmental factors. Just like having a genetic tendency toward high blood pressure—the actual problem may not surface until you gain weight, stop exercising, or face a lot of stress. You may not realize that you are susceptible until your life hits the right concoction of negatives.

It is also thought to be a 'whole body' disease, which simply means it is combined with abnormal variations in hormone levels, neurotransmitters in the brain, and daily body patterns. Thyroid disease has the ability to produce dramatic mood swings when the body produces too little thyroxine; even though it is a completely separate disorder, there is a connection between the two in some people. Seasonal changes seem to have a large impact on the severity of symptoms. The bleak, chilly days of fall and winter push our buttons, as well as hot, muggy weather. Some have found unbelievable relief by installing air conditioners or frequently taking cold showers.

There are unique hallmarks of classic bipolar illness. One common tendency is a denial of the illness. While some people think this happens because they are living in denial, doctors say this is actually part of the illness, like a paralysis in the brain. Dr. Xavier's book *I Am not Sick. I Don't need Help* gives many helpful insights on how to handle this kind of problem.

Another tendency is to be opinionated about who they like and their shifting moods (which may be determined by your acceptance or rejection) make it difficult to keep friendships. They may meet you at the door with a hug, or snap at you "What do you want?" insinuating that you are coming to hurt them. Even strong friendships shake under this kind of handling. When this kind of problem goes on for years, untreated and without adequate understanding, family rifts become deeply entrenched. Outside the plain communities, broken marriages are almost guaranteed. Inside the plain communities, marriages take incredible strain and sometimes permanent damage. To make things worse, family histories are often dotted with stories of suicide, drunkenness, and crazy episodes that are alluded to in hushed tones and knowing, but clueless, looks.

Along the way, I have met others dealing with similar things. Once while Christmas caroling, a particular lady caught my attention. Her animated expression revealed that she was totally absorbed in the mood of the moment as we sang. One child by her side had painted hair . . . a thick strip of red and green. His actions matched the color of his hair. (You are probably thinking—"No wonder he acts like a freak—he looks like one! "Maybe he looks like one because he feels like one?)

I made it a point to meet her, and was immediately drawn into deep and yet disconnected conversation. Her eye contact was as intense as her speech. I followed the trails and heard about extensive studies on Scripture, a sewing business, and the classes she offered. She exuded an independent stance to life, no doubt the result of a childhood that taught her to fight to survive. And then came the clincher. "By the way, my mom had bipolar disorder. Do you know what that is?"

I stifled the urge to hug her. Conscious of creating a scene in front of my startled church family, I calmly informed her that I did. Her son with painted hair appeared at her side and clutched her arm. "It's his social anxiety," she explained, and instantly a whole new ocean of topics opened up for us. But it was time to go. We said goodbye and agreed to keep in contact.

3. What is psychosis?

PSYCHOSIS is a state that sometimes occurs during a mental illness. A person who is psychotic experiences one or more of three basic symptoms: hallucinations, delusions, and disorganized thinking. These symptoms block their ability to stay in touch with reality and their own actions. One person described how this feels: "It's as if I'm flying a kite that is pulling higher and higher and the string slips out of my hand. There go my thoughts . . . I am helpless to pull them back down to earth again." It has also been described as 'looking on from a distance' or 'climbing or swimming upward' towards reality. Some people realize, at least to a degree, that something is wrong, but feel completely helpless. When they try to recall things that happened while they were psychotic, their memories are vague, exaggerated, or mixed up. The same lady says: "I tended toward psychosis when I lost too much sleep. I woke up so foggy- brained, I

> *Insane people are always sure they are just fine. It's only the sane people who are willing to admit they're crazy.*
> NORA EPHRON

didn't know what was real. Dreams, sights, and sounds blurred together, back and forth, from one to the other."

A HALLUCINATION is any sensory experience—sight, sound, smell, taste, and touch—not caused by an external reality. A person sees things that are not there, hears voices that do not exist, smells odors that aren't present, and feels nonexistent things crawling over them. These things are as real to them as the words on this page are to you. Some people learn to recognize that these experiences are different from reality, that it's simply a symptom of their illness, and ignore them enough to function normally. Others cannot tell the difference.

TEMPORARY FLASHES are mild hallucinations. Examples are seeing 'a knife' on someone's neck or seeing the road 'scroll up' in front of you while you are driving. As a child I felt persistent tickling sensations that I imagined were bugs. During the most severe phase of my illness, I experienced times when lighting changed, furniture shifted, and halls tilted. One time the baby I was holding seemed to slowly shrivel up. Things like this made me feel dangerous. Experiencing hallucinations or temporary flashes is distressing and needs to be shared. Even though we may know what we are experiencing is not real, it helps us relax if we can share with someone and get the help we need. Medication is very affective with this kind of thing.

A DELUSION is a false belief. People who are delusional may believe that others are trying to harm them, or that God is asking them to do things that are bizarre. They may be convinced that they have sealed their destiny by committing 'the unpardonable sin.' Religious delusions are especially distressing; often the person fears if the command is not followed through, God will punish them. Trying to convince them otherwise will often only strengthen their belief; they may even see you as Satan's messenger.

DISORGANIZED SPEECH reflects disturbed thinking and makes communication difficult. The person jumps from one topic to another, switching gears mid-sentence, answering questions only vaguely or maybe not at all. While some parts make sense, the discussion as a whole is incoherent. This is even more confusing if an hour later the same woman can sew a dress and explain what she is doing.

During psychosis, haunting things from the past may resurface; sorting past and present reality can be a real challenge. If this happens to you, write these things down and wait until you are well to analyze them. A wise counselor will not draw conclusions from what is said during times like this. TIME will help sort fact from delusion.

It should not need to be said if you or someone you love is psychotic, go for medical help immediately! Even though it may *seem* manageable, psychotic people can quickly become dangerous to themselves or others, and need careful medical supervision. Trying to handle the situation on your own is not wise. But be prepared—they may fight getting help, or at the doctor, shape up enough to avoid being admitted. Have your observations thought through and be ready to state them openly.

> *"I stopped and looked anxiously into the study. Dad was at his desk, muttering and scribbling nonsense on a paper. My heart skipped a beat; I knew this was one of the first signs. What shall I do? Call my sister? Call Mom? But Mom was shopping and I hated to bother her. The stress of the past days had been incredible and she needed a break. I picked up the phone and called my sister, who promised to be right over. I sighed with relief. There were many episodes like this but right now I was so tired. I knew what was next. Dad would become more and more agitated—mumbling senseless things, and throwing his weight around.*
>
> *But I knew at the same time that he was NOT fine. He seemed to know it too.*
>
> *I welcomed my sister, and we took Dad to his favorite rocking chair. He became very angry, threatening to hit us. We*

girls looked at each other, tears streaming down our cheeks. We couldn't believe that, once again, our life had filled with the drama of another spell of psychosis. How many more times will we have to go through this? Once before, we forced him into the car and went to the emergency room. When we finally got there, he sat calmly in his chair in front of the doctor and announced that he was just fine. Nothing is wrong with him! He acted so sane that the emergency personnel looked at us strangely and released him. Back at home, I cried miserably. What are we going to do? How long will we need to live with this type of stress?

Much madness is divinest sense
To a discerning eye;
Much sense the starkest madness
"Tis the majority
In this, as all prevails.
Assent, and you are sane;
Demur -you're straightway dangerous
And handled with a chain.
EMILY DICKINSON

Eventually we found answers for my Dad, when the fact that he needed help was obvious. It was amazing to see the change in him once he stabilized and I wondered why help had to be so long in coming! How did we get to this place? Couldn't we have caught the problem earlier? What could we have done different? How should we handle someone who fights the help they so desperately need? It felt like a cruel merry-go-around that was seemingly unavoidable."

-'Laura'

4. How can I cope with the swings?

Bipolar Illness is one of the more severe mental illnesses. The mood swings are especially disruptive and debilitating. They affect our relationships, how we think about ourselves, and our conclusions about life. Here are a few tips to help us keep our boat turned right side up:

If we see a light at the end of the tunnel, it's the light of an oncoming train.
ROBERT LOWELL

COMMUNICATE AND COOPERATE WITH YOUR DOCTOR

Follow your doctor's instructions (yes, I mean take your meds!) and stick by his side. Even though there may be times to ask for a second opinion, we should suspect ourselves if we keep jumping from doctor to doctor. Are we trying to avoid doing what we know we should do? Call him if your days are consistently low or if you are turning the house upside down in a high! He needs to know these details to make knowledgeable decisions on how to help you. We can't expect our doctors to help us if we aren't totally honest with them about what is happening, even when those details are hard to admit. (If you are the support person, take your responsibility to communicate seriously, even if it makes us angry at the time. It is well worth the risk!)

Because medication curbs our highs, and thus the bright, creative side of our personality, we need to keep the whole picture clear in our minds when we are deciding whether or not to stay on medication. I found that hypomania brought out and polished existing talents, but once the swings evened out and my illness receded, I painted less. The ideas, drive, and energy just wasn't there. Part of this may be because my energies were once again funneled into our family life, and I didn't need that type of outlet as much anymore. But I was still faced with a choice—my family or my art. Do I push to get off medication and pursue art, or do I take medication and fill my place in a functional family life? I still enjoy art, but in a sense I feel a loss; a missing of something that may have been. It was an aspect of my personality that could have blossomed had it not been so critical to remain steady for those I love. But Philip James Elliot was wise when he said, *"He is no fool who parts with that which he cannot keep to gain that which he cannot lose."*

Do we consider the input of those who live with us? We must try to grasp how our 'high and low times' affect them. What about the pacing at night, the flashes of temper, the disappearing money, the mounds of yarn in the closet, the animated, 'parrot-like' conversations? How about the uneasy worry at the edge of the mind that things will spin out of control? Living alone may avoid some of these problems—no one needs to be bothered by us and no one will be hurt—but even then we have the potential to be dangerous to ourselves and constantly in financial and relational crisis. Whether we are in a pleasant and productive high or in a crushing, suffocating low, it is difficult to reason properly.

"People think we would be delighted to return to normal, - but what is 'normal' after all? I hate the new, restrictive schedule and the medication that leaves me feeling less energetic. I feel like I lose a lot of time and a lot of ground. Other people tell me at least I'm acting normal, but I don't compare myself to that. I compare myself to what I used to be, to the 'best' of what I have been. I feel a loss—a slipping away of those glorious bright hours where everything shone and everything clicked."
'KERI'

Be sure you take the exact dosages of medication regularly. We are known for our irregularities . . . it is so tempting to start and stop at will. It is easy to think the problem is over once we start feeling better. But when we do this, it puts us at risk for the repeat of an episode; if medication is stopped suddenly, the risk of suicide increases. At first, we may be convinced we are better off without medicine, but remember—the lovely glow of success may simply be hypomania with a full-blown mania on its heels. Restarting your doses does not promise immediate relief because it takes a while for blood levels to stabilize. Sometimes it even loses its ability to help and you need to 'go fishing' for another kind—a process none of us like! We need to remember that getting help early and then STICKING with treatment helps to prevent our mood cycles. It is helpful to have an accountability person . . . someone who checks in occasionally to see if you really are taking your medication.

TRY TO RECOGNIZE YOUR OWN PATTERNS

What signals a high or low? Tuning into this can help you to counter the swings. For instance, connecting extra- super good days with a high prepares you for the disappointment you feel when you crash into the corresponding low. (The extra 'fluffy' feeling of a high has a way of making you feel like you've gotten over all of your problems. The low overwhelms you because all of a sudden those problems are back.) Be as realistic as you can. Try reasoning like this: Today I feel like baking 10 cherry pies. I suspect a high, so I'll only bake 3. Or Today I can barely function, so I suspect a low. I feel like sleeping all day, but I think I'll at least try to make a pie. There is something about this that helps you understand what is going on and protects you from feeling helplessly stuck. It enables you to face your problem realistically even though it doesn't take the swing away. I suspect in the case of true mania this kind of reasoning does not register at all.

> "*One key thing for me is to understand my sleep patterns. Too much sleep shuts me down. I lose vision for life and self-motivation. Too little sleep makes me more vulnerable to mania; I feel good, I'm more in control of my world, so it's commendable to be active and productive! To keep myself safe, I must know how much and what quantity of sleep I am getting. Since falling to sleep was slow for me, I have various aids. I have needed to use prescribed sleeping meds in extreme swings. In normal living, I listen to music, have twenty minutes of light reading, and do stretches and deep breathing to help my body relax. Since bipolar is a dysfunction in the front lobe of the brain, a warm wet washcloth on the forehead often reduces the pressure or tightness I experience when trying to sleep. Also, I learned to put weight, such as Stone Blankets or wet bath towels, on my restless legs or tight muscles that refuse to relax. I try to ignore their messages which dictate that I should "get going" which results in a lot of pacing. Lying flat on my back*

usually increases mind activity and nightmares. Finding good sleep positions has been very valuable."

-C. J. L.

HANG ON THRU YOUR HIGHS!

Are you feeling agitated? Are you sailing through with less sleep than usual? Are you waving your arms unnecessarily, or spitting out a steady stream of words? Does nothing move fast enough for you? If you see signs of an oncoming high slow down, and think. Have a well-rehearsed rescue plan in place and use it! Establish accountability people who help channel your energies the right direction. Little things, such as a regular quiet time, or simply saying less in a crowd does help. They highlight proper boundaries in your mind, helping you stay in touch with your emotions and actions. They keep you out of victim mode, reminding you to take responsibility where you can. Here again, if you lose complete touch with reality, this type of reasoning is out of reach.

Acknowledging what is going on is step number one and verbalizing it is step number two. And do take your meds faithfully . . . while they have the potential to cut back on the creativity and energy surges you experience, they also prevent the embarrassment and regret caused by your impulsive excitement.

HANG IN THERE THRU YOUR LOWS

Lows tend to creep up on us unawares; the lingering effects of the fading high blinds us to what is happening. The ugly, tired feelings that take over make us feel dangerous, lonely, and afraid. Recognizing these red flags helps us stay ahead of other problems. When they start waving, adjust your schedule and wait it out! When you wake up with that heavy feeling, and you simply want to bury yourself in a hole for the day, shift gears accordingly. A day like this is often full of tiny steps, doing things one at a time as you are able. Have a 'low-day' plan that allows you to cut corners, because everything you do will take longer. Don't become angry at yourself! Remember, if the downward spiral continues, you may reach a point where you are too low to go for help. Reach out BEFORE you get there.

Be aware of how your low affects others. It is easy to lash out angrily; we need to be very careful we are not taking our frustration and pain out on others. If you realize you are doing this, leave the room and find a quiet place where you can pull yourself together. Think about what you could do to alleviate the situation.

Put in positive time by doing something that relaxes or refreshes you. This may mean taking a walk, calling a good friend, or simply combing your hair. Keep your thoughts as positive as possible. When reality is painfully negative our thoughts naturally become negative. It takes special work to push them the right direction. Here again, severe lows can dip us beyond the ability to do these things. These are simple suggestions for managing *what you can.*

BE CREATIVE!

One of the beautiful parts of our intense and deep emotions is the gifts that come along with them. We can find expression in poems, art, music, crafts. If we are low, we often feel so helpless and tired that it's hard to think of things to do; when you are well make a list of ideas that you can fall back on! Paint pictures. Enjoy music. Write poetry. Visit your elderly neighbor. Make some fancy dishes. Pick and arrange some flower bouquets. Cut some garden lettuce and send it to a friend. Wash down the porch. Repaint that rusty, old chair. If we put these gifts to use, time passes more quickly and alleviates our pain. Life is full of opportunities, and thinking outside our own painful boxes eases our pain.

When you reach for the stars you may not quite get one, but you won't come up with a handful of mud either.
CHOP

BE PATIENT AND POSITIVE

The process of finding the right doctor and the right kind of medication or combination of meds often takes a long time. Half-hearted attempts simply will not scale the wall. Not only do we need to go through the poky process of finding which kind works, (and this may take years!) we often need to choose between positive results and negative side effects. Tune in to what your support people are saying! You may feel you can't stand the side effects, but they may be saying it is not worth going back to what it was like without the help of *any* pills! Please, if one kind doesn't work, don't say "we tried medication and it didn't work." I tried five different kinds until my doctor found one that worked well.

WATCH OUT FOR EXTREME THINKING!

I remember when I first became aware that I thought and lived in extremes. The pendulum swung back and forth . . . high or low, none or all, feast or famine, now or never, friend or foe. I started my quest for balanced thinking, which of course, I assumed would result in balanced moods. It didn't quite work that way; rather, balanced thinking became a result of balanced moods!

There are various reasons why people struggle with 'extreme' thinking, but it fits bipolar illness like a glove. It grows in the very soil of our mood changes. It is not something we deliberately learn or have been taught to do; it happens automatically. Accepting whatever kind of help we need to bring a balance to our moods eventually blends the whites and the blacks into more passive and tolerable shades of grey. And rest assured, I am not talking about compromising principle! I am talking about processing life in a realistic and normal fashion.

USE THERAPY ALONGSIDE YOUR MEDICATION

If our illness is severe, we may need a strong combination of both medication and therapy, which simply means learning to work with our thoughts about life and our way of relating to them. We may wonder why Christians need this kind of support. Our minds are very physical and mind therapy can be just as effective as muscle therapy. Learning to stretch our minds around new and effective ways of thinking encourages healing and gives us practical ways to 'rein things in' when we are about to fly out of control.

Of course, we need to be aware of the dangers we face in a secular world. There are mind therapies that a Christian simply cannot dabble with. If we scan over a list of self-help books, we may come across types of 'mindfulness' or yoga that simply do not fit with Christian principle. We may need to do some sorting in our therapy classes, and this can be especially dangerous for someone who is young and unstable already. Finding safe therapy is possible, and we should search our options with care and consider the advice of people we trust.

You may ask—what does therapy consist of?

- *Gaining an understanding of our specific illness*
- *Learning how to accept it*
- *Connecting with strong emotions and learning how to manage them*
- *What to do in a crisis*
- *Dealing with feelings of inferiority*
- *Exploring anger, how to manage it*
- *How to deal with difficult people*
- *Reducing relapses*
- *Uprooting and managing irrational beliefs and self-talk*
- *Personality types, exploring ways we handle conflict and communication*
- *The medicine of laughter—having a sense of humor*
- *Taking responsibility for our own life and mental well-being*
- *Learning to recognize unhealthy thought patterns*
- *Self- awareness—knowing our own emotions, understanding them, identifying our strengths and weaknesses, knowing what motivates us in life and an awareness of how we impact people*

> *If you fail to plan, you plan to fail.*
> UNKNOWN

- *Learning to overcome our fears; how to be vulnerable without fear*
- *How to stop panic and anxiety cycles*
- *Thinking about it—What is good about me and my life?*
- *Time inventory—what do we do with our time?*
- *Different types of stress and how to relate to them*
- *How to find a balance with our energy level*

Do not fear mistakes. You will know failure. Continue to reach out.
BENJAMIN FRANKLIN

As we do our therapy, we should never leave God out of the picture. Our thought patterns must always come back to the foundation of what He has done and is doing in our life. We need to pray about our problems and trust Him to help us find the answers we need!

RIDE THE WAVES AS GRACEFULLY AS YOU CAN!

The ride to stability can take much longer than we think. Even though we take medication, we may still experience a certain amount of rough wind. It is important to be able to sit back, accept, and appreciate the bursts of light and clarity that we find in and among the black clouds of our illness. Through it all, God is very gracious. He balances our suffering with unexpected pools of quietness in our hearts. We are blessed with abundant joy in the good days, and patience through the bad. When we reach out and embrace life in spite of our illness, rather than recoil in fear, we experience the richness of life.

The intensity of our perception and feelings can be positive! The depth with which we experience life gives us the ability to empathize with others who also face unique suffering. We comprehend pain and all its writhing questions, because we've experienced it. We also grasp the heights of ecstasy; it adds depth, zeal, and the power to move forward in thankfulness.

Our illness often brings about profound changes; life loses its predictability. If only we could prepare ourselves a little for the slam of stunted, weeping thoughts or look forward to the calm breaks of inspiration and clarity! If only we could know what to expect. But the coming and going of our illness is nothing we can put our fingers on, hold down, tie together, and box up. We learn to give ourselves over to the random waves, trusting that God will give us the ability to swim when they tower over us, and the courage to keep working on our 'sand castles' when the tide recedes. If the changes are coupled with an understanding of what is happening, resourcefulness, and discipline, something lasting and meaningful can come from our life.

At this point in my existence, I cannot imagine leading a normal life without both taking lithium and having had the benefits of psychotherapy. Lithium prevents my seductive, but disastrous highs, diminishes my depression, clears out the wool and webbing from my disordered thinking, slows me down, gentles me out, keeps me from ruining my career and relationships, keeps me out of the hospital, alive, and makes psychotherapy possible. But, ineffably, psychotherapy heals. It makes some sense of the confusion, reins in the terrifying thoughts and feelings, and returns some control and hope to the possibility of learning from it all. Pills cannot, do not, ease one back into reality; they only bring one back headlong, careening, and faster than can be endured sometimes. Psychotherapy is a sanctuary; it is a battleground; it is a place I have been psychotic, neurotic, elated, confused, and despairing beyond belief. But always, it is where I have believed, or learned to believe, that I might someday be able to contend with all of this.

No pill can help me deal with the problem of not wanting to take pills; likewise, no amount of psychotherapy alone can prevent my manias and depressions. I need both.

DR. KAY REDFIELD JAMISON
Taken from *An Unquiet Mind*
She is professor of Psychiatry at the John Hopkins School of Medicine

Lithium (Li mw 7) is a metallic mineral. It remains one of the most commonly used medications for manic-depressive illness. It is one of the oldest treatments for "mental illness."

Lithium is naturally found in grains and vegetables, and in some areas drinking water also contains significant amounts. Human intake varies, depending on location and diet. Evidence now appears to be sufficient to accept lithium as an essential (nutrient); a provisional RDA of 1,000 µg/day (1 mg/day) is suggested for a 70 kg adult. In humans there are no defined lithium deficiency diseases, but low lithium intakes from water supplies were associated with increased rates of suicides, homicides, and the arrest rates for drug use and other crimes. The biochemical mechanisms of action of lithium appear to be multifactorial and are intercorrelated with the functions of several enzymes, hormones, and vitamins, as well as with growth and transforming factors. (Fowler G. Crazy Water: The Story of Mineral Wells and Other Texas Health Resorts. Fort Worth: Texas Christian University Press, 1991)

Lithium was used in the mid-1800's by the famous English physician Sir Archibald Edward Garrod (1857 -1936), to treat the joint and kidney disease "gout" caused by the accumulation of uric acid. Dr. Garrod also talked of treating "gout of the brain" which likely included a range of mental illnesses. In the late 1800, lithium was being widely used in Denmark and France to treat bipolar illness. The first documented use of lithium to specifically treat acute manic illness in the United States was in 1871 by a William Hammond, Professor of Diseases of the Mind and Nervous System, at the Bellevue Hospital Medical College in New York. Regardless of a rich anecdotal history, there are few published medical reports about studies of lithium in groups of patients with bipolar illness before 1949 when John Cate, an Australian physician, described the remarkable effects of lithium upon 10 patients with chronic "psychotic excitement." Despite lack of FDA approval, lithium was increasingly used "off-label" in the United States to treat mania in the 1950's and 60's. Its reputation as a maintenance medication to prevent cycles of mania and depression was enhanced by observations of a single patient by Mogens *Schou* (1918 – 2005). He was a *Danish* psychiatrist in Denmark that said, "When we gave him continuous lithium treatment to keep away the highs, we saw that also the lows disappeared…"

In the early 1990's lithium began to fall out of favor, in part, because of the effective marketing of valproic acid as a mood stabilizing drug. Other mood-stabilizing medications, which were also anticonvulsants, followed - carbamazepine (Tegretol), and later lamotrigine (Lamictal). Patients often, 60% of the time, discontinue lithium because of side-effects; weight gain and mental dullness are common complaints, but the need for periodic blood tests, the potential for dangerous interactions with many medications and naturals, and the risk of kidney damage also makes lithium a difficult medication to use safely.

My remarks about treatment of bipolar illness must include a subject that is understandably often avoided---suicide. Dr. Kay Jamison in her remarkable book about suicide and bipolar illness, *Night Falls Fast*, provides a sobering statistic: *Over the 10-years after the Vietnam War more people died in the United States from suicide associated with bipolar illness than were killed in the Vietnam War.*

Suicides are overwhelmingly the result of impulsive "attempts". If a gun is used in the attempt, then morbidity & mortality are high. In the United States there are 89 guns per 100 people and the suicide rate for bipolar illness is 7.9 deaths/100,000-patients-per-year. In Australia there are 14 guns/100 people and suicide rate for bipolar illness is 0.8/100,000-per year. In the Netherlands 3.9 guns/100 people and the suicide death rate is 0.28/100,000-per year. Gun laws in the United States will not soon change. The suicide rate from this illness would likely be reduced by the routine removal of guns from homes of individuals diagnosed with bipolar & depressive illnesses.

Once bipolar illness is controlled by medications, patients typically want to stop lithium and other mood-stabilizing medications. They report they feel well, don't like side effects, and believe they no longer need medication.

Patients who give-up medical treatment do often seek alternative treatments using amino acids like tryptophan, tyrosine, methionine, or the OTC derivatives of these chemicals, combined with high doses of vitamins, special diets, steroids, exercise regimens, trips to Mexico massage & spa-therapeutics – some of which are more expensive and demanding than the medical therapy that was stopped. Despite the initial success of alternative remedies, cycles of mania and depression predictably recur, followed by recurring *real-trouble,* and despair.

After medications are stopped, suicide attempts and hospitalizations are more common. I am aware that many lay-counselors, chiropractors, naturopaths, well-intended family members and health care providers at times encourage patients with these illnesses to stop lithium and other medications. They must be aware of the risk and consequences of recurrence of illnesses.

Moreover, after discontinuing lithium, rates of suicidal acts rose by 7-fold and 16-fold within the first year, and fatalities increased by nearly 9-fold...... Lithium maintenance treatment in recurring major mood disorders has strong evidence of anti-suicide effects not demonstrated with any other mood stabilizer.

(Night Falls Fast, Dr. Kay Jamison)

-D. Holmes Morton, M.D.

BIPOLAR

I walk alone
An uncertain Road
My shoulders bowed
With cumbering load.
My heart explores
Each wearisome pole;
While thorns pierce deep
My anguished soul.
My untold pain
They cannot see
Their hearts denied
True empathy.
But oh! They care
When my path is dim
I may never know
How they pray for me.
Lord, when storms rage
Lift me above
And shelter me in
Your arms of love!

-Ruth Nolt
(used with permission from
Pathway Publishers, and paraphrased)

THANK YOU . . .

As I ponder the journey we have stumbled through together,
I am deeply moved.
I owe you a debt of gratitude for allowing me a window into
your life.

From you, I learned that pain can be a companion,
one we cannot always run from in spite of our best efforts.

I learned that a human being can endure suffering way
beyond what I thought possible.

I learned that trust and love are at the same time the most
fragile and the most powerful things on earth.

I learned a deep respect for the resilience of the human spirit.

I learned a new definition of reality.

I learned that when someone has totally lost control of their
mind, who they are doesn't really change.

I learned to walk beside insanity and
mental illness without fear.

I learned that often strength is weakness,
and weakness is strength.

I learned how much I had,
when I saw how much you didn't have.

I learned to see people for what they are,
not what they seem to be.

I learned how powerful unmet needs are,
driving us to actions and beliefs totally outside of reason.

I learned what happens when parents refuse
to look at their own pain.

I learned that no matter how major the crisis,
the sun will always come up again tomorrow.

Truly, you have been my teachers through the most intense
schooling of my life. From my heart, thank you,
and don't forget. . . .

I Love You.

-'Amanda'

SOLO

A tree on a hill
Bends low in the storm.
A hill full of trees
Breaks wind into breeze.

Alone is not good
When trouble rolls in.
We fly all apart
From strain at the heart.

-Anita

PIECING THE PUZZLE . . .

I believe in the sun even if it doesn't shine

I believe in love even if I don't feel it

I believe in God, even though He is silent.

---

1. What will understanding my illness do for me?

Acknowledging that you are ill and taking an honest look is probably one of the toughest, most courageous things you will ever do. Most of us fight this realization with all we have! The feelings of being overwhelmed and out of control are incredibly painful. However, sooner or later we realize the best choice is to face our problems and persist in finding answers.

Keep going, and the chances are you will stumble upon something, perhaps when you are least expecting it. I never heard of anyone stumbling on something sitting down.
CHARLES KETTERING, *Inventor*

Learning about our illness encourages acceptance. As our understanding grows, our fear lessens. Slowly we learn that the sun will rise tomorrow, that others live with similar thorns and lead a meaningful and productive life. We gain a sense of direction, just like a compass charts the path of a ship. This process may include adjusting our schedules, shuffling our priorities, and learning new ways of handling stressful situations. As we take these steps, we slowly crawl out of victim mode, strengthened by the knowledge we *can* do something about our struggles. That strength gives us courage for the times we don't like what we find. Sometimes we are told, "You have to WANT help!" While this feels like a slap in the face, we need to be sure we really are open to the help that IS there. Our own mental blocks can be a big obstacle! Nobody can do for us what we need to do for ourselves.

Finding our way back to health is a process. Just like a puzzle, each piece helps to clarify the big picture; when one piece fits, it provides a place for the next. Missing a piece can stall progress for years. One of our doctors compared it to opening a door with combination locks. Where should we start? Picking all the locks unlocks some, but it locks others. Gentle prying reveals which bolt is under strain; as we release that one, another one may become obvious! Some 'lock combinations' are really complicated, but focusing on the most obvious issue, one at a time, encourages progress. In our search for answers, we will discover many factors: from genes, chemical imbalances, food allergies, diseases, the effects of drugs and alcohol, to abuse and neglect, death, coping methods, family rejection, financial disasters, and spiritual havoc. Genetic and environmental combinations vary as much as the snowflakes tumbling through the sky on a winter day. Identifying our specific 'combination' takes determination, but it leads to healing.

2. Can emotions really be a blessing?

Sara's sister had an illness called schizophrenia. As a child, Sara knew what it was like to play quietly in the corner of the yard, while her sister screamed for hours. Other days, she tiptoed quietly past her as she wept in a corner of the sofa. She learned to avoid the terrible rages that left her sister exhausted, and everyone else close to tears. To her, emotion of any kind seemed a terrifying thing. At a young age, she learned to stuff her feelings, to stay calm when she felt terrified, to bury her disappointment when one of her sister's "fits" sent them home from the school picnic right after lunch, to forego her own urge to cry on Mom's shoulder when she saw Mom's tense, haggard face.

As Sara grew older, this way of relating to life began to take its toll. She began to struggle physically and emotionally. When she finally reached out for help, it took a long time for her to learn to feel again. When she did, it wasn't always easy for her to identify what she was feeling. Sometimes she felt things with extreme intensity. Learning appropriate emotion and how to express it in healthy ways was a journey for her. Sara is not alone.

> *Hope is the feeling you have that the feeling you have isn't permanent.*
> UNKNOWN

When we live with the drama of mental illness, it is easy to start suspecting all emotion. But stripping life of emotion would be dismal and unnatural. God created us with emotion; in fact, it is one of the ways we are made in His image. Some people think only positive emotions are acceptable. However, avoiding or denying our negative feelings jeopardizes our ability to experience positive emotions. Why do we love to read the book of Psalms? David, a man after God's own heart, beautifully narrates his own emotional journey through life. In this world we find solace and the reassurance that we are not alone.

As plain people, we tend to struggle with emotion. Many of us share German ethnic roots that influence us to be stoic and practical, uncomfortable with displays of emotion. This tendency does not relate well to the strong emotion that comes with mental illness. It compounds the sense of being different or not understood in our battle to control our emotions. Men may get the distinct feeling it is manly to be strong and silent. Women may bottle their emotions to appear serene and self-controlled. People may make us feel guilty for what they feel are inappropriate or defective feelings. "You shouldn't be feeling depressed . . . Good Christians feel happy and peaceful all the time."

Differences in emotional makeup vary greatly. Some of us are born with sensitive makeups, which is no different than being born with red hair. Not only are our emotions stronger and more chaotic, they linger longer. Their overwhelming strength tends to affect the way we perceive things, which may be different from everyone else. People may accuse us of lying or exaggerating, when it truly is how we see things at the moment. We often struggle with impulsivity, jumping from crisis to crisis and relationship to relationship.

"Navel gazing"—focusing so much on the emotion of the moment that you miss the step of moving on . . .
UNKNOWN

We relate to strong emotion in different ways. We may push them under until they suddenly get the best of us! We may run along with them or away from them. And sometimes we don't run away at all.

We turn them off and remain stoic and unfeeling. Extreme lows and highs are hard to deal with, and tend to leave us feeling betrayed by our own emotions. We may try drastic ways of punishing ourselves (cutting, binging, purging, or 'spiritual' exercises such as extensive fasting) in an effort to control or ease our emotion. These things may seem to work, but are very damaging.

Emotions seem very real, but they do not change facts. While we acknowledge them, we realize they are not ultimate truth! When we surrender to God in spite of how we feel, we move beyond our emotions into the solid world of truth. You may ask, "How do I know what is truth? My mind tells me one thing and my friends another. It's dangerous to believe myself above everyone else, but it's also dangerous to believe people I don't trust!" Yes, it is. But we still need other people. We need to learn to trust *somebody.* And to the 'somebodys' out there, please be trust worthy!

It is damaging to grow up in an environment that degrades emotion, or accuses us of inaccurate and unrealistic feelings. Not only should we learn how to express our emotions without fear, we must learn how to deal with them in a positive way. Others can help us with this. Ignoring negative emotions wears us down, enforcing a negative atmosphere. We must seek the help we need! Doing this blesses us with a positive reality and strengthens correct perception.

When illness is common in our family, unhealthy ways of handling emotion can be deeply ingrained. We need people around us who model emotional health. Do your friends relate to emotion in a healthy way? If they do, it helps you accept the 'feeling' aspect of your illness, and provides a safe place for you to find support when you feel out of control. Do you avoid socializing because you are worried about having a meltdown, losing your cool, or overreacting in a way that is unconventional? Healthy friends encourage you to be yourself—they are unembarrassed by emotion, gently help you connect to reality, know how to enjoy a good laugh, and place a caring hand on your shoulder in the face of a meltdown. In this way, they surround you with stability.

Through it all, learn to laugh—especially at yourself! Proverbs tells us "A merry heart doeth good like a medicine." A good laugh keeps us from taking our feelings too seriously. That is why I keep a magnet on my fridge that says—if it weren't for mood swings I wouldn't get any exercise at all. Humor relaxes us!

3. Why is honesty such an issue?

Honesty is very healing. God wants us to be honest with Him, even if we are angry at Him! He wants us to face the way things are, even if it scares or embarrasses us. Who are we fooling when we refuse to be honest with God? Honesty helps keep us linked to reality, especially when our ill minds are distorting things. Trying to evade stark reality or insisting that others hide what is going on, brings unnecessary grief and stalls the wheels of progress. It brings damage to the healing process.

> *It's not denial. I'm just selective about the reality I accept.*
> BILL WATTERSON

Being honest encourages us to get on with life. Some of us stay stuck, whining the same sorry tune over and over again. It brings attention our way and helps us avoid hard work or taking responsibility for our own mistakes. Sometimes we remain stuck at difficult parts of our stories because making progress will mean looking at things squarely. Refusing to face our hurts is cowardly. We often need help to do this; hurts caused by relationships will only heal in relationships. Sometimes we do look at these hurts, but persistently lick our wounds. This keeps us victimized. Accepting God's redeeming love and forgiving ourselves and others moves us into the power of love, joy, and peace. It gives us the ability to do different.

Does being honest mean saying everything we think or

know? Not necessarily! Imagine the chaos to any church or family unit where everyone would be totally frank with each other at all times! Sometimes in our zeal to be honest, we damage relationships and create a lot of havoc. Honesty must always be coupled with a commitment to the good of others.

4. How do I relate to unreasonable fears?

Anxiety can be a normal and beneficial part of our lives. It heightens our awareness of danger and prepares us for action. It can also become an overwhelming condition that produces unreasonable fear without cause. These disabling beliefs block our ability to think rationally, making it difficult to make decisions and solve problems. We may even panic, doing something crazy and impulsive. Soon after I got my license, I got lost on the roads. In my excited state of mind, I stopped in the middle of the road and backed into another car. A furious lady emerged and stood in the middle of the road, screaming. Thankfully, I had a calm brother along, but to this day, I take pains to know exactly where I'm going. A single happening like this has the potential to lock us up for life. Viewing ourselves as incapable and the world as a dangerous place to live in makes us more vulnerable to an anxiety disorder!

Nothing in life is to be feared. It is to be understood.
MARIE CURIE

Since most types of anxiety disorders are tied to a genetic predisposition or brain chemicals that are not working in balance with one another, they respond well to medication. We should not resist this kind of help. One woman said vigorously to her doctor "Medication will not fix my problem!" The doctor wisely responded, "No, it won't, but it will help YOU fix your problem." Anxiety disorders are generally treated with a combination approach involving not only medication but also therapy. This simply means learning new ways of thinking. *A* very basic help is sharing our thoughts and feelings with people who are supportive: another is practicing relaxation techniques every day until they become automatic. Stay active. It is easy to simply avoid or escape anxiety-provoking situations, but this will only heighten your fear. Instead, work toward facing the fear in a way that is tolerable to you. (If you are afraid of driving, pick a time when there is less traffic and take the time to look at a map! Or take a friend along . . .)

Phobias and fears wear us out emotionally. Some live in the shadows of old traumas, others fear new traumas and worry they will be pushed over the edge.

> *"Early in the morning, my husband and I were taking a walk. We both heard a gunshot. He didn't think twice about it, but I imagined him lying on the ground, blood running out of his mouth. I pictured myself calling 911 and an ambulance pulling in the lane. I saw our blissful time together turning into a living nightmare."*
>
> -*'Keri'*

If past trauma haunts us, it does not necessarily mean we have not worked through it. It may simply be a symptom of our weak emotions at the time and focusing on them will only aggravate the fear we are struggling with. If this is the case, share with a friend, and then distract yourself by doing something you enjoy. You may need to distract yourself again and again until you can bear remembering those things again. Ask for what you need, such as someone to talk to, some information, or suggestions on how to relax. Call your mom or dad, a friend, your counselor, or your doctor for help; asking for help is not a sign of weakness! It is a sign of courage and strength.

Trying to understand the different factors that enter in will help you know what to do different. Clue in to what triggers your fear. Was it the look on that person's face, the feeling you had inside, the 'not knowing' or the exposure to a certain atmosphere? Then look honestly at how your fears are affecting you. How much power do they have? Are other emotions hiding behind them? Asking these questions wakes us up to areas in our lives that have been hampered or affected in negative ways. Confronting our specific fears with the truth replaces these negative messages with affirmation and confidence. Asking God to help us build trust in Him and others, and handing our insecurities over to Him, slowly stretches us until our fears subside.

What Exactly is OCD?

As the name implies, OCD is a mental disorder characterized by recurring, uncontrollable obsessions and compulsions. When professionals classify mental illnesses, OCD is lumped together with conditions such as phobias and panic attacks in a category called anxiety disorders. Such disorders involve excessive fear or worry that lasts a long time or keeps coming back. The symptoms cause distress or interfere with the person's usual activities and social relationships.

Of course, everyone worries from time to time. For most people, though, the worries change along with whatever is going on in the person's life at that moment. Obsessions, on the other hand, are more enduring. The same unwanted thoughts keep repeating themselves over and over. Although the exact nature of the thoughts varies from person to person, obsessions often involve concerns about being diseased, dirty, or sinful. Each time the thoughts return, they stir up feelings of fear, distress, disgust, all over again. When people repeatedly try to neutralize these thoughts or images with another thought, image, or action, a compulsion results. Compulsions often involve rigid routines and rituals that seem nonsensical to outside observers. But to the person with OCD, they have a purpose, because they counteract the anxiety that comes from obsessive thoughts. The problem is that they're only a temporary solution. The thoughts soon come back, and so does the desperate need for relief.

It's a vicious cycle that is very difficult to break through sheer force of will. In fact the more you command yourself not to have an obsessive thought, the stronger and more intense it tends to become. Fortunately, there are effective treatments that can help you break free of the cycle and take charge of your life again.

-Jared Kant, Taken with permission from *The Thought That Counts*

5. How shall I relate to painful things from the past that mental illness tends to stir up?

When we are mentally ill, everything present, past, and future is wrapped in pain. Painful things are a part of life for all of us. If we have strong relationships and caring people who help us process these things, we are better equipped to face mental illness. If we have lots of emotional baggage, we need to deal not only with the present pain of the illness, but past pain crying for attention. This can be completely overwhelming. But many times we struggle to look at past pain through lenses that are foggy, scratched, and distorted by our illness.

> *If you can go through life without ever experiencing pain you probably haven't been born yet.*
> NEIL SIMON

Why do things from the past often surface when we are ill? One of the reasons is that our illness has a way of crumbling any existing defense mechanisms or protective walls. It causes earthquakes in our carefully stacked closets, leaving the sealed packages strewn hither and yon in bits, their contents exposed to curious eyes. Of course, this leaves us vulnerable and exposed.

Where do these packages come from and why are they there? Maybe when something bothered you, you just told yourself, "It's just me. I'm too sensitive; it's not nearly as bad as it seems." Or maybe when you tried to share, someone responded sarcastically, "What ails you for making such a big deal out of such a little thing?" Maybe they suggested, "If I were you, I wouldn't look at that corner of my life." Or maybe they sweetly said, "God knows all about it. Just tell it to Him and He'll take care of it." Maybe they didn't say anything, just gave you a blank look. Maybe they quickly changed the subject. Maybe they really cared, but didn't know what to do for you.

That's why you needed the scissors, the scotch tape, and some wrapping paper. "Just wrap them in pretty paper and tape shut some of the holes," you heard them say. So you did, and carefully slid the package back on the shelf. . . . Now the earthquake and the pieces . . . where do you begin to put it all back together again?

Facing these hurtful experiences is healing even if the tiniest, hardest, dustiest package lying in the farthest corner is the fact that you have a mental illness. It is a blessing to have someone you trust and respect at your side . . . someone that cries with you when you open the package with a slip of paper inside that reads, "Never cry . . . It is childish and useless." Someone that laughs with you when you read, "Don't laugh. . . . Life is very hard and you just might not make it thru." Someone who is a trustworthy adult when you read, "Don't trust adults. They always let you down. You must learn to be stronger and smarter than they are."

> *Pretending to be a normal person day after day is exhausting.*
> FOUND ON A MUG

Not only do these painful memories and deeply ingrained beliefs trigger feelings of anger, blame, and loss, they are intensified by our struggle with mental illness. Our *feelings* may mushroom until they have taken on immense proportions of hurt; at the same time, these feelings may be based on things outside of reality. Beware of psychotherapy that asks you to empty your mind and imagine what may have happened! This form of therapy is risky at best, falling flat and hard under a mind that is already full of unreal perceptions. It takes you in dizzying circles, exhausting everyone and stirring up false accusations. It is easier to see the trouble other people have caused than to accept the presence of an illness. Not only does an illness make us more sensitive and vulnerable, it often magnifies and distorts reality. If you find painful memories surfacing, write them down or share them with someone else. But be willing to wait *until you are stabilized* to draw concrete conclusions about these things.

Do take the time to look at stressors, especially if they keep resurfacing! We tend to acknowledge them when we crumble, but as soon as we feel better, carefully stack the closet and shut the door. We blame our fragile health for the disturbance and go on with our lives. It is true, our illness has the power to magnify or distort memories, but living with unresolved pain can also aggravate our illness. Even though medication alleviates the symptoms of our illness, these persistent 'thorns' may keep surfacing in times of stress. We need to acknowledge and eliminate them. God's power can change them.

> *The work of dealing with memories is essentially a search for truth. The fact that a memory has surfaced does not guarantee it's truth. The fact that a memory has been repressed for years does not mean it is untrue.*
> DIANE LANGBERG
> *Counseling survivors of Sexual Abuse*

How should we relate to people we feel are or were abusive? First, we need to be sure our perceptions are correct. Reading graphic books on abuse can play with our minds until we come to false conclusions; we need to be sure we are not exaggerating or misreading the situation. At the same time, those who have been abused often downplay the seriousness of their situation. If we feel someone has been hurtful in the past or persists on being hurtful, we need to ask for advice from people we respect. They can help us sort through our perceptions and decide what to do. We may need to communicate limits or put a relationship on hold, at least until we are strong enough to relate to the extra pressure. While we need to relate respectfully to all, we do not trust someone who hasn't proven to be trustworthy!

Our beliefs about life follow us right into the tussle with mental illness. Normal struggles intensify as new struggles pop up. Instinctively, we fight or flee, and it only makes sense that this urge becomes stronger when problems multiply and feelings intensify. Living fiercely independent of others and denying our own problems makes recovery very difficult.

"It was unsafe, very unsafe to be shown wrong. I became arrogant and unteachable. It was wrong, wrong, and wrong to

ask questions, to depend on someone else's judgment, to honor someone else's conclusions. Subconsciously, I believed being without situations where I needed to figure my way of survival would have been boring and without challenge."

-C. J. L.

Our attitude toward pain is very influential. Dr. Paul Brand devoted many years of his life to the dreaded disease of leprosy. What he learned dramatically affected his outlook on pain. Leprosy attacks the nerve endings of the limbs and various extremities of the body, making it impossible to feel pain. In his book *The Gift of Pain*, he explains how this "numbness" makes lepers indifferent to the way they are destroying themselves. He watched them hobble around on shortened limbs that were oozing blood. He removed embedded tacks and thorns and watched in horror as they reached into fires barehanded. He noticed missing fingers that were intact the night before and discovered that rats were actually the culprit. While most doctors assumed the disease was doing the damage, Dr. Brand discovered that they were actually destroying themselves because they had nothing to warn them of danger. It didn't hurt, so why did it matter? He taught them to be diligent and careful with their unfeeling bodies.

As a doctor, you will be treating their fears as well as their organic illness or injury.

After a career spent among leprosy patients, who are made to feel uniquely cursed by God, I know well that guilt compounds mental suffering.

DR. PAUL BRAND
The Gift of Pain

It is a blessing that emotional pain alerts us to areas in our life that need attention. Tuning in to it's cause prevents more problems. *Pain whispers before it shouts. Gentle persuasion works far better than violent correction. (The Gift of Pain)* Our emotional health hinges on our ability to respond in a healthy way to painful experiences.

Responses such as helplessness, anger, fear, guilt, and loneliness intensify the pain we are already experiencing. Facing these feelings and doing what we can to alleviate them removes some of the pain. Fear is the strongest intensifier of pain, both physical and emotional. For some, the pain of growing up in a family where mental illness ruled creates intense fears. Many of these fears are reduced by studying the illness and planning a different course.

As we learn to relate to our illness, a good fear keeps us from pushing our limits too far and undoing covered ground. Silencing negative signals without changing our behavior can invite a much bigger problem . . . we may feel better while we are actually getting worse. At the same time, we need to overcome the 'bad' fear that keeps us sitting in our house day after day when we *are* capable of weeding the flowerbeds. This line may be fine, but maybe not as fine as we think! We need to be willing to step out and do our best even when we don't feel like it. Active distraction helps to keep us out of victim mode. While medication is very helpful, the actual work of getting back into real life is on our own shoulders!

When we are surrounded by pain, condemnation, or rejection, we often develop a negative concept of ourselves. For instance, if we feel rejected by others, it is easy to reject ourselves. If we feel worthless, we act worthless and see everybody else as worthless, too. These outside influences warp our view of God and how He sees us. We hear much in our world about self-esteem, and need to counter these humanistic views with a Biblical view of God and ourselves. While it is unscriptural to say that humanity is basically good, it is also unscriptural to believe that we have no worth before God.

There are other wrong concepts of God that fuel our pain. We may feel like He is hovering over us with displeasure, finding a certain amount of glee in our suffering. This type of struggle can be a result of relating to authority figures that were unreasonable in their demands or did not express care for us as an individual. If you are helping someone who is struggling, remember that simply reading Bible verses and expecting it to reprogram them is unrealistic. You will need to be 'God with skin on' to them; how *you* value them and how *you* relate to God will go much further than any 'theory' you may be trying to drill into their head.

Taking your own life is something you can't afford to gamble with.
DR. JOEL YEAGER

6. What about suicide?

The number of suicides rises each year. Our world is full of people who struggle to cope with the strain and stress of daily life. The pain of living saps their desire to live, and they begin to see suicide as a way out. Like a drowning man, they grab for something—anything that will relieve the pain they are going through. Among those who struggle with mental illness, suicide is a very real risk.

> "*When I was ill, I used to really feel that I should hurt myself or end it all. I was persuaded that hell was ahead and if I do my part to get there sooner, the punishment wouldn't be as severe. I tried eating things like dog food and laundry soap and started to stick things in outlets. I was desperate! I thought—I've got to do something. God and others would be pleased if I do. Yes, I had a fear of hell from my upbringing, if I would actually die; I wanted to, yet was afraid, yet hated myself for being bound to that fear and not just simply doing it.*"
>
> - *'Esther'*

Because of the sacredness of the life, suicide is a very sensitive topic. God is the Giver of life. He has breathed a bit of His own life into each one of us in the form of a soul. He alone holds the key of life and death. How does He look at someone who takes his life into his own hands and commits suicide?

By looking with compassion on this struggle, we are in no way providing loopholes for a person who is contemplating suicide. Suicide is not an option. Faulty reasoning says "God made me this way. If I take my own life it's His fault." Or maybe "If God is this cruel, then I don't want to live for Him." Living with the "hell" of mental illness can convince us we are destined for hell or pushes us towards finding quick relief. This type of reasoning, fueled by an irrational and sick mind, is a dangerous thing.

What is the right thing to say or do when we realize someone is struggling with suicidal thoughts? First and foremost, remain calm and don't act shocked. Encourage open and honest discussion. Ask specific questions: "Do you have a plan? How much do you think about it? How do you think suicide will help your situation? How will it affect those you love?" You may think asking them whether they are suicidal will 'put it in their heads' and make them do it. This is not so. When those who *are* self-destructive verbalize their thoughts, the chance that they will act on them decreases. Hearing their thoughts out loud might wake them up, helping those thoughts lose their power. These are difficult conversations to have, but don't put in the 'back forty' issues that belong in the 'front ten.' Never tell them that they are just trying to get attention. They may take this as a challenge, or it may push them further into feeling misunderstood.

> Studies show the majority of suicides are not done by a psychotic, delusional person; they are people who have concluded their illness is something they are not able to escape. *It is so important to help them find a way to live with their illness!* Condemning them subconsciously pushes them toward the conclusion that their situation is hopeless. If this is so, why continue living?
> 'KERI'

They are sharing with you because they trust you and want your help! Listen to what they are saying and try to understand what they are feeling. Help them find a way to safety—practical things that will put a hedge of protection around them, like staying with them overnight, or helping them to call the doctor. If it is serious enough, take them to the hospital!

Help them to find a place for their children if you or they feel they are unable to take care of them at the time. Try to divert their attention to other things . . . go for walks, visit friends they feel comfortable with, curl up with blankets and drink tea, and help them do simple jobs around the house.

Just because someone expresses their struggle to you, does not guarantee they are safe. Swift action and close attention is always necessary. Someone who is suicidal often drops subtle signs. These may include a sudden personality change, withdrawing into a shell, or erratic behavior. Prevention and awareness of what can happen goes a long way. Ignoring the crisis of the hour and refusing to go for medical help are ways to invite results that are irreversible. Instead of judging, condemning, or belittling the person who is struggling, can we look at ourselves and do all we can to alleviate the situation before it is too late?

When we have done all we can possibly and humanly do, we need to put them into God's Hands. The horrible does happen, the irreversible is hard as stone, and the grief is killing.

"Comments others make when we are struggling with despair can cause us to shut down verbally and emotionally. During my struggle with suicidal thoughts, I was always told '*It's wrong to feel that way—that is sin.*' I felt unheard. Only years later, while going through a time of counseling, did closure come to that dark time. It involved many different things . . . one was forgiving those who tried but did not understand the struggle and left me alone. Another was confessing my desire and plan to end my life to God as wrong, and seeking his forgiveness. And finally thanking Him for intervening and bringing a stop to my plans one black night. I praise my heavenly Father for the healing he has brought into my life. He overruled and gave me a new chance to choose life." Deuteronomy 30:19 says "*I call heaven and earth to record this day against you, that I have set before you life and death, blessing and cursing: therefore choose life. . . .*"

'MIRIAM'

Losing someone we love in this way is indescribably painful and life-changing, but blaming ourselves will get us nowhere.

There are no simple or sure answers for our questions, and we do not need to be ashamed to admit this. We aren't God, nor should we be trying to be Him by supplying concrete answers. The best we can do is minister while there is life!

TO THOSE WHO STRUGGLE

Do not feel alone or ashamed of your thoughts about dying. This is a common struggle among those who struggle with mental illness. Sometimes the messages of wishing to die are muffled and almost gone, and sometimes they become loud and insistent, making us feel like we need to do something. We need to fight suicidal thoughts when we are rational enough to realize what we are thinking. We can live with and suffer the pain of our depressions if we have the hope that there is an answer to our problems. It's the feeling of no escape that often makes us feel so desperate.

We need to hang unto hope like a drowning man grabs a rope thrown his way. This takes deliberate action on our part . . . tuning in to the positive messages and avoiding the negative. Avoid those who say "Are you sick again? I thought you were over it!" Or "did you say you tried three different kinds of medication? Then you must be medication resistant." These kinds of responses only cement the feeling that our pain is permanent. Like one lady said "My fate is sealed. I've had my last chance at life. My opportunities are gone and my life is wasted." Sharing these negative feelings with someone hands you hope; it gives you the strength to escape them.

You are at a greater risk for suicide if you. . . .

- *Are male*
- *Refuse to take your medications or regularly seek help from others*
- *Drink alcohol or use drugs*

- *Suffer from panic attacks or severe anxiety*
- *Have a tendency toward impulsive actions, like reckless driving or violent outbursts*
- *Your family tree is dotted with suicides or violent, unpredictable acts*
- *Are living in isolation*
- *Do not have any connections with a good doctor*
- *Have a specific plan in place as far as how and when to take your life*
- *Have recently been hospitalized or tried to kill yourself*

When you sense your thoughts becoming more insistent, changing from "I wonder what it would feel like to die" to "I want to kill myself, I just don't know how to do it,"—take action! Have a plan in place, like removing the things you think of using. (Guns, pills, etc.) Find someone safe to be accountable to, and hand these things over. If you can't discuss this kind of thing with your parents, find a friend, or a sibling, or a coworker—anyone you trust!

Talk to your doctor! Set up an appointment immediately and ask them to help you take precautions. Sometimes we suffer our suicidal thoughts alone, because we are embarrassed to admit our struggle. Maybe we fear the response our confession may trigger. Maybe we fear that we'll be sent straight to a hospital. So we ignore the problem and in the process miscalculate our own weakness. Refuse to play around with the suggestions that enter your mind . . . you may do something on impulse that you can't reverse! Reach out for help while you can!

At what point we lose our ability to decipher and control what is happening is something no human being can know. Reverently and respectfully, we put all of this into God's Hands. We know they are very good hands. We know He does understand, we know His gentleness, and we know His justice.

CHOOSING LIFE

"The depression wasn't lifting. At first I didn't even know it was depression. Life seemed hopeless, it was difficult to eat, and I was too anxious to fall asleep. When I could eat, it was difficult to swallow the food, and then I sometimes threw up afterward. I would lay awake for hours each night and daytime was just another struggle to be endured with no relief the following night.

All of life grew dark and hopeless. The winter was an unusually cold and long one. As my body became progressively weaker, I was unable to assist with the farm chores. My family tried to involve me in things I could do, but most things were impossible. I was either too weak, or because of the depression unable to concentrate except for very simple tasks. This contributed to the feelings of worthlessness, for instance—'I'm just in the way, my family would be better off without me.' It was difficult to trust in God; I struggled with 'Does God really love me, do my parents love me?' These questions were asked repeatedly.

Partway through my deep depression, my doctor diagnosed it and started me on an anti-depressant. My family assumed I was starting to recover, but I was not sure I would ever be well again.

While deeply depressed, there were frequent thoughts of death and dying . . . morbid thoughts like imagining how I would look in a casket, and how my hands would be folded. Sometimes I would simply lie on my bed and wish to die to escape the emotional pain and misery I was suffering. The house we lived in was moderate size, but it seemed as if all the walls had moved inwards by 2-3 feet and left me feeling trapped. At times it was almost overwhelming—"I simply need to get out of here!" It felt like wearing dark sunglasses all the time, even indoors. Sometimes I shared my feelings of despair with one of my parents. It was good for me to share, but the response did not really help.

When sharing my thoughts of feeling that life wasn't worth living anymore, people would say—"but, it is wrong to hurt yourself! That would be murder and someone who does that will go to hell." These thoughts were not incorrect, but it did not give me the support and affirmation I needed at the time. My greatest need was to be allowed to verbalize my feelings, bring them to God, and simply be affirmed in my parent's love for me. They did reassure me of their love time and again and did much more for me than I can recall.

In the depths of my depression, although the thought often came to me of life not having meaning and value, the thoughts and risk of it was higher after I was recovering. Everyone around me saw improvement, however I felt hopeless—locked in the pain and darkness of despair. By this time my depression had lifted slightly and I was strong enough to attend church again. But one evening I had a plan, and last minute stated that I did not feel well enough to go along to prayer meeting. I thought finally I will be alone, and then . . .

Graciously God intervened, an emergency arose in the barn and at last minute my father needed to stay home. There was a strong feeling that somehow God worked things out to destroy my plan—I was not at home alone and my father did not know about my intentions. After that night I no longer felt as suicidal, and I shared it briefly with him several days later. The depression did not lift suddenly. But the experience left me with a feeling of awe—God must have seen and cared. He stopped me from fulfilling my intentions. Gradually over several months, the feelings of despair lessened and I began to enjoy life again."

To onlookers, the thought of taking one's own life may seem remote. You may wonder—why would anyone think that way? Don't they know it's wrong? Don't they know they will soon feel better again? What does a person who is struggling with suicide need from family and friends? What should you do when someone confides in you—"Life isn't worth living anymore." We must remember we are not experiencing the depth of emotional pain, rejection, and despair of life they feel. They may feel numb and see life and their circumstances as one big black hole with suicide as the only escape.

What can friends and family do? Take threats seriously. Comments like "I'm not worth anything, I'm just in the way—the family would be better off without me," are serious. The individual truly feels worthless, and may be secretly contemplating suicide. Warning signs are offering to give away cherished belongings. I recall telling a parent, that my siblings could have some of my belongings (I said, "I don't need them anymore.") If the person suddenly becomes very quiet and withdrawn, the risk of suicide may have increased. The opposite can also be true, some people suddenly become quite energetic, because now they have a plan for escaping the pain of depression. The risk is higher when there seems to be no way out of the depression and pain it is causing. Even when others see improvement, a depressed person's perspective may see no change.

The caregiver needs to allow the person to express their feelings, even if they have heard the same pessimistic comments many times and reassure the person of God's love and their own love and support. Sometimes the unconditional love and support of one or two close friends can help lift a person from depression. Be careful of your response. Simply telling someone what they are struggling with is wrong will not help; it isolates the person and makes them feel unheard. Their unusual comments may be a desperate cry for help. They may not share their struggles of feeling life is not worth living with you or anyone else again. Allow them to share and remind them, "I love you, I care about you, and God loves you. Things will get better again." If a person is seriously depressed do not leave them alone. The risk heightens if someone feels alone and unsupported. Give them your telephone number and have them promise to call you any hour of the day or night before they would ever do anything to harm themselves. Reassure them that you are available 24/7. Never promise to keep such thoughts a secret and if the risk seems high do not leave them, call for help while staying at their side. Offer to accompany them to a doctor's appointment. (It does not hurt to call the doctor's office beforehand and warn them of the person's true condition. A person can put up a false front in a doctor's office or minimize their illness, weight loss or difficulty coping with life.) No precautions are too great when a person's life is at stake.

-by one who was there

What do you do if you know something is deeply wrong but you don't have the strength to ask for help?

Here are some things that have worked for me:

1. Make a pot of tea. Clear a spot on your messy table. Find a pretty napkin. Drink your tea.
2. Make your bed every morning.
3. Read your Bible, even if it is just a few verses. Your soul needs nourishment.
4. Eat an egg and an apple.
5. Take a walk.
6. Call an elderly person whose life is so pitiful compared to yours that you can't help but cheer her up.
7. You know there are things you should do. Break them down into little steps. Put on your walking shoes. Plan to reward yourself with something for every five minutes you walk—if that's what it takes. Write down the phone number you should call. Plan to call at 1:00. Reward yourself with more tea after you call.
8. Keep a journal. Write down what you are obsessing about. Also find three things to be thankful for and write them down. Write a prayer for the day, even if it is only one sentence.
9. Give yourself credit for surviving. Survival is good.
10. Promise me and yourself that if you are ever a danger to yourself or your children, you will call someone right now. You know the 911 number by heart. Call it if you need to.
11. Look up NAMI online. Learn a lot. Call them if you should. I promise they will not make you feel

stupid, even if you don't even know what question to ask.

12. Tell your spouse, friend, mom, someone, what a hard time you're having. Ask them to help you get help. Plan ahead how you will do this. When will you bring it up? What words will you say? Then open your mouth. Say the words. Tell them you need them to give you a hug and pray for you. If they won't, find someone who will. And then let them lead you to the help you need.
13. **Believe that there is help and healing for you.**

-Dorcas Smucker

FIGHT ON

It takes effort . . . not that slump
Not that sliding over bumps.
It takes stopping, looking, hearing
Facing truth without fearing.
It takes calmly looking back
At the present- at the lack.
Things that others may be saying
Those we love, who keep on praying.
Can it be that they may see
Things we can't while poised to flee?

It takes effort . . . not that sigh
Not that always wondering why.
It takes thanking, love. Acceptance
Of the things that still surround us.
It takes reaching out for guidance
Even though suspicions bind us.
Not just floating on the tide
That will fling us far and wide.
It takes fighting . . . but be sure
You are headed for the shore!

-Anita 2016

SURRENDER

Surrender is not a spineless bending to any ill gale;
A weak flattening of dreams.
It is an inward strength—
Flexible, pliable, tender, in the face of adversity.
Strong enough to stand, but soft enough to lean
In the direction I am to take.
Seeking not to lament the past
But to better the future.

Surrender is being as willing to take a detour,
As to descend a mountain.
As trusting in a meadow of thorns as in a garden
Of roses.
A sweet knowledge that regardless how yesterday's
Echoes haunt,
Today's winds blow, and tomorrow's clouds loom
God will lead me nowhere that I, through Him,
Am not able to navigate.

-unknown

I WANT TO BE A GOOD PARENT!

The secret of caring for your children
Is Caring For your children.

Borrowed from Francis Peabody's saying:
"The secret of caring for your patient is Caring for your patient."

Looking at an illness that has genetic origins would be incomplete without looking at how it impacts our homes. We have all heard the question, "Which came first, the chicken or the egg?" In many ways, watching mental illness cycle through a family leaves us with a similar question. A parent suffers, and their children suffer because of it. The children grow up and become parents. Their losses from childhood follow them, and their genes follow them as well. They suffer, and their children suffer . . . and the ball rolls on.

1. What happens when a child's needs are missed by an ill parent?

> *"I didn't see a doctor because I thought medicine would be dangerous for my babies. So I continued in a state of severe depression. I did not want to live anymore. I knew it would be wrong to take my own life, but I wished someone would take my life. I had four young children and I did my best to carry on, but I am afraid they weren't properly cared for because I was often in another room crying."*
>
> *-'Kayla'*

Children who grow up with a parent who is mentally ill and does not get the help they need have much in common with children whose parents are emotionally absent for other reasons. You may know someone like this. When you relate to them, you wonder, "Why is he so childish?" I will assure you, inside that person is crying, "When may I simply BE a child—the child I was never able to be?" But they seldom voice that question, even to themselves. They simply press on, living in an adult world with an adult body, but relating to life in a childish way.

> *"Because of the damage my Mom's illness had on my identity and worth, I believed the lie that I don't matter to others. I am not important. I still sometimes struggle to allow others to care for me at a deeper level . . ."*
> 'KENTON'

Enter the world of this 'adult child'

for a minute. For one reason or another, necessity thrust them into an adult role at a very young age. They got themselves out of bed and made their own breakfasts; they rocked themselves to sleep, put their own bandages on, patted themselves on the back, figured out life's myriad of problems alone, and cried their tears silently in dark corners. They stuffed their own fears and sorrows under carpets, while they gathered their siblings around them. They washed their faces, dried their noses, put bandages on bloody knees, and kissed them goodnight. Outwardly, they soothed and comforted; inwardly they shivered and shook with fear. They gave motherly advice in a childish tone, said "It'll be okay" in a shaky voice, and wrapped their small aprons around bodies nearly the size of their own.

The years passed, and they survived . . . their shoe sizes changed and they graduated from school. They developed an 'aura' of maturity that caught people's attention. They looked at the world solemnly, with a caution that becomes the mature. They comforted and guided until they were satisfied that they had fulfilled their responsibilities world around. "How perceptive," some people said, nodding their heads approvingly. Others saw deeper and wondered.

Some of them married. They birthed babies, and wrapped their patched aprons around them. They rocked, sang lullabies, smoothed out wrinkles, and filled bottles. They settled squabbles, helped with school lessons, gave back rubs, and applied salve. They washed mounds of clothing, planned meals, sewed clothing, and balanced budgets. They did the best they could, learning a lot from watching others.

The touch of human hands-
That is the boon we ask
For groping day by day
Along the stony way,
We need the comrade heart,
That understands . . .
And the warmth,
|the living warmth
Of human hands.
THOMAS CURTIS CLARK

And then, sad to say, to the surprise of many, they gave out. The truth unfolded slowly and dramatically, while they shivered helplessly beside their shattered castles. Where a pillar of strength once stood, they found vulnerability and helplessness. Woven in and around their needs, they found coping methods that collected over the years – things that helped hold them together under the pressure and pain of things that were too big for them. They missed the blessing of a carefree, sheltered childhood where questions were answered, fears were calmed, emotions were guided and hard things were broken down into feasible pieces. Without these important things, they were more vulnerable to the storms of life, including their own genetics!

In an ongoing illness, it is very difficult to keep the family intact. The whole family suffers. There are many needs, even though everyone is doing the best they can! Where can we halt this ball with help and hope?

An *awareness* of these needs enables us to hold out hands of comfort, hope, and guidance! Always, we need to *support*—doing the little we can, in whatever way we can, for as long as we can. But a large portion of peace comes from *acceptance.* One of my doctors said, "It's simply life on earth." There are some things we can't do anything about. Helpers must consider the whole picture, the suffering of the parents as well as the children. They must focus on *restoration!* Do not do what some people do—destroy the already shaky parent-child relationship! Instead, help the children love and respect their parent for who they are, looking beyond the crippling illness to their heart of love.

2. How DO *you fill your child's cup if your own is dry?*

I want to be little, but I am a Mom
Who's feeling so tired and sad on the run.
I grew up too fast, was too old too young;
I wish that the past would once again come.

A candle loses none of its light by lighting another candle.
UNKNOWN

This little poem expresses the sentiment of an adult who felt pushed into life unprepared. This happens for different reasons. Maybe the parent was selfish and careless. Maybe they were a workaholic, an alcoholic, chronically ill, or died when the child was young. This leaves children longing for the opportunity to return to childhood days . . . they mourn what they never had, what they never will have, and what they find very hard to give. They ask themselves the question "How can I be a good parent if I was not parented? How can I give to my own children what I have never experienced myself?"

Believe it or not, the best place to start is to look at what you missed as a child. Asking this question is not about blame, revenge, or pity parties. It's about acknowledging truth so we can move forward in a positive way. Realizing our loss invites healing and growth. Choosing to deny these losses makes it impossible to give our children any more than what we have been given. We naturally tend to parent the way we were parented, even though we may not want to. Looking back to these things connects us with the power to do differently.

Another way that God heals our needs is through positive relationships with other adults. Treasure and cultivate relationships that fill your own cup, especially with other parents whom you can observe and learn from. We already know no home is perfect, but we are blessed with many hap-

---

What did it do to us to have a parent with mental illness? Yes, we had longings for a normal home, but, we, as children, learned to cling together with a fierce loyalty to each other. Adversity does draw a family closer and make everything taste sweeter, just because you're facing it together with courage and loving hearts. Our hungry hearts reached out to anyone who took time to shepherd us. Our Christian school teachers filled an important place for us. Much of our spiritual nurturing came through them. We thank God for His providential hand in this. Through our affliction we learned compassion for others. Just as God comforted us, we want to reach out and comfort others. **To pity is human, to relieve is divine.**
ANNA P.

---

py, functional two-parent homes that anchor those of us who face unique challenges. This is a priceless gift in today's mixed up world!

We can also find the answers to our unmet needs in a meaningful relationship with God. Our needs draw us to Him—only He can meet them perfectly. Understanding this frees us from a demanding attitude and keeps us from resenting those who have 'failed' us. It does NOT free us from our own responsibility of doing the best we can with our own children.

Some counselors say you will not be able to be a good parent until you have received good parenting in some form or other. You can go 'dad or mom' hunting, but you may find people who are unavailable, people who misread your intentions, people who are spooked off by your needs, or people with imperfections just like your own dad or mom! For a relationship like this to do what it is intended to do, the person we are reaching out to will need to understand what we need from them, and insist that we respect their personal boundaries. Throwing ourselves on them in a demanding way will not bring us the results we need. While a supportive close relationship with a healthy parent figure can provide a major source of healing and support, it is important that we don't despise or neglect the parents we do have. We need to respect them for who they are and acknowledge the good they have done.

Never accept the message that if your needs were unmet as a child, you are hopelessly and permanently disqualified to be a parent. Parent, and do the best you can! Most of us don't fully wake up to our own needs until we cradle a little newborn or guide a toddler, and then we feel trapped! We can receive a lot from others, but focusing too much on our own needs will only frustrate us and will certainly not meet the needs of our children. By recognizing their needs and seeking to meet them to the best of our ability, we are also acknowledging our own needs. God can fill in our own empty spots and those of our children. He can help us connect with them in spite of our physical, emotional, or mental needs. Good parenting is not about having a problem-free home; it's about facing our problems honestly and seeking the help we need, even if it means allowing someone else to step in and fill in for us at times.

It is not hopeless! We can move forward, learning how to be an *adult* adult who is there for our children. We begin by recognizing what we have lost, seeing what we have gained, and clearing the slates of those who 'failed' us. As we accept healing and help, we don a new and better apron—the apron of stable adulthood, which is broad enough to cover and comfort our little ones, and mature enough to help us face life's responsibilities.

3. Can I be a good parent if I struggle with mental illness?

When I realized I was ill, I was terrified that I had failed as a mom. We've all heard the saying, "Like parent, like child." I didn't want my children to experience having a mom with mental illness, or fear they would be like me some day. I cried a lot, overcome by feelings of remorse, afraid that I had scarred them for life. I repeatedly said to my doctors, "But I want to be a good mom!"

My doctors reassured me. One of them told me he knows it is a lot of hard work, but he also knows women who have done it. The other one told me that simply understanding and facing my illness will keep me from repeating the things I don't want to repeat.

> *Who then can so softly bind up the wounds of another as he who has felt the same wounds himself?*
> THOMAS JEFFERSON

We worry that our illness will estrange us from our partners, from our children, and from our friends. We have seen this happen to others. When we discover we have the same weakness, it is easy to feel trapped in a mound of unanswerable questions and tottering problems. In our struggle to make sense out of our own lives, we often miss important things in the lives of our children. Sometimes we feel so inadequate and drained that it seems impossible to think we can be anything for our children other than a living grief. We are afraid we will never be able to trust ourselves or relate to our children in a caring way.

What makes a good mom or dad? Isn't it simply doing the best we can with what we have? How do I relate to my illness? Am I trying to understand it, and do I accept help from others? Do I care enough about my children to find the help I need to be able to live and love in a way that blesses them? We should not be teaching our children that perfection is possible in this world. More important than perfection is handing them the tools they need for a challenging job! For instance, have we showed them how to say, "I'm sorry"? Or have we taught them to deny the way things really are?

Even though parenting through an illness is difficult, we need to embrace the challenge. Here are a few helpful goals:

Make sure your children understand that your illness is not their fault.

Do not just assume that they know that. By nature, children see themselves as the cause of everything that is wrong in their world. We reinforce these feelings by saying things like, "If *you* would just behave for once, I could think clearer! *Your* noise is making me so tired. I could function better if *you* would just stop asking me so many questions!" Never put this burden on their small shoulders. Normal children have needs, and they should not feel guilty for that! Find ways to give them space to be children. Communicate things they can do to help you out. Try saying, "It's just too noisy, please quiet down!" Or "Can this wait till Dad comes home?"

Try to monitor your repulsions over touch and noise. We squelch our child's desire to communicate when we shove them off our lap with a "Please don't touch me, I can't stand it!" Children do not find it easy to understand this kind of behavior, even if it is explained to them. They need a lot of reassurance and comfort in this area; even subtle messages leave them feeling very insecure. One child yearningly said to her mother, "I waited and waited for you to hug me good-night, but you were always in bed." It is tempting to be defensive when our child makes a confession like this, but we should acknowledge their loss in spite of all the excuses we may have. Be thankful if your child acknowledges and expresses this kind of thing! They can and should learn to express their needs in a respectful way. Instead of shaming them, we should encourage open sharing and work through the impact of their losses. Relating to them wrongly in this area will affect them for life; their childhood years form the rules and beliefs they will carry into adulthood.

Deliberately leave positive messages for your child: make an effort to smile at them, reassure them that things will be okay, (even when you aren't sure yourself), give hugs (even though you are exhausted and foggy). Focus on showing them your unconditional love in a 'language' they can understand!

During Mom's well moments, she read to us for hours . . . we never tired of listening.
-'SARA'

As they grow older, help them understand the nature of your illness. Doing this helps them separate you from your illness. They will not be as quick to blame themselves when things are going topsy-turvy. Communicate. Don't make them guess at things or hide things. Sometimes silence is golden; sometimes it is just plain yellow.

Encourage your children to have positive relationships with other adults. This is good for any child! People like this provide a buffer in their lives when you are low, and also are able to offer feedback and accountability for you. Children can emerge intact from a lot of chaos if they have consistent places of light and stability to turn to. Make sure they know you are okay with it if they want to discuss with safe adults what is happening at home. Teaching them that no one else can be trusted is very crippling.

Are you leaning on your child in unhealthy ways? It is not their job to 'parent' you. Children can do a lot to help with the day-to-day workload, but they should not have too much responsibility placed on their shoulders, such as disciplining younger children or managing finances. When your illness keeps you from your normal duties, reassure them that they don't need to fill in all the gaps. If you are the parent who is not ill, make sure your child is not carrying you, either, especially emotionally. We need to work together as a family to cope, and be humble enough to go for help from doctors, friends, family, ministers, and neighbors.

3. What are the blessings and challenges of a struggling parent relating to a struggling child?

"Susie? Susie? Susie? Susie? ". . . finally Susie answers from her corner of the sofa, where she is staring vacantly up at the ceiling. " I want you to sweep your room, no, I guess you should set the table first, but I really want you to bake an apple pie right now." Susie jerks to life. "What do you really want me to do?" she demands, stamping her foot. "Please be respectful," snaps mom, "and come make this pie."

Susie stares at the recipe lying on the counter. It has ***apple pie filling*** *scrawled at the top of the page.* ***1 cups diced apple, 1 tab. Cinnamon, 1 ½ tsp. salt, and 1 cup flour. Mix together. Put into one 9 in. (or two) pie shell, top with margarine and bring crust up around the apples. Bake unto apples are soft.*** *Susie sighs. I am sure mom means sugar where she wrote flour . . . not? She reads on:* ***Crust—1 ½ cups flour, ½ salt, and mix. Mix 1/3 oil and 4 tb. ice water and put into flour.***

Susie explodes. "I can't understand half of this," she yells. "What in the world are you trying to say?!"

If our illness is genetic, it should be no surprise when the same weakness shows up in our children. Wondering where we went wrong is a fruitless question; if it's in our genes, it's bound to be in theirs! When this happens, what are some things we need to keep in mind?

A child who mirrors our own weakness is often the most difficult for us to relate to. But they need our input the most! We need to hug them, laugh with them, and assure them things will be okay. They need to learn to trust and depend on others, welcoming their input in their lives. We won't teach them this if we resent them or turn down the help of other people. We need to be an example they can trust and follow.

Do you take advantage of the good times? Instructing your child when you are both foggy and disconnected can be very frustrating! It steps on short fuses and stirs up disrespect. (When my daughter acts just like I'm feeling inside, it's easy to lock horns with her.) Stick to the basics when either of you are low, but be as consistent as you can. They have enough to work through without your own directions bobbing in all directions.

I don't know why (these special children) come and go upon the face of the earth, but one thing I do know, they change the lives of those who know them.
DR. HOLMES MORTON
Clinic for Special Children

Routine provides comfort. When a 'foggy' adult is trying to communicate with a 'foggy' child, they often miss what each other is saying. If you are giving instructions, look directly at the child and insist they do the same. If they look away, get their attention and start all over again. Have them repeat the instructions until you're sure they got it. This is hard work for both parties.

Respect their needs; ask them how they are feeling and talk about it. . . . Maybe sending them to bed for a nap is better than forcing your way through the fog, even if you won't get done what you were hoping to. If your child knows that you respect their limitations, it will go a long way in helping them to give you space.

You likely will have horrible, incoherent moments where you clash with them, but do your best to curb your frustration.

When you realize you have hurt them, be quick to apologize and reassure them of your love.

Having the same struggles as your child can put you in a good position to help them. Teach them some of your own tricks! Children respect parents who are big enough to help them to absorb their problems, handing them the tools for their journey. It blesses them with a sense of security.

Children need models more that they need critics.
UNKNOWN

4. How do we help a struggling child?

When we reach out for help with a child who has unique mental health needs, we find an amazing variety of approaches, from diet to exercises. These children seem to need higher doses of everything! What works in one situation will not always work in another, but there are foundational principles that can be applied to each and every child. What are some of these?

Every child has worth. Love them for who they are, and let them know it in a 'language' they can understand.

What does it mean to love our children? We LOVE when we accept life and our dear children no matter what. Doing this provides a sense of security and safety that surrounds them in a cozy embrace. They find themselves covered with support and attention and guidance. Under this kind of environment, they develop the ability to receive love and eventually give it as well.

We want to love each one of our children, even those who do not perform well. But sometimes we relate to them in a way that says something different. What if our child fouls every ball or spoils the beautiful singing with a monotone hum? How do we react when he is constantly shuffling his feet, losing his pencils, or looking out the window instead of following directions? What does the speed drill chart say to Johnny, whose dyslexia makes it hard to follow the neat, straight rows of math facts? Children who always fall short of the ideal are often labeled as stupid, clumsy, fat, or bad. This teaches them they are worthless. Depression reinforces the belief that they were born bad and will always be bad. They feel like misfits, born to disappoint and cause trouble.

Is the answer to ditch the speed drill chart? Do we decide to banish normal childhood competition from our classrooms? Is it our job to shield them from the normal flow of living? These aren't questions with easy answers, but we must ask them! We will need to learn how to be creative in our teaching and parenting! We can't just assume that the way it works for everyone else will work for us. God created each child with unique gifts and weaknesses; it is our job to discover both. To be able to do this, we need to see each child as an individual, not just another child to fit into our cookie cutter mold. Often in our zeal to be efficient and consistent, we run right over innocent children whose needs are being misunderstood and overlooked. Can we accept that different is not inferior or abnormal?

When we ourselves understand love and acceptance, we unconsciously surround our children with it. But sometimes it takes deliberate effort to express our love in a way that it is understood. Do you know the 'love language' of your child? I would encourage you to read Gary Chapman's book on *The Five Love Languages of Children.* Speaking our child's 'love language' gives us a strong foundation in navigating life's storms, including a strong backbone that will do wonders in the struggle with mental illness. Not only will our children trust us, our discipline will be more effective.

Every child needs a balance of love and discipline.

Do you, like I, tend to see discipline as a negative thing? If you do, you are vulnerable to negative child training practices. These negative feelings do not prepare us for the long, all-absorbing task of guiding our child from infancy to adulthood. The path to adulthood is a lot harder for some of our children than others. Yes, life isn't fair. Is that okay? Are we giving our children positive messages of hope, propelling them forward with the assurance that they can do it?! Do we smile ourselves and enjoy the process, or do we let the anxieties of training cloud our faces?

> *"What can I do to correct my child's behavior?" often leads to thoughtless punishment. Asking, "What does my child need?" lets us proceed with confidence that we will handle the situation well."*
> THE FIVE LOVE LANGUAGES OF CHILDREN

A child who is poorly loved is just as handicapped as one who is poorly disciplined. It is our job as parents to discipline, but that discipline must grow out of a love for the child. This means we will discipline in light of the child's good and not for our own selfish reasons, like being embarrassed of how they act. Our child forms his concept of God from the way we relate to him. When we disapprove of an action, this does not change our love for them as a person. When we properly balance love and discipline, our child reaches adulthood with the ability to come to God in his sinfulness, receive His forgiveness, and accept His work of love. When parents don't walk this tightrope wisely, children find they are unprepared to face the storms of life—especially the storm of mental illness.

All children need the security of structure and a framework of rules to be able to function at their best. Rules that function in a healthy way have four basic characteristics:

1. *Firm rules* get a fixed consequence when they are broken; obedience brings affirmation.
2. *Consistent rules* won't shift or change from day to day.
3. *Clear rules* will be easy to understand and possible to see through. The ability to understand what is being required will vary greatly from child to child. Just be-

cause it is clear to you or another child, does not mean it is to them.

4. *Predictable rules* are made before, not after the misbehavior.

Some parents are able do this without much sweat, but not I! Sometimes I even wonder if it's possible. When I am focusing on something, the family jokes the house could burn down and I wouldn't even notice. I have made great efforts at being consistent, but that itself created inconsistency because my mind eventually jumped the groove so I could focus on other important things. It seems to work better to be consistently inconsistent! ☺ I am so thankful my husband covers for me, but I am convinced his clear, predictable thought processes make it possible.

Sometimes we mothers are too gracious with our children when they could be doing better than they are. This protective way of 'covering for' them creates its own havoc. Unsettled problems are left to simmer and stew till Dad steps in the door, and then he has the dirty job of pulling everything together. Dad seems mean and the children come sulking to mom for pity and protection. We must back up our husband's efforts, and express any concerns about unreasonable demands in private instead of letting it show on our faces and actions at the moment. If our children sense we are not working together, it makes them insecure and encourages them to take sides. They may even try to pit us against each other in an attempt to get what they want.

Being pleasant but firm not only conserves your authority, but it enhances your authority because you are gaining your children's respect and love as well as their gratitude.
THE FLL OF CHILDREN

Do you treat your child with respect, even when you are making a request? In our effort to teach them obedience and responsibility, we need to communicate that their feelings and opinions matter. If most of our conversation consists of pleasant chit chat, they will respond positively to the times we need to give a restriction or demand. It will also help them to respect other adults.

Punishment is hard to handle in a responsible way when our methods bob up and down according to the mood of the day. If we feel horrible, it is easy to punish severely, much worse than they deserve. When they can see by the look in our eyes that we are out of control, they feel insecure and frightened. If we are going through a relapse, we should focus on getting the help we need and be slow to punish until we have recovered. While this leans towards inconsistency, it is more important that we do not lose control (even for a moment) and inflict irreversible damage. Consciously expressing our love to our child before and after a correction helps them understand it was for their good.

5. Other practical helps:

The tongue has the power of life and death.
AN ANCIENT HEBREW PROVERB

It is difficult to accept that your child is struggling with a mental health issue. Many times the onset is so gradual that we don't notice what is happening. They often can't or won't express how they feel; this means that parents need to be sensitive to things that signal that something is wrong or unusual. Food may be gross, noise may put them over the edge, or touch may irritate. Maybe they wander from one partly finished job to another. Maybe they just "can't think," or act long before they think, and don't seem to be able to grasp consequences. It can be a real challenge to sort between deliberate, bad behavior and innocent behavior, but close observance will give us an answer with time. The way we handle their negative behavior will go a long way in helping them to relate well to their own unique makeup. If we shame them and punish them for things they can't understand, we teach them to hate themselves and life in general (including the people in it).

How can we teach them to be responsible for their actions in spite of their illness? How can we tell what they are responsible for? Sometimes we can't. Some of our work is a stab in the dark, but one thing we can do is be a good example. If we slam the door angrily on a bad day, do we turn around immediately, apologize, and close it softly? If we find it impossible to manage our own frustration, are we willing to go for help? Example goes a long way, but finding ourselves under the pressure of a relapse makes this a challenge. We may shrug off their hugs, become impatient or over reactive, go to bed early when we would normally read to them, or verbalize the negative messages that are churning in our heads. Why should it surprise us when they become insecure and demanding themselves?

Sometimes their crazy behavior may simply be an unspoken message: "I need help." We need to be careful that we don't jump to conclusions that are harmful, such as deciding they are being manipulative when they need attention! Manipulation is an unhealthy way to react to unmet needs, but maybe they don't know how else to get their point across! We also need to be careful that we don't accuse them of 'not trying' when they have had several successful days succeeded by a slump. People ask "Why can they do a good job for a while? Isn't that proof that they can do it?" Maybe, maybe not! Someone explained it this way: "I can 'swim' for a while, but then I tire and start taking in water." We must remember that a lot of these children work *much harder* than the average child. And they get tired!

Many times others aggravate their sensitive areas without realizing what they are doing. It puts us, as parents, into a real dilemma. If we run to their rescue, they blame others for their problems. If we ignore their vulnerabilities, they become the victim of merciless hands and mouths. We are responsible to protect our children, but also need to teach them how to respond graciously to pain and frustration. Do we help them understand that expressing themselves in the right way is good, but that lashing out and hurting someone else is unacceptable? There may be times we need to talk to the parents of the children who are being hurtful, or make deliberate effort to stay close and intervene should trouble start.

Other children will relate to them in a way that humiliates or brings the worst out of them. 'Sophie' was a child who struggled with ADHD. Things blew up to immense proportions and she was often accused of lying or exaggerating. But in her mind she was saying things just like they were. One day after she told a story, the little girls that were with her ran into the house to ask her mom if it was true. She smiled and explained to them that sometimes Sophie exaggerates things. Before she realized what was happening, they approached Sophie with their accusations. "You lie! Your mom said so! What you say isn't true, and now we can't believe you!" Sophie took it for a while. Then she lost it. She left her friends know that what she had said *was* true and said some things that were ugly. Upon her mom's request, she apologized for her ugly reaction, but the damage was done. In their minds, she was not only a liar, but an angry liar!

Are you helping your child to understand their illness? Be matter-of-fact about the label and point them to others who have struggled and related to it well. Your positive attitude will do wonders in giving them courage! It will lessen their sense of doom. Work together to avoid triggers and find creative ways around trouble spots. . . . Be open with their siblings, teachers, and even close friends about what is going on. It is important they know you aren't ashamed or afraid of them, but are going to relate to their problems just like any other problem in life. Being secretive or refusing to acknowledge what is going on locks children into a sense of shame that is extremely hard to break when they are older.

Carefully observe your child and the patterns of their illness. Your job is to learn, usually by trial and error, what is most effective in the long run. There are enormous variations in patterns and it may be hard to put your finger on what actually helps. But intervening as early as possible minimizes the length and severity of their problem! Cut out stress, late nights, or specific things in their diet that aggravates their symptoms. If you are doctoring, stay in touch with their doctors and communicate your observations. Avoid degrading remarks about doctors and medication. Help them to relate to the mocking remarks of others about "those stupid pills they must take for their brains every morning." Be a good example! If they see us freely disregarding our doctor's orders, we can't expect them to cooperate either. With children, more is caught than taught.

Tips on how to handle aggressive behavior:

- Isolate the situation and remove the audience.
- Get them to talk and listen carefully.
- Identify and sympathize. Help them feel understood.
- Speak calmly and firmly. Sound confident.
- Say very little and give them time to process.
- Remind them of their limits.
- Do not allow them to shift their primary complaint to other people or things.
- Invite positive feelings and outcomes.
- Give the child time to process, don't rush them.
- Do whatever you can to bring them back down to a place of rest.

When they find themselves locked inside an uncooperative body that runs them into all sorts of trouble, they face a lot of anger and frustration. Children act how they feel. They do not stop to try to understand why they are feeling the way they do. As adults, we can help them do that instead of reacting out of frustration. This only deepens the problem and causes unnecessary guilt. For instance, when they struggle with an overwhelming need to do something—in obnoxious ways such as shuffling feet, breaking pencils and shredding paper and plants—we usually apply discipline. They seem like mini volcanoes constantly brewing fresh trouble and conniving ways to explode. We become consumed with controlling and subduing 'the monster.' However, this stance does not and cannot work; these situations can't be hammered out with a spanking every day.

Think about it—are you simply in a power struggle? Some children will fight while others slowly become voiceless and dull, retreating further and further into their shells. They may not be able to connect the dots or communicate what they are feeling. We often reach the conclusion that this child is extra bad. This mentality does not go undetected.

When a child is upset, try not to take the things they say personally! Doing this blinds us to the real issue. Demanding that they treat *us* fairly is making them take responsibility for actions that they may not be able to help. Why do they say "Everybody hates me." "I want to die." and "I hate you"? Do they really mean those things? They probably don't mean it the way it sounds, but it is one way to get your attention! Address it in an active but calm way. Sometimes they use words to manipulate, but usually they talk like this because they truly feel terrible. Don't be slow to reach out to others for help when relating to them becomes overwhelming! Therapists can give you excellent tools to help you diffuse their extreme states, instead of adding to them.

. . . words that give positive guidance all say, "I care about you." Such words are like a gentle, warm rain falling on the soul; they nurture the child's inner sense of worth and security.
THE FIVE LOVE LANGUAGES OF CHILDREN

Affirmation is another powerful way to communicate love and it includes both your words and your demeanor. Exhaustion tends to blind us to the good that is there. All children treasure compliments, even if it may appear they don't. Deep down, they are struggling for air. They want to believe that they can learn how to live! They are also quick to discern if we are praising their performance or if we really value them as a person. Do you make them feel guilty for things they cannot help . . . a scattered, one-tracked brain, or the inability to sit still and focus? Do we accuse them of being lazy and undisciplined? Consider consulting a doctor about these problems. Medication can stabilize some of these things. Steady the ladder for them, and they just might surprise you with their 'apple-picking' abilities!

If you are given to criticism, work hard to change this habit. Have you listened to yourself lately? Apologize for cutting words! While it does not completely erase the hurt, it lessens the pain and invites their forgiveness. Nothing feeds the silent 'crying of the soul' like the loud, consistent dripping of criticism. Actually, in time, it may drive them crazy!

At times loving a difficult child means serious heart work for parents. Filling your place can seem worse than thankless. We need God's grace to consistently mirror His unconditional love to our hurting children. Children have a way of knowing how to push our most sensitive buttons, quickly exposing areas where we have heart work to do.

Guide your child to something they can do—especially things that serve others and bring out and expand their talents. Help them to focus outwardly instead of only on their struggles. One good way to divert extra energy is to channel it in positive ways. Make rice crispy squares for neighbor Anna who can't even get out of bed! Monotone Willy who "does horrible in Math" may do a great job milking the neighbors' goat while they are gone on a trip! Doing this successfully brings them the joy of accomplishment, and feels like a drink of cold water on a sultry day! There is nothing as killing as getting the feeling that everything is wrong and always will be.

We learn to highlight the good times so that those memories can build a walkway over the bad times.
'KERI'

When service is your goal, your children will pick it up. You may ask—How can I serve others if I barely keep afloat myself? What do we have to offer other people when the house is a mess and our child throws tantrums every fifteen minutes? It is true, we have our bad moments, but we can also have our good moments. Are you allowing the negatives to cloud over the positives? Service gives life meaning . . . not only to you, but to your child.

And last, but not least, NEVER GIVE UP!

ISAIAH 45:9-12

Woe to him who quarrels with his Maker . . . does the clay say to the Potter "What are you making?"
Does your work say "He has no hands?"

Woe to him who says to his father, "what have you begotten?" or to his mother "what have you brought to birth?"

This is what the Lord says "do you question me about my children, or give me orders about the work of my Hands?"

"It is I who created the earth and put mankind upon it."

THIS THING OF TRUST

Trust is a choice . . .

a commitment—not a feeling.

1. Why is trust a special challenge?

Trust is one of the basic stepping stones to healing. But it can also be one of our hugest hurdles! Mental illness often makes us suspicious and aggravates our fears. Relating to people who misunderstand us reinforces our belief that others aren't safe. But following our instincts or refusing to trust can keep us locked in a cycle that will prolong our pain and eventually destroy us.

One of the most frightening aspects of mental illness is realizing that we cannot trust ourselves. When we lose the ability to think clearly, we also lose the ability to trust our own perceptions and sometimes even to control our actions. Because of explosive, hurtful words, we often reap strained relationships. In our enthusiasm, we may tackle three times the amount of work we are able to handle or lose weight till we are dangerously thin. What seems perfectly logical to us is sometimes perfectly irrational. This realization leaves us feeling powerless and vulnerable.

> *It is sometimes an appropriate response to reality to go insane.*
> PHILIP K. DICK

Fear is the opposite of trust. Because our illness aggravates all our emotions, we face fears that are intense, irrational, and pervasive. We tend to suspect others without even realizing it. What does it mean to trust in the face of that kind of fear? Does it mean to just do what others tell us to do?

Trust is much more than just a feeling. It is a choice, a commitment. It may feel like holding a nail while someone else brings down the hammer! But when we are already vulnerable and hurting, we try to avoid pain at all costs. It is hard to hand the controls over to someone else and allow them to make decisions that affect us!

"Sometimes I feel shot at from all sides. It seems like God and everybody else is against me. All I want to do is crawl

back into the 'tunnel' to protect myself. The tunnel feels secure because it keeps me from becoming a target for all the sharpshooters . . .it is a place where I am not expected to function, I can think without interruption, I don't feel dangerous, others don't feel threatened and I can rest from the demands of life."

-'Keri'

When we are in this state, we often want to be left alone, but I have been blessed by those who have persistently made their way in through the tunnel to find me and bring me out. They kept me in touch with real life, something very necessary for a mom with five children. It helped me to unwrap from my own world and its concoctions, it exercised my muscles of endurance and perception, and it strengthened my ability to trust myself, others, and God Himself.

To those reaching in: Please nudge your way in . . . barging in forcefully is rude and frightening. You will often need to make the move before we reach out, but if you become too aggressive, we might slam the door on you. If this happens, keep trying slowly and carefully. Remember that trust cannot be forced—it must be earned. If you can't get anywhere, talk to others who are close to the situation and share your concerns. At times the need becomes so critical that others must forcefully push their way in, but this should not be done rashly.

Is there a place for protecting ourselves when we feel vulnerable? While we need to live carefully, our 'caves' can be dangerous. Just like freezing to death in a snowstorm, we may slowly shut down on the world around us. We may understand our own limits better than others, but the choices we make to protect ourselves often cut off the lifeline of relationships that we so desperately need. Our SAFE barricades may protect us from harm, but they will also block the help we need. We need to accept help even if we feel paranoid. If those who love us are disagreeing with our conclusions, we need to pay attention. In order to find healing, we often need to do exactly the opposite of what we feel like doing. This is what I call the "Art of Reversal." Following our initial feeling will usually prolong the healing process. Just like a mother in labor, we need to invite our pain rather than fight it. What is it teaching us?

2. What are some wrong ways to handle pain?

Mental illness is very painful. It is only natural to shield ourselves and make exhausting attempts to control our own lives. We may feel we need to stay on top of everything! So we live in a nervous state of mind, unable to enjoy life and others. Sometimes the pressure to perform drives us, and we crave the approval of others. Every time we fail we hate ourselves, and become even more controlling. More control leads us to being even more out of control and our existence soon seems hopeless. We think "If only I was stronger, braver, or smarter, maybe I could outwit everything."

> *All men should strive to learn before they die, What they are running from, and to, and why.*
> JAMES THURBER

As children, we naturally fight to survive. We react to the hardships of life with an inborn determination to make it! We may find ourselves fighting alone, doing the best we know how. At a young age we learn to distrust and intimidate others, escape into a fantasy world, and control others. We wear masks to hide what we are feeling and appear as we are expected to appear. We hide our pain and emptiness with a steady stream of jokes or fascinating stories. We lie to protect family secrets. We may even 'steal watermelons' from the neighbors to still the 'hunger pangs' of our brothers and sisters. We don't think of these things as sinful; we are simply surviving. But when we move from childhood to adulthood, we discover that these patterns don't pan out. We heap more hurt and pain upon our own heads before we realize what is happening.

Our pain and confusion cloud our perception. Our suspicions multiply rapidly. "He didn't smile at me thus he doesn't like me. She didn't call me thus she just doesn't want me to come. Why are you looking at me?–Probably thinking about how horrible I am." We interpret everything based on our belief "Nobody likes me. They're out to get me." We may become very difficult to live with, resisting help, clinging to unhealthy relationships, hating life, and living resentfully.

I'm afraid of making a mistake. I'm not totally neurotic, but I'm pretty neurotic about it. I'm as close to totally neurotic as you can get without being totally neurotic.
BRIDGET FONDA

Our pain easily seeks relief in sundry addictions. What are some of these?

Manipulation only makes sense to a person who is in a lot of pain and confusion. "I'll never let others hurt me again!" We manipulate for two reasons: to avoid more pain and to get our way. But it really doesn't get us anywhere . . . it just digs our hole deeper. We become controlling and demanding, self-willed and stubborn. We hurt others, deceive ourselves, lose money, kill good friendships, and nourish bad ones. We get what we really don't want, and want what will hurt us in the end.

Fantasy is soothing and sweet. It is soft, airy, and promising! It plays out our dreams and soothes over our disappointments. It dulls our pain and paints things our way. But it is fake and often lustful, and consumes mental energy and time that should be devoted to the real world. It can also mold our thinking and perceptions to the place that we become distant, unrealistic people that live in a concocted world. This kind of coping is dangerous!

Emotional dependency is especially sly. Because our relationships with God and those closest to us often become weak and wobbly, we may blindly reach out to others in unhealthy ways in an effort to ease our loneliness. We funnel our energies into this 'new', meaningful relationship which gives us a reason to live! In the process, we often ignore personal boundaries, violating principles that would have been clear to us in a healthy state of mind. Our need has a way of fogging our 'windshields'. Just like ants love sticky syrup, we crave attention, approval, and protection from the horror of our tormented minds. In its own crooked way, we are often drawn to other needy people. The feeling of mutual assistance ties us together. In time we may find ourselves doing things that would horrify us in a clearer, more lucid state of mind. We need to be sure we are connecting with are people who are well, have solid principles, and point us the right direction. If your relationship with someone is taking on a shade of secrecy that excludes others and demands intense involvement, stop and look at the possibility that you are in a dependent relationship that brings about more damage than healing.

These wrong ways of relating to our illness make things worse. They snowball our problems. Clinging to an addiction for relief is natural to our sinful nature. Anything can become an addiction, even good things, such as work. We may pig out in the pantry, tune in to the wrong kinds of music, soothe ourselves sexually, or read novels, trying to block out the harshness of life. It becomes a vicious cycle- we hurt, we addict, we feel guilty—that hurt causes us to addict and we wallow in guilt again. How can we break this cycle?

I was blind to the truth because I could only see what I wanted and expected to see . . . I might have saved myself months or years of suffering.
BOB OLSON
Winning the Battle

As responsible individuals before God, we need to recognize these patterns and choose differently, which may mean unlearning habits we used for years. This can look daunting, even impossible. It is easy to lose our sense of direction spiritually which makes us even more vulnerable. In our vulnerability, we give in to things simply because we feel lonely and exhausted. They become our 'pacifiers' of comfort. But relying on these things only clouds the water and stalls our progress. By allowing others to walk closely with us through accountability and an open relationship, we can see the areas where we are cold and hard toward God and others.

3. What are some other barriers to trust?

The wounds of life betray us. While some are harsh and cruel, others are subtle forms of neglect that escape the eye.

BETRAYAL IN ANY FORM

God intends that parents provide safe and sheltered relationships where children can learn about themselves and life without heart-breaking damage. Under their parent's umbrella of protection, they learn to make sense out of life, moving gradually from dependence on them to dependence on God. They thrive in the soil of their parent's unconditional love! When a parent ignores needs, mocks mistakes, nags constantly, or punishes mercilessly, a child retreats into himself and stops growing. When parents are aware of abuse and do not interfere, or demand that children be quiet and ignore it, the child's ability to trust dies. When a parent does the abusing, the very foundation of trusting relationships is broken.

> *God loves me, no matter how others treat me. He wants me to bring my pain to Him.*
> ANONYMOUS

When involved adults are aware of abuse and doing nothing about it, their SILENCE is a double betrayal. In a sense they are joining the abuse, because they are looking away when something should be seen and recognized. We need to realize the seriousness of being witness to trauma in another person's life and doing nothing to acknowledge or stop it. Our lack of response communicates to children that their experience is normal and worse yet, that God is distant and uncaring.

If experiences like this shape a childhood, children usually deny what happened, but the sickness spreads the whole way through them. They carry a deep distrust of all adults, and even God. They develop a hatred for the way they are made, despise their longings, and distrust anyone who offers them unconditional love. Sometimes they put on a tough front and choose relationships that are mechanical and emotionally detached.

Even though they long for intimacy, they are terrified of it and believe they don't deserve it. They may feel more comfortable in relationships where they are ignored or shamed, or desperately needed.

> *"For years, my mom struggled with depression. We had our happy times, but the relapses always came and she withdrew into her bedroom for hours at a time. During these times, I did my best with the wash and the dishes. I even combed myself, but my school mates made fun of me. I hated going home to a weeping mom who was touchy and distant. And Dad always looked worried . . . I started having nightmares and problems with concentrating at school. My teacher, who insisted on perfect papers and conduct, targeted me. He even called me stupid! I know I was sensitive, but I believed it. I didn't tell my parents about my problems because I didn't want to add to their worries. Life became a thing to dread."*
>
> *-'Doreen'*

If this young girl was genetically predisposed to illness, she was already vulnerable to stress without the extra trauma of neglect and abuse. These two negatives feed each other, and we are left with a conglomeration of problems.

When an illness is present, how do we sort out whose perceptions are right? This type of conflict has ripped many families apart. It is not always possible to know, but there are times both parties need to agree to meet in the middle. The focus must be on healing, not on being right! The feelings are real and can be dealt with, even if the happenings and memories are garbled. If no one takes responsibility for the damage, whether it was done knowingly or unknowingly, relationships remain in shambles. Issues need to be looked at, acknowledged as far as possible, and forgiven so healing can take place.

We need to step over the shame and terror we feel, and reach out for help, whether we have been abused or been abusive. When a parent *does* remember and admits to abusive behavior, he is throwing a life-line of healing into his child's reach. If you are a parent whose child is accusing you of being abusive, it is never wrong to say, "I am sorry you feel this way. What can I do to help?" Many parents fall flat in the face of these type of accusations, and stay stuck there, trying to prove their innocence. Please remember, whether you are innocent or not is beside the point! Your child is hurting, and you must make their well-being your utmost interest, even if it means accepting false blame. What is more important—a relationship with your child, or vindicating yourself?

Our hearts bleed for those who are suffering at the hands of an abuser and don't know what to do. Maybe you fear your abuser or think no one will understand your predicament. Maybe you think it's your fault. This is a lie. Please talk to someone! God is real and loves you. If you are a bystander observing such a situation, DO SOMETHING!

Sometimes the abuse is exposed and the illness ignored. Counselors without medical training are especially prone to pin- point abuse without considering the presence of a genetic illness. They may falsely conclude that counseling will take care of everything! It may take a doctor or a therapist to identify this segment of the problem. A genetic vulnerability can complicate things and take counselors and counselees in circles for years.

Our distrust of others, especially those nearest us, sometimes springs from hurtful ways they have responded to our illness. They often mean well, but don't understand what we are facing any more than we do, and come to wrong conclusions. They may unknowingly provoke us by their actions, and then condemn us when we lose control. They may push us into public situations we can't handle, and then wonder why we make a scene. And there may be people who *don't* mean well. They may embarrass us in front of a crowd by exposing our weaknesses. They may scold and intimidate us every chance they have, making us feel stupid and simple. They may live under the pinching fear of what others think, and insist that we walk the line. They may suggest that we "just need to get over it" and point us to God, but this just puts a bitter churning in our stomach! Instead of protecting and supporting us, they add to our pain. Even though they talk about God, they aren't showing us what He is like.

"Sometimes I fear mental illness . . . I worry that I will have that kind of struggle. I desperately don't want my husband to have to go through that. One of my friends told me, "If you ever face it, you will learn to work with it." That was a real comfort. God, help me be pliable in your hands!"
'WANDA'

AN OBSESSIVE FEAR OF MENTAL ILLNESS

Many times our fears stem back to the helplessness and frustration of watching someone else struggling with their mental health. Especially for children, not understanding what is happening, feeling too responsible for what is happening, or feeling unseen in the struggle has a big impact on them later in life. This fear of becoming like mom or dad needs to be dealt with; it has the potential to do exactly what we don't want it to do. We need to face our own fears and come to a place of rest.

> *"The stress and memories of my own mom's illness left its mark on me. I determined that if I was ever faced with something as serious as mental illness, I would go for help right away. But I prayed over and over that such a thing would never happen.*
>
> *It was after the birth of our third child that these memories reared their heads in an ugly way. We were happily married for years and life had been fine. But all of a sudden, I was experienced combinations of strange things, including anxious feelings, dry mouth, and diarrhea. I started to overreact to things that were happening and thinking bizarre things that didn't really make sense. I felt panic in public settings and worried that the stove might not turn on at the right time at home. My*

meatballs would be cold when we got home. The vivid terror of childbirth flooded my mind. Memories of the stressful times at home when my own mom was ill haunted me. They came back with startling clarity and fear took yet another grip. It whispered "You're becoming like your mom!" I was horrified. I was afraid that my worst fear was becoming reality. I looked numbly into the face of the dark monster that caused my mom to do all those strange things. Sleep at night was becoming difficult, and I took warm baths, trying to relax. But one morning I was gripped by a full-blown panic attack. I responded instantly by calling my husband who was already at work. We left the children behind and went to our family doctor for help. He talked with us and gave me something to help me relax. Relieved, we returned home and the children stayed with their grandparents. Someone brought flowers. I felt surrounded by love and care.

In the following days, I settled down to a slower pace. As a couple, we looked together at our schedule, our past, our future, and our fears. I struggled with a bitter angry feeling toward God. Wasn't it enough that I had been there faithfully for my mom? Exactly what was mom struggling with and why? Why and how am I repeating the process? Am I helpless or is there something I am doing wrong that I can change? Where do I go from here? Will I be this way the rest of my life?

It took days for me to reconcile myself to the idea that I was struggling the way I was. People helped out in different ways. A friend of mine was dear enough to share her struggles with anxiety. She handed many tips over to me that had helped her along the way, pointing out the anxious thoughts about my mom. It helped me to realize that fearing becoming like her would worsen my problems with anxiety. She encouraged me to 'flow with the tide' and stop fighting it. She told me accepting my illness for what it is may not take it away completely but would keep it from getting worse. She helped me realize I am not helplessly doomed to repeat past memories . . . I have positives my mom never had! I can learn healthy thought patterns that relieve a lot of my fears! At the same time, she reassured me that medication was not a shameful thing.

There are many things I admire greatly about my mom, and I mourn the years she had to suffer from her illness. Help is available! How is it that I have the privilege of getting help early, learning to work with my weakness at a young age? I feel blessed beyond measure, especially as I look back over what was. I can't erase the trauma of those years from my mind, but I can use what I learned in the darkness of those hours. I can thank God for making the way easier for me, and I can also thank Him that I am my Mom's daughter!"

-'Virginia'

THE 'DEAD LOCK' OF MENTAL ILLNESS

The following article illustrates how the aftermath of mental illness leaves trust issues in its trail:

Jerry's dad struggled with an illness for years. Jerry knew something was wrong with dad. Mom did too, but didn't seem to know what to do about it; she either covered the problems or ignored them. And she never discussed them with Jerry. At church, different families seemed to be at odds with each other and there were many critical, cutting remarks. Jerry even heard some discussion about his dad. "What is wrong with him anyway? He doesn't know anything about finances! And I think he's just plain down lazy!" And the farm did suffer. They lost some crops because they were on behind. Broken machinery piled up alongside the shabby farm buildings, tools cluttered the shop, and the bags of miscellaneous revealed his dad's love of farm sales. During his school years, Jerry faced a lot of mockery. He often arrived late at school, exhausted from shouldering too many chores. As a youth, he struggled to fit in with the youth group.

I am making a way in the wilderness and streams in the wasteland . . .
ISAIAH 43:19 B

He didn't have any friends to confide in and the older men did not seem to see him. He existed on an island of loneliness, feeling confused and helpless about life in general.

After a few years, Jerry married. He was shocked at the strong feelings that eventually surfaced towards his own wife. He became angry and controlling, frightening his wife and children. To make matters worse, he began struggling with episodes of depression, just like his own dad. In these depressions, he became even more controlling and distrustful of the people around him. His wife did not know what to do. She concluded her husband's illness was her own fault.

They were facing a deadlock.

While it may be easy to see answers from this angle, people who are in the middle of a situation like this find it hard to pinpoint the actual problem. They may not understand their own genetic vulnerability. They also may not see how their inability to trust the adults in their lives as a child freezes their ability to trust others and lead out later in life. As a result, they become distrustful and controlling. While proper treatment may alleviate part of the problem, trust issues will probably continue until they are honestly looked at. Understanding why we find it hard to trust can bring a fuller and swifter recovery.

4. How do we try to control our situations?

BY BEING THE BOSS . . .

In our desperate struggle to feel secure, we often go through hell and high waters to remain in control. We may not cue in to or understand our actions; we do know we are fighting for our lives! When we become argumentive, others do a huge favor by refusing to argue or prove a point (it's so pointless). We do ourselves a big favor if we realize we are not the only one that understands what is happening in our lives.

This kind of hefty, stubborn independence often stems back to childhood habits.

> *"After all, wasn't I the one that held things together, explained things to siblings, and forged ahead on my own? Didn't I always manage to have everything figured out about the time the others were only waking up? Hasn't it always been up to me to 'make things turn out right?' Isn't my organized, logical way of looking at life proof that I am able to manage my own life plus the lives of the people around me?"*
>
> -*'Marla'*

Firstborns are especially prone to this way of thinking. They may have needed to carry large loads of adult responsibility, such as caring for younger siblings when a parent was ill. Younger, smaller, or weaker ones may set out to prove that they can do everything themselves. "I don't need mom's help anyway."

> *Happiness is having a large, loving, close-knit family in another city.*
> GEORGE BURNS

They may feel responsible to hide their parent's behavior and become good at controlling situations to meet their own needs, or to hide the 'secret'. Or they may hold everyone hostage with their strong will. "After all, mom is too weak and ailing to do anything, and dad is too busy taking care of mom."

If abusive, dysfunctional, or absent authority figures are present, distrust has legitimate roots! A woman may find herself in a 'boss' position early in her marriage after years of relating to an authoritarian dad. It feels right and good—because that's what she was used to—clashing horns with her dad. Or she may have had a dad that who was very permissive. She learned to lead out on her own. After all, aren't men "too slow and dull to figure things out?" If you, as a marriage partner are too aggressive or too passive, your partner may feel driven to disrespect you. Could it be you yourself are looking to them to replace an absent or abusive parent figure? Worse yet, are you refusing help or do you treat them in a way that accelerates and intensifies their problems?

Combinations of personality and life happenings can also create a platform of independence:

> *"During my first year of school, my mother was diagnosed with cancer. Her illness sapped lots of energy from my parents. During that time, my independent tendencies worked in my favor. I pulled my own world together. It didn't even dawn on me that my parents were less present for me. I had already figured life out, or at least life was to be figured out! Also, at the same time, I was violated in ways and involved in things too large for a child to process. My self-interpretations and conclusions about life were the safest and most available resources for me. I learned to live in hiding."*
>
> *-C. J. L.*

Intimidation is another 'boss' method which makes others feel like they are walking on ice. When we allow our moods to rule the roost, we keep everyone's eye trained on our latest need; doing this gives us the security that things will go our way. This breeds anger and resentment in those around us, and encourages weak behavior. A spouse may think "We really don't have the money to do that kind of shopping, but I'm afraid she will have a bad day if I don't let her go." Seeing others live in fear of our reactions can be a source of comfort to us when we feel threatened and insecure. It makes us feel powerful, and not as alone.

BY PLAYING THE VICTIM . . .

"Why don't we wash the dishes together before supper, Sara", Marge suggested. Sara tucked her yarn into a bag and slouched down on the sofa. "I'm just too weak to do anything . . . too foggy. I can't think," she responded. Just then a neighbor called on the phone "I'm going over to the "News Nook" to look for a book. Does Sara want to go along?" A smile spread over Sara's face. "Sure thing," she responded happily.

Karla struggled with an anxiety disorder and was glad for the slow paced, predictable schedule at Yoder's fabric. But lately she hated her job. A new girl who was aggressive and outgoing had started working there. Everyone seemed to like her, but she made Karla feel dull and stupid. "I don't star in anything when she's around," Karla moaned. "I can never think of what to say to customers. At least not in the cheery, confident way she does. If I'm not the best, I guess I'll be the worst." Karla became sullen and unworkable. In her anger, she worked slower and slower. When her employer asked her if she liked her job she admitted she didn't. "My OCD is making it hard for me," she said.

You can't keep a bird from flying over your head, but you can prevent it from building a nest in your hair.
MARTIN LUTHER

Joe smiled as he paid for the brand new grill. It was a good day, wasn't it? He knew his bank account was scraping bottom again, but he just had to buy something to fit the mood of the day. He couldn't help himself! But when he got home, he stopped at the shocked look on his wife's face. She laid a bill on the table and looked up into his face. That was all it took. "Stupid bills!" he yelled angrily. "They ruin our lives!"

How do I know if I am in victim mode? Here are some questions to think about: Do I feel I have a problem that I simply can't help? Do I hang my diagnosis around my neck and use it to excuse my behavior? Do I feel like I have legitimate reasons to 'hang it up' and quit living? Being a victim is tempting, because it excuses us from the hard work of living. It places blame on our circumstances and other people in our life. "I want to change but I can't help the way my teacher treated me—it's their fault I am this way." If a problem is genetic, a 'victim' tries to shove blame unto God's shoulders—"It's his fault. Why did he make me this way?" It is true we are not responsible for our genetics or past abuse, but we *are* responsible for the way we choose to relate to it.

Struggling with mental illness often leaves us feeling weak, unable to get what we want or think we need. So we try to get our needs met in indirect ways. We may expect others, who we think of as strong and capable, to do things that we should be doing ourselves. Instead of communicating our needs directly, we send others to speak for us. What drives these actions is the feeling that I will never be able to gain control of my life on my own, anyway. I will always need other people, situations, sickness, and tears to get me out of the latest pinch.

This indirect control manipulates the emotions of our helpers by either making them feel guilty or giving us the excuse to bail out of the relationship. We may become infuriated and portray them as heartless and cruel people, when in reality they are recognizing our ugly ways of seeking relief. Or we may get 'sick' to control the amount of stress that comes our way. When we use our illness to bring relief in the way we want it, we are being controlled by our illness. When this becomes habitual, it is very difficult to sort what part of the illness is authentic and what part is used to meet our own needs. Using our illness as an excuse can become so engrained that it clouds the truth of our actual condition. We may even confuse ourselves. This is very frustrating for helpers and doctors alike.

If we find that the people around us are handling us with gloved fingers, we need to take an inward look. Am I a pale-faced, whimpering person that sprouts headaches whenever something looks a little too daunting? We may be secretly using our illness to avoid doing what we don't feel like doing. If we struggle with feeling like our life has been ruined and that we have nothing left to offer the world, we are on dangerous ground. When we lean on the people around us all the time, we can't exercise our own 'muscles.' Wise helpers *will* back off in an effort to help us get our own feet underneath us. We may panic and be tempted to manipulate to keep these securities around us, but it is much better to communicate in a direct, open way about what is frightening us, and consider their encouragement and affirmation.

5. Can I learn to trust God?

One of the most tragic results of our illness is the feeling that no one can understand our inner struggles. Sometimes we feel that the past and present will keep us from being able to love or be loved. In our inner hurt, anger, and confusion we feel that our Heavenly Father doesn't really care about what is happening. How can a loving God allow this kind of suffering? Is He trustworthy?

> *Never be afraid to trust in the dark what you saw in the light.*
> UNKNOWN

Wrong attitudes about life often find their roots in a warped concept of God. If we see Him hovering over us menacingly, just ready to let His big stick fall on our heads, we become obsessed with trying to appease Him with our outward performance. We try to earn His acceptance. Surely if we would pray more or confess enough or spend more time with the Bible this wouldn't be happening! We develop a 'super-spiritual' approach to life in an effort to relieve our guilty feelings and to elicit God's help. God can and does help, but He doesn't need to be convinced to do so. Praying obsessively and clutching our Bibles in a desperate attempt to feel better becomes a meaningless ritual. Behind this type of living is the false belief that if we could *perform* spiritually, none of this would be happening. Often this belief is reinforced by well-meaning friends who offer pat 'spiritual' answers.

In fact, while we are concerned about our spiritual lives, becoming overly preoccupied about spiritual things while we are mentally ill can actually work against us! When our minds are not functioning, we are not able to tell whether God's Spirit is telling us something or if it's our own notions or deliriums. One young girl makes this comment about her schizophrenic mother, "Some of mom's spiritual thoughts are wacky, but so are her thoughts about everything else!" Another young girl writes:

"Sure, you can eat it," Dad said. "I'll go to hell if I do," Mom answered worriedly. "Don't believe those thoughts, just eat it," Dad insisted patiently. With that mom slowly brought a spoonful to her mouth. She stared at it for a while, and then slowly stuck it into her mouth. "This life is a battle," she sighed. "Will I end up in heaven or hell?" Then she suddenly pushed her bowl of barely touched food away and mumbled," I just don't feel right eating this, the Holy Spirit is telling me not to!"

When our minds are ill, they are capable of interpreting Scripture in damaging ways. We may become convinced that God is trying to tell us something that is not true. Stay close to others who understand your weakness, people who know God and love the truth, people who can consistently show you a right view of God and yourself. Borrow their faith and hope; ask them to read Scripture to you, and pray with you, rather than trying to do it alone. Also remember—God never asks us to do something that goes against His Word, against the voice of His children, or against His character. *Left alone* we can be very self-and other- destructive people.

> *Why is it when we talk to God we are said to be praying, and when God talks to us we're said to be schizophrenic?*
> UNKNOWN

When we learn to trust others, we learn to trust God. The ability to do this hangs on two 'nails' . . . we need people who care about us and show love to us, and we need to have a right attitude toward what we are going through. Harboring bitterness and self-blame, believing our own suspicions, and giving way to our fears will not encourage trust.

UNSINKABLE

The torrents, long for me too strong,
Out-drown my will to think,

And the swell of life, in mist-capped waves,
O'er-fills me with its drink.

My struggle's this—to gasp for air?
Or welcome sleep in sweet despair.

But Bouyant and Eternal Hands,
Upbear me, lest I sink.

-Becky McGurrin

IT IS OKAY

It is okay
that I don't know
what thing is next
the way to go . . .
To have no plan
all set in place.
No guarantee
No promised pace.

It is okay
To hold out hands
that tremble with
confusing strands
and shattered bits
of broken plans.
Of troubled water
that sloshes by
and tumbles o'er
each boulder high.
No inlet quiet
No tranquil trickle
No soothing light,
No sharpened sickle
to cut a path
clear and well-known.

It is okay—
I'm not alone.

-Anita

SURROUNDING WITH SUPPORT

1. What is it like to face mental illness in our own family?

When someone we love displays the symptoms of a mental illness, we feel confused and afraid. We feel like saying, "Will you just get over this please? It's embarrassing the whole family!" or "What ails you? Can't you just stop washing your hands all the time?" or "Just eat! It's as simple as that . . . why wouldn't you want to eat?!" As the changes creep over our loved ones, our pain and concern increases. The one who is ill may be oblivious to their problem; they may even think *we* are the ones who need help! Whether we are the one in trouble or the one looking on, the pain is real.

> *You can get the monkey off your back, but the circus never leaves town.*
> ANNE LAMOTT

We may struggle to admit something is wrong, until we are forced to. Watching someone we love turn into a stranger leaves us grieving a major loss. Working through the stages of denial, anger, and sadness takes time . . . often much longer than we wish it would!

> *"I had just gotten home from an afternoon of babysitting and was relaxing on the couch when I heard mom coming down the steps. My heart quickened—How was mom? "Serena, what shall I do with this?" Mom asked. I turned to look at her and saw an empty pretzel bag in her hand. I stared at her, baffled. When my younger brother Seth whispered "She was like this all day", slowly the reality sunk in. The thing we greatly feared WAS coming upon us. Mom was having a breakdown."*
>
> *-'Serena'*

The stress of mental illness affects the whole family. Life becomes unpredictable and unsettling; it is difficult to prepare for the changes because no one knows what's next! The 'real' person comes and goes. Our hopes come and go with them. Life becomes an endless emotional roller coaster. We learn to expect the unexpected.

> *"Over this difficult time, Aunt Abigail came for a week. She was a tremendous emotional and physical support to us. "Well, Kaitlin, shall we go for a drive?" Aunt Abigail asked mom. "The girls . . . they . . . don't . . . want me . . . to," Mom faltered. We looked at each other blankly. What had we done to give Mom that impression? A few minutes later the door slammed shut; Jana and I looked at each other for a long moment, and then simultaneously burst into sobs. Why did this have to happen to us? I stared into Jana's face which mirrored my own red eyes and tear-streaked cheeks. "What's wrong with us?" I giggled. "All we've been doing since Mom left is cry!" We began to giggle, though nothing was funny. Why are we crying anyway? I giggled harder. Cause we need our REAL mom!" Jana choked, and the sobs started all over again.*
>
> *I rolled over in bed. Was I dreaming? Mom was calling! There was mom, smiling and normal. "Mom, you are better!" I yelled. It was not a question, it was the obvious truth. I wrapped my arms around her in a tight hug. Our family rejoiced, enjoying the warm baked oatmeal that was proof that our mom was back! Only yesterday, she would not have been able to do something like that herself. But that afternoon the clouds returned as we realized mom was having a relapse. I sobbed my disappointment into Grandma's understanding ears. "That's how it will be, Serena," she encouraged. "There will be ups and downs before she's better altogether." "But, Grandma, will she ever be better?" I sobbed. This fear was first and foremost in my mind. After Grandma's reassuring words soothed my soul, I got up ready to face life again.*

Avoid thinking you need to have concrete answers. Keep the goal in view and see every inch towards it as progress.
UNKNOWN

The next week mom changed into quiet mode. We heard little or nothing out of her. No more "I guess Joey isn't a devil, is she?" The week slowly drug by and one evening mom started to act her normal self again. We rejoiced, but were afraid to hope it would stay this way. But the next morning I woke to the sound of dishes being washed. That day was the best day of the year! We had so much fun laughing, talking, and reconnecting with mom again. "I forgot it was this wonderful to have a mom," I whispered to my sister as we listened to mom preparing supper. "Please, tell me I'm not dreaming!"

-'Serena'

The stress of relating to someone who is mentally disturbed puts pressure on our own equilibrium. We struggle to return to normal life. It unnerves us when an irritable, depressed mood flips into a giddy, engaging one. Angry accusations make us doubt our own ability to make even simple decisions. Feeling lost and confused, we make desperate attempts to bring them to their senses. We begin to question our own sanity! What happened just a half hour ago, or were we just imagining things? Why do they change like that? How responsible are they for their actions? The questions seem endless!

We cannot do great things. We can only do little things with great love.
MOTHER TERESA

2. What can we do to halt the downslide of an illness?

1. DO something! Learn all you can as quickly as possible. Look into genetics as well as other possible stressors.
2. Talk to others who have worked with something similar.
3. Make an appointment with a doctor as soon as you can. You don't have time to go to college or sort

thru the terrific maze of 'cure all' suggestions. Don't wait till it's an emergency to make an appointment. You will often need to wait several weeks for an opening. In critical situations, fax basic information ahead of time so the doctor has a little background.

4. Let your doctors know how serious things are . . . you won't be able to do this if you are in denial yourself! If you are unable to say everything in front of the one who is ill, write details down and give them to the doctor.

5. Try to remain open-minded. When we are desperate for answers it is easy to go in circles or get hung up on our own conclusions. Stick with your doctor. Research on your own, but ask his opinion on what you read; you are not there to educate *him!*

6. Do your best to provide stability for any children involved; arrange for them to go to other families if needed.

7. Surround yourself with support people.

8. Follow through with the decided-upon plan. It should not be your goal to reduce their medications as soon as possible. Do whatever it takes to help them live profitably!

We love quick-fix answers, molds, and predictable outcomes, but most of the time, Life simply doesn't work this way. Our efforts often feel like a 'stab in the dark' and sometimes a 'stab in the back'. While we learn a lot from each other, situations vary greatly and applying conclusions from one case to the next can be very harmful. However, getting help as early as possible and not giving up easily goes a long way:

"Last summer my fifteen-year-old son began to act strange. We recognized the symptoms and took him to a psychiatrist. He acted very normal at the office, so the doctor decided he was just being immature. However, sometime later he began hearing things, like me calling him or the phone ringing. He was afraid of windows and doors, thinking maybe someone would come in and get him. I was alarmed, but I also knew medicine could help. I took him back to the psychiatrist who prescribed lithium. He improved immediately, reinforcing a bipolar diagnosis. He is doing very well. I think it is good that we caught it in the beginning stages. A doctor explained that each time a person has a major bipolar episode, it affects their brain and increases the likelihood that they will have another one."

-'Kayla'

Plain people are strong believers of brotherhood and support which is an invaluable gift. However, in this type of situation, this trait can quickly become a serious complication. What we see as truth can block our ability to provide the safe and loving relationships we so desperately need. Working through the maze of advice while figuring out how to keep things from getting worse can be completely exhausting.

"The 'verbal war' raged on about what would fix Charlotte. The arguments were long and loud. Fingers pointed here and there. Some quoted scripture, others watched over her like you would a naughty child. Some suggested herbs. Others felt she needs more of a schedule. I could hardly bear to watch it."

-'Tabitha'

"Make her rest—work her hard—take the children—let her have the children—let her talk all day—-make her be quiet—her mind needs a break from thinking—stabilize her

> *with meds—no meds, they mess up the brain—separate her and her husband—give her nutrition—have Bible studies!"*
>
> -'Susie'

> *"I was told I need more sunshine- the moon affects me- I need my colon cleansed. My daughter, who struggles with the same thing, was told to pray the sinner's prayer or go to someone who deals with demons."*
>
> -'Kayla'

The strain of this kind of nightmare has torn even strong families apart—if not literally, figuratively. Family relationships are often ruined by dogmatic opinions, well-meaning endeavors that only complicate things, or other important issues that fall through the cracks.

To make things worse, the one who is ill may not recognize the symptoms for what they are. Some are delusional but think things are fine. They secretly throw their medication into the trash. Convincing them help is necessary seems impossible. Try anyway! Tap into anything that gives them incentive, "Will you do this for the sake of your family?" If they endanger themselves or others, we need to act, NO MATTER WHAT! Enforcing help takes extreme courage and support, but refusing to do this only prolongs the suffering and may result in something drastic and devastating! It is easy to forget *they* are suffering, too, and getting help is not only for the good of those around them.

3. What **positive** *input can we give?*

Relating to someone with a mental health crisis has a way of exposing our own weaknesses, and tests our ability to love even when the return is small. When they get angry, we take it personally. We allow them to control us and then resent the way they are ruining our lives. We blame ourselves for their problems, and forget the many factors beyond our control. We feel victimized when they target us and forget that hurting people hurt others. Instead of being honest, we try to normalize bizarre behavior. Our useless actions only snowball the existing problem.

In spite of our helpless, out of control feelings, we can respond in helpful ways. What are some of these?

LOVE THEM UNCONDITIONALLY

"I knew I had it good. Still, the feelings of frustration grew. I began to try to fix Mom. "That's ridiculous!" I would argue. I would try to get it through her head how she was wasting her life worrying. I used verses or my own made up psychology. I thought I had the key because I could be honest with her in a way others weren't. It seemed like everyone was depending on me to fix up this poor mortal being. Dad seemed helpless to know what to do, so somebody had to do it, I thought. People seemed to notice and sympathize with my efforts, so I knew I was on the right track. She just needed someone to watch her and help her think right!

"Remember—it's not the person's fault, so don't get upset with them! You can't always expect to understand mental illness . . . what you CAN do is try to help . . ."
'KERI'

Then one day Mom stood near me and said, "Well, you can plan my funeral." "Why?" I asked, irritated. "I'm gonna die," she said simply." " Why is she like this?" I thought. "Why can't she just be normal, cleaning the house and cooking like other moms? Why do I have to put up with this?"

"I'm sure your Mom doesn't want to be like that." My friend's words broke into my thinking. It wasn't a totally new thought, but more new thoughts began to form. My mom is sick. She doesn't want this life. She wishes to be normal. She really can't just "will" to do differently. "God, help me to just love Mom instead of judging her," I prayed. I began to see that Mom's first need was simple acceptance from those closest to her."

-'Tabitha'

Unconditional love does not come from our own hearts, but from the heart of God. Our relationships must clearly reflect God and His heart for them. This is a tall order, but ignoring it will drive our efforts into the ground. How can I know if I love them in my own strength or from a wrong motive?

1. I am continually frustrated by the daily wear and tear of the situation, and take it out on the person or others I love.
2. I begin to see them as an object or project rather than a human being.
3. I become impatient with their progress and insist on things changing when and how I think they should.
4. I am offended when others try to help and seem to make more headway than I have.
5. I refuse to look at the needs of my own life that are exposed in the process.
6. My own emotional state begins to rise and fall with their ups and downs. I feel overly responsible for the situation and lose my ability to leave them in God's hands.

Unconditional love does not mean ignoring important issues. Doing this leaves us both feeling used and angry. Expressing legitimate concerns needs to be accepted and practiced by both parties. Concerns should be expressed only in a spirit of humility, prayer, compassion, and courage. It should *not* be an attempt at 'taking each other by the horns', or throwing personal opinions around;

Don't let the unknown twists and turns of the future rob you of your present joy. Let go of your goals and dreams and just be okay with the way things are right now.
SHERRI R.

it demolishes any good we may have accomplished. Evaluate honestly and often your relationship with them. If you see red flags, back off and go to God with your need. Remember, if you are serving them out of a need to be needed, your tank will eventually get empty!

LEARN TO TRULY 'KNOW' THEM

> *"During my mom's depressions, she buried herself in books or took long walks or called her friends to talk. In her good times, she had interests in many areas like flowers and grocery shopping. She loved children and was an excellent story teller. Everyone depended on her to be the brave lady who drove the school children in snowy weather. She wasn't afraid of driving faraway new places. But in these dark depressions, she seemed to care about nothing. It seemed you could have pushed her right over the edge."*
>
> *-'Tabitha'*

We learn to truly know them by asking questions that help us see the whole picture. Even if we think we have it all figured out, we should ask anyway! Not only do we need to know them, they need to know us. Our honesty encourages their honesty. Shallow or intimidating ways of relating encourage denial. Work with them to find root causes instead of trying to control them, accuse them, or being embarrassed by their condition. This will take time, money, and lots of hard work. In our attempt to piece the situation together we need to allow God to direct the process. If a certain instrument is effective, thank Him.

Ministering to the loneliness of a suffering person requires no professional expertise . . . usually . . . a quiet unassuming person: someone who was there whenever needed, who listened more than talked, who didn't keep glancing down at a watch, who hugged and touched, and cried.

DR. PAUL BRAND
The Gift of Pain

Explore other resources, read books, talk with doctors, and contact others who have gone through similar experiences. Become familiar with the mental health care services in your area. Even though your situation seems manageable, be knowledgeable of what they offer. It gives you a leg up if you are abruptly slung into a crisis. Teams such as *Crisis Intervention* can tailor the kind of help you need.

We will not always have an answer, but that is fine! Our ministry is much more about the journey than the destination. Giving them a safe place to express themselves helps them process their thoughts and feelings. Answers may be unwelcome for a long time! Instead of taking this personally, use the time to pray, do your own heart work, and tap into helpful resources of information. Loading ourselves with miracle promises does not prepare us for the long haul and fuels unrealistic expectations in those we are trying to help.

OBSERVE PATTERNS—DO WHAT YOU CAN TO HEAD OFF OR ALLEVIATE PROBLEMS

> *"Charlotte was only fourteen when she became very withdrawn, never smiling at our laughter. She loved to write riveting stories, but there were no more stories. She often sat soberly in a corner. We weren't sure what was wrong. After a while, she returned to her normal self. Again, at age sixteen there was the extreme quietness, sad, sober eyes, and withdrawn expression. She answered questions in a short way. Her mother heard her pleas in the attic to God. What did it all mean? Once again, the spell passed over. One day Charlotte married a young man. Soon after the birth of her first daughter, the shadows fell again. She became sober and withdrawn just like she had earlier. This time I felt even more confused, seeing it up so close. She held her baby close, not letting anyone hold her at church. To many of us, it felt like she disapproved of us. Were we doing something wrong?*

After her baby girl was diagnosed with cancer, everything seemed fall apart. Her thoughts became confused and her talk made little sense. She stood or sat like a statue- with no expression. In the darkest hours, she curled up in a fetal position, feeling utterly apart from God and condemned to hell. We could not let her alone."

-'Tabitha'

> *People don't care how much we know, until they know how much we care!*
> UNKNOWN

Simple observation teaches us a lot. What are the initial 'red flags'? Are they themselves able to recognize them? How do they ask for help? Do they express their feelings verbally or are they quick to 'act them out?'

Don't be shocked by crazy words and actions . . . the state of mind can block their ability to rationalize. Intense feelings that change quickly leave us stunned and confused, while these same feelings leave them frightened and ashamed. 'Holding up a mirror' for them encourages recognition and contact with their own feelings and actions. Help them verbalize what they are feeling by asking questions or suggesting what you suspect may be going on. Expand their 'feeling' vocabulary. "What does "I don't feel well" mean? A gentle attitude keeps them from becoming discouraged.

Be alert to impulsive behavior! It may show in simple things—open windows, doors, drawers, or kettles cooking unattended on the stove. When emotions are high and self-awareness is low, the emotion of the moment is the only reality they can see. An illness can be so severe that they feel "soulless, animal-like, or terrifyingly dead." They may say things like "I don't know why I did that." Or "Who am I?" The loss and shame these feelings trigger has no bounds. It drives them to find answers, and their unstable minds often lead them to false conclusions. Many things happen under this pressure, often in the form of violence or escape. The same escape route may be used over and over again without a thought of the consequences.

"I knew Mary biked a lot when she felt disturbed. It was as if she 'biked' her emotions out. One day when she felt pressured, she grabbed her bike and headed out into the rain. It rained the whole time she was gone. After several hours, she came home drenched, but subdued, with some MacDonald wrappers in hand."

-'Keri'

This ability to function and yet be so sick can be confusing and dangerous! Some can't read a recipe, others sew and cook like normal; this baffles us and deceives us into thinking that nothing is amiss until they melt into uncontrollable crying spells or expound on specific delusional hang-ups. They do strange things, attempts at getting the help they so desperately need:

"Charlotte stood rooted to the floor, gazing at me. I had learned to accept this and no longer felt uncomfortable. I smiled and gave her a hug. She smiled, too, and then it was gone. We went for a walk, climbing the hill behind the house in silence. Suddenly Charlotte climbed up a snow bank. I turned and saw her bend down to put snow in her mouth . . . so unlike the 'real' Charlotte who was always full of grace and dignity. "You're eating SNOW?" I said it as a question. Charlotte's eyes looked oddly hopeful. "Maybe it will help me," she said simply. A light clicked on in my head. All those strange things she does—putting strange things in her mouth, standing on furniture . . . it always has a reason. In her mind it makes perfect sense! She is, in her own desperate way, trying to find a cure to this grueling experience. I hugged her. She stared back at me blankly."

-'Tabitha'

Noticing their symptoms helps us be slow to judge their condition. Is it possible that a troublesome behavior is a *char-*

acteristic of the illness instead of a character flaw? These may be things they cannot help. Their weakest spots magnify under the effects of an illness and so would yours! This perspective keeps you from resenting them or placing unreasonable demands on them.

ACCEPT THEIR LIMITATIONS.

"My father had his second breakdown fourteen years after his first. This time we were able to care for him at home, with medication. His brother took off from work two weeks to come and help. Some of us children also helped take care of him and took our turns watching him at night. This time his healing was more gradual, a slow, uphill climb. He didn't work well on his own; mom had to work with him and coach him in the greenhouse. Daddy found joy in making simple wood crafts, marble rollers, kites, etc. He struggled a lot with depression and feelings of worthlessness. Mom took him along when she visited friends and relatives because he enjoyed visiting and it helped cheer him up. We were blest with answered prayer; in his later years he recommitted his life to God and found peace. He stayed on medication the rest of his life.

The best thing loved ones can do for those who are hurting is show them acceptance and tender, loving care. Be patient with the slow healing process! Even the longest journey begins with a single step."

-Anna Putt

Every inch of progress is a mile.
ANNA PUTT

Those who are struggling often do not communicate effectively. They may be unaware of their condition, unable to think rationally, or feel emotionally 'paralyzed'. When they do express themselves, it is easy to become frightened and angry by what we hear. We grab for our toolboxes and try to fix their faulty thinking, when instead we should continue listening. *Validate! Validate! Validate!* Thank them for giving you a glimpse of their inner struggle. Deciding they just need more self-control or will power throws another 'dagger' into the ring. Your condemnation will be felt.

Expect off-the-wall feelings and comments! If feelings are strong, negative, or weird we tend to downplay their messages. It is quite an art to stop, listen, and read between the lines. What are they trying to say and how do we echo reality back to them? While we help them curb their extreme thinking, we must not teach them to discredit *all feeling.*

> *"I feel like I should pay Lois!" Mom announced from her spot on the worn, tan sofa. "Why?" Jana questioned. "Because I am sitting here on this couch," mom answered with a concerned look in her eyes. As Jana reassured mom, we girls tried to keep a straight face from our spot in the corner where we had an intense game of chess going. "Funny thing is," I told Jana, as we were getting ready for bed that evening, "a few days ago we would have run to our room bawling." We were learning to laugh at mom's abstract comments. We were learning to accept our circumstances and make the best of them. We were learning how to relate to this 'strange' woman, who was our mom!"*
>
> *-'Serena'*

Be careful to avoid long discussions which tire their already exhausted minds or reinforce their delusions. Having Bible studies, in-depth evaluations of their childhood, or even simple charts simply will not penetrate! It often makes them worse. Not only does it reinforce their warped beliefs, they may come to false conclusions about what you are trying to tell them. Someone described this as, "The gray wall that won't let me understand anything," and then sighed, "I guess it means I am just not disciplining myself like I should."

We all face a strong desire to restore reason by reasoning, but arguing with a delusion often merely entrenches the belief!

> *"I had some conversations with her on the phone. She appeared so normal, and an unsuspecting person would not have picked anything up. I thought I would try to reason with her and I specifically remember a two hour conversation where I got nowhere and ended up feeling frustrated with her and with myself. I dished out love and listening and she just took me in circles. The more I tried to reason with her and make sense of things, the more confused I got. Then our counselor told me, "I wouldn't go into those kinds of conversations with her. Just keep it light and cheerful."*
>
> -*'Wanda'*

Expect havoc in your relationships, but don't be the source of it, be the constant. Understanding they really do want to have a relationship will help you persist. Every time their behavior severs a tie, it feeds their fear of being deserted again; they develop patterns of control, such as calling you five times in the middle of the night. At the time, they simply do not have what it takes to understand this is what drives people away. Being patient with them saves them from another bead in the string of broken relationships.

Sometimes we go in circles trying to figure out how responsible they are for their actions. Those who are suffering often feel like they are being carried along where they don't want to go. Some slouch into victim mode while others adamantly fight any help that is offered. Helping them find a balance isn't easy!

When in doubt, it is better to err on the side of compassion. Being critical and judgmental is easier than looking at the whole picture.

FOUR CRITICAL LIFE MESSAGES:

I believe in you.
You are listened to.
You are cared for.
You are very important to me.

IF YOU CANNOT REDUCE STRESS, HELP MAKE IT DOABLE

The story is told of two sisters who survived the Holocaust. Seren was the oldest and the strongest—Esther, however, was gentler in nature, extra-sensitive to the inhumane things they were experiencing. One terrible night the air raid sirens screamed on and on. Esther started screaming too and couldn't stop. In desperation, Seren took the dish towel she had in her hand and told Esther to tear it into strips until the bombing stopped. It worked. Every day after that, Seren salvaged scraps of material and hid them under her pillow. When the sirens began to scream, Seren grabbed a piece for her sister as they ran for the shelter. Her diligent efforts to protect her sister paid off. They both survived.

What you can't help them avoid, help them survive! Do not minimize their pain! A lack of empathy leaves them feeling even more alone. Stuffing the reality of their feelings only encourages them to blow up later, hurting themselves or other people. Help them learn how to live with pain. They may ask, "Where is God? Why? Why? WHY?" We can assure them God has not forsaken them. "We can't explain why God has allowed this. Can you be okay with that?"

Healthy food, personal love, and structure provide a strong backbone for our homes. This is true for everyone, but *especially* for those prone to mental illness. Diet, exercise, schedules, time for hobbies, and spending habits are all included. If Matthew gets up at ten, drinks mountain dew for breakfast, skips lunch because he isn't hungry, eats a bag of chips mid afternoon and reads book until midnight, is it any wonder his mental health suffers?

Protect them from specific 'triggers'! Triggers are situations or people that excite them. Even birds can experience a 'trigger.' We bought a beautiful, smart parrot when it was six months old. Frank gently tried to catch it with a black glove while it flew wildly into the sides of its cage. Once it got used to being held we stopped the 'glove' sessions. But it did not forget that glove! For months our parrot hated the color black, from the socks on the table to the hot pad in the drawer. Triggers are also common for people who are in emotional distress. Avoid causing unnecessary agony by doing things that remind them of past pain or trigger strong emotional responses.

We also need to protect them as much as possible from the stigma of mental illness, careless remarks, and critical eyes. This may be difficult to do.

> *"Again, it is hard. People don't understand why one so young needs to be on medicine and think that in a little he should be able to get off it. I am weary of trying to explain that he might need to be on medicine for life, like a diabetic. At least he is mostly normal now and I don't need to explain strange behavior. There still are times though, when he is either depressed or enthusiastic. Sometimes I allow him to stay home from church or stay in his room when other people are here. I allow him to eat his meals in his room, because he is unable to deal with people at the table. I am sure people would not understand this, if they were to know about it. They would think I am being too soft and not disciplining him properly. They would think it's because there isn't a father in the home. (My husband died from cancer.) I never know what to say when people ask where he is. I try to tell them that "he isn't feeling well." Often they want to know what it is and start asking if it's the stomach flu. Sometimes we tell the people who know more that "he isn't doing well." They still think it's something he will get over."*
>
> *-'Kayla'*

Your zeal for an issue should not leave a trail of hurting people.
'BARRY'

SPEAK INTO PROBLEM AREAS AND COORDINATE PLANS

First of all, gird yourself with an optimistic, cheerful attitude! Open your eyes to the growth that has already taken place. While helping them form goals, we don't always know what to put on the front burner, nor do we know how capable they are. We need to remember—what may be a simple matter to us may be hard work for them! This keeps us from resenting the need to monitor details we feel they should already know. One of the most important goals is to rebuild their belief that it *can* be done!

> *"I had been feeling bad for several weeks. One morning my friend called and asked how I was. She was quick to decipher the truth. She asked if I called my doctor yet. I said I simply didn't have the strength to pick up the phone. She encouraged me to do just that! "I want you to call him as soon as we are finished, and I will check up on you later to see how it went," she promised. It was just what I needed."*
>
> *-Lorraine W.*

Doctors need to know little, everyday details so they can give tailored assistance. Information needs to be complete and clear. If the one who is ill is unable to give the true picture of how things are, someone will need to do this for them. Do not rely on them to communicate the need to the doctor, or to communicate the doctor's orders to you! If you are the go-between, use the expression needed to convey your concern. Saying in a flat voice "I really should talk to you sometime because Erica needs a little help," is an understatement when she is violent or suicidal. Don't try to butter up a serious situation— Instead say, "Can you call me right away? We need help now!"

Make sure medication doses are being taken, pills have a way of disappearing mysteriously into trash cans. Foggy minds find it easy to skip doses. While controlling minute details is exhausting and frustrating for both parties, they need to be responsible to someone. We will need to win their respect and cooperation.

If they are prone to manipulate, firm limits need to be set on acceptable behavior that are clear, consistent, logical, and enforced promptly. Agreeing on a plan and sticking to that agreement when someone is argumentative and antagonistic can be very difficult. How do you stick to your guns without becoming a control freak? Being consistent even under resistance assures them that their actions will not destroy the relationship as it has so often in the past. If you do not want their 'craziness' to destroy them, you must first of all refuse to let it destroy you.

Being able to control our own emotions in a crisis situation is extremely important. We need to practice regulating our own emotion *outside* of crisis situations. Doing this helps us internalize the problem; helping someone who is out of control feel UNDERSTOOD goes a long way in bringing down the heat of their emotion. We need to allow compassion to take over our reactions. Say "I can see why you find this so hard." It does not mean saying "It can't be that bad. You are blowing things way up." Give time and space and then offer your help. Together, come up with a solution for the present problem, allowing them to pick an option that they can connect with and support.

Being proactive may prevent a crisis. Look ahead and discuss things that may make it difficult to follow through with the agreement (such as the habit of ignoring calls or texts when upset, or sleeping in really late.) Are there ways you can help them meet their goals? Ask them to report back . . . stay connected!

Even as helpers, we need to consider carefully who needs to change. As we help others on their journey, it is not uncommon to uncover problem areas in our own lives. Is my way of relating making things better or worse? Am I impatiently demanding instant change? Are we willing to work just as hard as we expect them to? It is so easy to polish, trim, evade or dye what we find to justify our own wrong attitudes or failures. This is when a 'team' of helpers can be useful! Alone, it becomes difficult to see the woods for the trees!

4. How should we relate to unhealthy responses?

Laura listened half-heartedly to the discussions going on. She hoped they noticed that she wasn't saying anything. Saying nothing was one way to get their attention! Sure enough, Betty finally stepped up and asked how she was doing. Laura responded curtly and sourly, "As good as can be expected," and began to enumerate the latest trials. Bitterly, she talked on and on.

Kate sat on the sofa and gobbled down a box of chocolates. Eating helped her forget her misery and boosted her tired spirits. For a little she felt good! For a little she forgot the awful drag of another boring, horrible day. For a little, she felt a burst of energy. She knew she was gaining weight, but she felt helpless . . .

Instead of pointing to the obvious needs of these girls, why don't we look at ourselves? Are we meeting their needs where we can? Is our lack of attention driving them to demand our attention? Are we falsely accusing them or being impatient with their needs? How can we help them avoid the traps of their condition?

If my devils are to leave me, I am afraid my angels will take flight as well.
RAINER MARIA RILKE

Remembering they are surrounded by pain, physical and mental, helps us sympathize with their drive to feel better. Naturally, they will try to find ways to cope with the horror of their condition. Maybe they summed up the courage they needed to survive from a young age! Maybe they faced their battles alone for years, doing the best they could. But as they move from childhood to adulthood, they will discover many of their 'survival methods' actually hinder their spiritual growth, making it impossible for others to help them.

Self-protective maneuvers or a demanding attitude can be really irritating, especially if the road has been long and we have sacrificed a lot! They may be super –vigilant, use intimidation tactics, lie, live in a dream world, battle false guilt, feel overly responsible, horde, or hide family secrets. Our job is to help them sort what serves them well and what hinders. There is a big difference between boundaries and walls. Boundaries are used to avoid relapses, maintain respect, and keep relationships healthy while walls encourage distance and close doors. Hard work and open communication coupled with patience for the long haul can break these ingrained habits or ways of coping.

Manipulation is a twin of self-protection. Derailing it takes a lot of hard work. Because of our sinful nature, we are all guilty of manipulating in order to get what we want, when we want, and how we want. A toddler quickly learns if pouting gets him the lollipop at the store. Even adults resort to childish and immature ways of bringing relief to their immediate needs. Disappointment, fear, or loss makes them susceptible to this form of staying in control because they are determined to protect themselves from further hurt.

When our children manipulate, we address it quietly and firmly, giving them clear instructions and backing them up with consistent actions. We encourage them to take responsibility for their actions without placing *too much* on their little shoulders. We need to be sure we ARE doing what we can to alleviate what they can't help. If children can get us to act like they are, they can excuse their own behavior. By refusing to 'catch the ball' or engage in the tussle, they are left with their problems in their own lap. Doing this may make us "the meanest parents on earth" but it encourages them to take responsibility where they can. It takes Dads of steel and velvet and Moms of velvet and steel to know how to relate in a calm but firm way to the push and pull of a child who wants to force things to go their own way. It also takes strong adult figures to relate to other adults who are acting this way.

Hurtful parents or authority figures that are focused on control themselves often overlook or intensify these ingrained responses. When a child pouts, the parent quietly snarls "okay, and then be that way" or shouts "if you don't stop it, something dreadful will happen to you!" This teaches them to respond out of fear instead of love. It teaches them that misbehaving is one way to get the attention they so desperately crave. Hurtful authority may be defensive, demanding respect from others and ruling over them with an iron hand. It gives them a feeling of control and excuses them from looking at their own issues and winning the respect of others rather than demanding it.

When we find ourselves 'locking horns' with our own children we need to look at ourselves first. Are we guilty of being too controlling? If we are, we *better* their skills of manipulation and self–protection. Not only do we give them our poor example, we give them practice! If we talk our heads off, they turn their minds off. We may even use scripture to try to get our way. This is very harmful, turning something pure and holy into a fearsome and twisted tool. We need to make sure our own hearts are healed and healthy. This lays a secure and stable platform for our children or anyone we may be working with.

5. Is this my fault?

"What did we do wrong?" "What brought her to this point?" "How could we have avoided this?" We can waste a lot of time and mental energy hashing over misconceptions, missed opportunities, and bad turnouts. Not only do we have our own guilt to work with, we may face hateful accusations from the one who is ill who is also trying to figure out what went wrong.

We instinctively feel responsible for those we love and for everything that happens to them. Guilt over someone's illness can be very unreasonable. Bottling up our struggles and questions only intensifies them. Being open about them and sharing them with people we trust helps us identify the false thinking that drives our guilt. People who are not as intensely involved will have a perspective that helps *us* to reason rationally. Even though the flood of perspectives can be completely overwhelming, we may find hidden answers. If we can wrestle with and disengage the grip of false guilt, we will have the power to help our loved ones do the same. It is amazing how they mirror us and our own attitudes in their helpless condition!

It is easier to feel guilty than to accept the way things are . . . guilt at least allows us a sense of control. We *could* have done something! Dwelling on what we may have missed in the past saps our ability to be of much help in the present. This, ironically, provides more to feel guilty about in the future. We need to live as fully as possible in the present, working with what we do know, instead of becoming frustrated over questions that have no answers. This is a good long-term goal to have—much easier to talk about than to do!

> *. . .we can be as separate as the fingers, yet one as the hand in all things essential to mutual progress.*
> BOOKER T. WASHINGTON

6. How can I survive?

"I looked around and the sight that met my eyes overwhelmed my tired body. The house was a sight to behold! There was clutter everywhere . . . stacks of dishes, baking supplies, stacks of cookies to put away, a dirty floor, piles of wash waiting to be brought in and supper waiting to be made. And my aunt told us to take mom on a walk every day. We hadn't done that yet! (Mom couldn't be trusted to go herself. We didn't know where she would go!) I stared at my sister in despair. Suddenly we missed our normally ambitious mom very much! That night, I pulled the fuzzy blanket over

my head and thought back over my day. My heart swelled with thankfulness to God. . . . He does care about every detail of our life! Just at the most overwhelming moment, Dad walked in the door and he and mom got the wash in. Then Dad took her on a walk. Anne and her three girls walked in the door and it didn't take long till all the work was done. "Thanks so much, God, for true friends who are there to support us!"

-'Serena'

It is almost impossible to stay intact without the support of family and friends. Those of us who have faced this type of struggle in our family unit testify to the simple things that others have done to bring relief to our own emotional and physical needs.

"God, you are powerful and we know you can heal Kaitlin. . . ." Anne's voice broke, and she fumbled for a tissue. I clutched my mug of tea tighter and took a deep breath in an effort to calm my emotion as I listened to Anne's prayer. It meant much, SO MUCH, to have people say they care and show it.

Slowly I opened the creaky mailbox and peered inside. . . . What was this? A card addressed to me! Yeah! I clutched it tightly, dug my other hand deep into my warm pocket, and ran . . . somehow I felt it was something special. Later, in the privacy of my own room, I opened it carefully. "Dear Serena," I read, "I know you are going through a lot right now. . . ." I could read no further. I buried my head in my grey jacket sleeve and let the tears fall. . . .

"Hard times help us grow," my aunt was saying. "This experience will make you stronger. . . ." "But she's not our real mom, it's like we have to learn to relate to a totally new person," I wailed, and then glanced at the clock. It was eleven o'clock!

My aunt grabbed me in a tight embrace. "Sleep well, Seree, remember, me and many others are praying. Your mom is just like someone with cancer . . . they can't help they have cancer any more than she can help how she acts." That night I once again drifted off to sleep with a wet pillow . . . but this time there was a spark of hope in my heart."

-'Serena'

The stress of mental illness tests a family from all angles. Even though siblings come from the same family, the way they experience life may vary greatly.

"Although my sister and I are from the same home, I don't think we had the same emotional experiences. For one, while she was quiet, I talked my problems out with my Dad and other trusted adults. I also cried easily when the stress was high. It took a lot of pressure off me. My sister's tears stayed frozen and I imagine her pain as well. I was talkative and had many friends, and school work was easy. For her, school was a trial. I think these factors contributed to her depression in later years."

-'Sara'

If you are the marriage partner of an ill spouse, you will find yourself busy with the needs of your spouse and your children. This will be completely exhausting, but listen to what the following writer has to say about her dad:

"Dad was a busy, hardworking farmer who was often stressed out from the pressures of caring for his wife, yet he did not forget his children! Looking back, I am amazed at the pressure he was under. In spite of this, he was our hero! We followed him everywhere. He had a marvelous sense of humor that often cheered us up no matter how sad we were feeling. Life often felt very unfair, but he taught us that life isn't fair. It doesn't have to be fair! God has lessons for us to learn, and someday He will reward us richly. Dad encouraged us

Helping children understand how mental illness affects their parent is a golden opportunity. It gives them the ability to see beyond the illness to the love that is there!
'KERI'

that God loved and cared for us. I learned at a young age to pray for our many needs. And God often answered our prayers; this gave me a strong feeling of connection and dependence on God. Everything we needed to know, from manners to Christian convictions came from him. I am sure God was helping him or he could have never done it. We are very loyal to him and come to him with everything, and in return receive wise advice. I wish all children had a dad like him!"

-'Sara'

It can be very easy for a family to 'drown' in the desperate needs of an ill person. Unless we continue to replenish ourselves and go at a speed we can tolerate, we will collapse. Keeping our own friends and activities apart from the one who is ill helps keep a certain amount of padding between us and the situation. It gives us a chance to evaluate things from a different angle and keeps it from swallowing us up.

"Carmen followed me around in my kitchen all morning. We worked together, talked together, ate together and took walks together. But I always blocked out some time in the afternoon to rest alone. It was a reprieve—a place where I could refocus, clear my brain, and plan the rest of the day. One day I wearily withdrew, lying down to rest. Suddenly, an odd feeling crept over me—I sensed I was not alone in the room. I turned, and there beside me, her head on MY pillow, lay Carmen. I felt like I was going to lose my own mind. It was the crest of a wave of suffocation that had been sweeping over my whole life.

I became aware of the way not only our own problems, but other people's problems, take a toll in our life. If we aren't careful, everything revolves around the latest crisis. Everything, including the most precious and private times of our life; such as those precious fifteen minutes hubby and I have together before sleep takes over. Guess what we're thinking about and hashing over?—Carmen and her latest need. She literally crawls into our bed in more ways than one!"

-'Amanda'

This is why we need boundaries. If we find this hard to stick to, we need to check our motives. Do we fear their response or feel too responsible for their condition? Are we trying to look good to others or filling our own needs in some way? True love is active and purposeful, not stagnant and permissive. It has a way of keeping its eyes open to wrong doing and staying engaged in spite of it. But staying engaged does not mean carrying them every step of the way. We have our own limits, and maintaining those leaves us with something to give.

Violating our limits may permanently damage our relationships! Silent resentment without clear confrontation destroys years of mentoring. We can communicate our own needs without transferring a message of rejection. Validate their need of support, but explain honestly what you are doing and why. Be willing to take it on your own shoulders. Say "I have plans today and can't spend the day with you"—even if the plan is to go for a bike ride! Don't say "I need a break from you or I will go crazy!" Remember it is for your own good; don't feel guilty about it! Help them find other ways to pass the time. "Why don't we check if you can visit Aunt Bertha

---

"Throughout my adolescent years I had to dodge the monster of self-pity. Why did I have a mom who was mentally ill? Not only did I worry over her, I had so many responsibilities! The other girls my age were so carefree! However, I tried to count my blessings whenever I was tempted to feel I had it tough. I was quite successful because I did have a lot to be thankful for. It was a way of coping and helped me a lot. Later, people told me I'm so optimistic that I'm not even realistic. I didn't like that accusation, either!"

'SARA'

---

for a couple hours this afternoon?" If you feel there is no one else who can relate to them, it's probably time for a reality check!

If stating a limit upsets them, don't give in! It will push you toward 'burnout', and cost you their respect. Keep in mind that it is painful for them, and tell them you understand that. Repeat your limit. Treat them like adults by explaining the pros and cons—don't simply demand compliance and threaten punishment. Calm their anxiety by explaining it in a way that they can grasp. Limits are not meant to be hard, unshifting walls . . . they openly consider the immediate needs. Healthy limits bend and flex, understanding that things do shift with time, people, and situations.

Some people believe seeking outside help is a sign of weakness. Believing this leads to a lot of unnecessary suffering. It is almost impossible for families to handle these things alone without the input and support of others who care. Deciding we can't talk about the most significant parts of our life is bound to take its toll. It leaves us feeling isolated and resentful and cuts off valuable input. Considering what our friends say is one way to avoid bad outcomes and overwhelming guilt. Our blind spots as a family can keep us from seeing something very important!

It is true; prejudice and overall ignorance about mental illness are major stumbling blocks. People find it easier to support a cancer struggle than a mental illness struggle. Our friends may feel awkward about the situation and, with the best of intentions, say or do the wrong things. We may even hear gossip and personal opinions expressed in a condemning way. If mental health needs *are* mentioned at prayer meeting, people tend to skirt around the concern or pray fervently that the person repents or learns to trust God. They also tend to shy away from us and those who are struggling, thoughtlessly feeding the family's fears and feelings of guilt. It is unfortunate that on top of everything else, we need to educate others, with the realization that what we are saying may still be rejected. People have no idea how much this hurts. I have been guilty of praying—Give it to them, Lord!

We need to be willing to share the diagnosis, prognosis, and any information that is helpful with friends and family. Not only this, we should openly share the confusion and heartache we experience! This type of openness is very freeing! Our firsthand experience puts us in a position of being able to speak with authority and compassion. Those who truly care will pay attention to what we are saying because they are concerned about our needs and the needs of our family. Also, people usually follow our lead regarding how much to discuss the situation. Do not expect them to ask how things are if we never bring the subject up ourselves! However, a large amount of misunderstanding and condemnation tends to close us up. If this happens, we need to find SOMEONE we can trust and not become resistant to all outside input. It is wise to assume there are people who care!

Church friends, mostly,
they wave from a distance.
They say nothing.
Or they say "We can't imagine."
And they can't. It's true.
They can't imagine what it's like
To see a loved one
Broken and lost,
Wandering about in an effort
To find sanity.
They can't imagine
The loneliness
We feel as we look across
The divide.
The divide that defines "normal".
The divide that causes them
To back away
And wave from a distance.
ANONYMOUS

When a loved one faces severe depression, it touches your life in a very deep way, in some ways more painful than death. Not only does it unsettle your whole life, it makes you feel inferior to other families who look like they 'have it all put together.' I faced the questions, "Why did this happen to my brother instead of me? Why does this person I love so much have to fight and struggle along, always on the edge of despair, while I live a relatively normal life?" (Even though riding their emotional roller coaster feels pretty far from normal sometimes!) These questions snuck guilty feelings into my heart. I also felt frustrated and confused because even though we were siblings, we couldn't understand each other's worlds. I needed to remember that I wasn't responsible for my brother's problems or actions, but I could still do my part to help him understand himself and seek help.

Also, how can you love someone so much and at the same time distrust them? We love the person for who they really are and yet distrust the 'stranger' they have become. A certain amount of distrust is not a bad thing! At the same time, you need to do your best to let them know they can achieve; they can learn how to move forward in life! It is also easy to distrust others. I shared some of our families' struggles with a friend, only to hear my own comments come back to me from another route in a blown-up version. Another time I shared with a friend and she looked at me blankly. She obviously did not connect with my situation. It was easy to go away discouraged, determined to keep things to myself.

Sometimes amidst the distrust and stress I began to wonder, "Is our family dysfunctional?" This 'suspicious' feeling often comes from other people and we pick up on it. After all, doesn't problem after problem speak of dysfunction? Yes, it can. But that is not the real test. My parents taught me the real test is what I do with my problems. Are you embarrassed of your families' struggles or are you accepting the fact that mental illness is part of life on earth and you need to be open to talk about it? Even though some people do not understand, it still doesn't need to be a shameful thing.

Control is the last thing you feel like you have on a roller coaster ride. You never know which way you may be thrown. All you can do is hang on and grasp for control tactics. If you aren't careful, you will quickly become a control freak. My brother's illness made me feel very out of control of my life. I dreaded the ups and downs because I knew the higher we went, the harder we crashed to the ground. It took me a long time to realize he wasn't on the roller coaster by choice, but I was. I was making my own life miserable.

It is a fact that mental illness brings extreme stress to family and relationships. As a family, it is your choice to allow it to drive you apart or bring you together. There were times we felt we were being driven apart, but God always brought us around to realize that we've got to do this together! Being able to laugh together over seemingly un-humorous or embarrassing episodes was one of our major helps! The best gift you can give to a suffering loved one is your love and affirmation. Let them know you will be there for them through all the tortures of their illness. Let them see you believe in your heart that the small light in their bleak midnight is not just a taunting dream. Keep them looking up!!

The path to recovery can be so loopy and confusing. If our trust is based on human, earthly help, we <u>will</u> crash with the roller coaster. We must continue to trust that God is working in and through all the disappointments, and our trust will stand.

-By a Sibling

GUIDELINES:

- Ask a family what you can do for them rather than telling them what you would do, especially if you have no experience with the illness.
- *When you call on the phone, ask if it is an appropriate time to discuss their needs. They may have a hard time handling extra phone calls and many visits. They are too fragile to handle a lot of noise and excitement.*
- Avoid disturbing the family, especially for the first week after the person comes home from the hospital unless you are called for. The family needs to work at building a trust again, which is very strenuous.
- *Ask the caregiver how the person may feel about a visit from you, especially if you haven't had a previous caring relationship, or you are an authority figure. They do not reject authority necessarily, but may carry strong and unusual guilt feelings.*
- Allow the family to protect bizarre behavior. It's not kind to reveal what they did in a 'dreamlike' state.
- *Do not believe everything they say. They often don't know what is real and what is not real, but it can sound nearly right.*
- They may laugh and laugh even if you feel like crying or are discussing something serious. They can't help it.
- *Be aware that they often repeat certain statements over and over and over again. And they are usually* relationship-breaking ideas. *This is extremely taxing to a family.*
- Expect disjointed conversation. We call this *leaps in logic*. They are hard to follow in their conversations and may

have very convoluted reasoning and grandiose ideas. They may also not be able to concentrate on what you say, nor remember what you have said. This all gets better with healing.

- *If you visit them alone, please discuss your conversation later with the caregiver. We are often very sensitive to what they might have said.*

- A care and a compassion for their torment and an understanding for their capacity to *fluctuate* will go a long way toward our being able to trust your friendship.

    e.g. If you make a visit they may be tired, and say things like, "*my parents spoiled my evening, or my wife lied, or my husband is looking at the neighbor's wife, or I need to smoke.*"

- *Do we act on these statements? No. Once the mind heals, these thoughts are replaced with good ones. Do we blame them? No. Again, in their well moments, they no longer believe or say these things.*

- If you can't offer years of close support, please be slow to dig for information and offer advice. It feels like spying and then our loved one's care is dropped like a 'hot potato' when your way has not worked.

- *Please do not discuss excommunication or church confessions until they heal and are ready. They likely feel very wicked and may think of suicide. Be willing to trust the caregiver to eventually discuss issues that might need church oversight. Right at the time of crisis there is so much to get straightened out that you work a little at a time.*

- Be very slow to blame a husband, a wife, or a parent. We as caregivers are not perfect.

- *Give the family space. Many times they know much more about the person than anyone else and should be respected.*
- It is very important to get help at the first sign of a difficulty. If there is damaging behavior on the part of a parent, help should be sought, especially right away. Too many children are suffering, and letting these things get worse makes recovery very difficult.
- *Anyone who chooses to see the doctor should be respected for doing so. Healing is possible, especially today with good health care.*

-By a Caregiver

DREAMS REBORN

Oh, the barren, empty fields—
Little breezes filled with chills.
Few remain of crackly stalks,
Few their rustly, whispered talks.

Fall has harshly bid the leaves
Drop from all their dappled trees.
Harvest moons must slip away
Leaving shadows at their play.

But within the wind's a note
Trilling songs of dreams, remote.
Dreams of buds, yet sweeter still
'Cause they had bare trees to fill.

-Marlena M.

TAKEN FROM PSALM 41

Blessed is he who has regard for the weak; the Lord delivers him in times of trouble . . . the Lord will protect and preserve his life . . . the Lord will sustain him on his sickbed.

My enemies say of me in malice, "When will he die and his name perish?" Whenever one comes to see me, he speaks falsely, while his heart gathers slander, then he goes out and spreads it abroad.

All my enemies whisper together against me; they imagine the worst for me, saying, "A vile disease has beset him; and he will never get up from the place where he lies." Even my close friend, whom I trusted, he who shared my bread, has lifted up his heel against me.

But you, O Lord, have mercy on me . . . I know that you are pleased with me, for my enemy does not triumph over me.

Praise be to the LORD . . .

COMMITMENTS FOR COPING

1. How can I learn to stay well?

ACCEPT YOURSELF AND YOUR STRUGGLES.

Variety is God's specialty. He did not shape us all with the same cookie cutter for a reason! The story *You are Special* by Max Lucado depicts Him bent over his workshop table putting us together—eye color, hair color, shape and height, emotional makeup. In and through that variety he mixes specific needs- things he *allows* for the purpose of drawing us to Himself. This concept may be hard to grasp, because most of us do not enjoy or appreciate our struggles at all. In fact, we tend to think God made a mistake somewhere. We are not the only ones that struggle from diseases that cripple, distort, maim, and debilitate. We learn a lot from watching others relate to their challenges. Just like the cripple, we need to come to an acceptance of what God has allowed.

Doing what you can-
Being what you are,
Shine like a glowworm
if you cannot be a star.
Work like a pulley
if you cannot be a crane
Just be a wheel greaser,
if you cannot drive the train.
UNKNOWN

Originally, man was created PERFECTLY, reflecting a perfect Creator. But when Adam and Eve sinned, we all took on the consequences. Sin brought pain, deceit, death, and diseases. From then on, man found himself in a flawed condition, living flawed lives in flawed bodies. God created us with the ability to make our own choices even though He knew what would happen. But He also cleared a pathway through the resulting chaos. He sent the best He had—His son Jesus Christ. Through His death on the cross—at the hands of His own creation—and our acceptance of His forgiveness, we find life and hope.

Those of us who have received Christ as our Savior have experienced both our fallen state and our redeemed state. When we love God and submit to His authority, He transforms us in beautiful ways. God allows questions, but He does not always give answers. When we live in anger over our flawed lives, we reject Him. When we demand death, we are telling Him He is not worth living for. We need to be willing to embrace pain, sorrow, and suffering, believing that He will make a way for us.

Sometimes we try to define who we are outside of God. Defining who we are must include facing God's divine authority in our lives. Some circumstances and experiences He has allowed are much harder to accept than others. When we reject ourselves, we accuse God of making a mistake. We accuse Him of flawed work, when in actuality these flaws are a part of the fall. In His great kindness, He stoops down and helps us to live and love well in spite of physical deformities, mental weakness, and sinful tendencies. In fact, He often uses these very things to bring glory to Him!

We LOVE to learn all we can about staying well! This is good, but how does it affect our attitudes if, in spite of precautions, we become ill or have a relapse? Are we able to accept what happens *in spite of* our best efforts? Shame has us hiding behind masks, excuses, and camouflages. This hinders God's ability to bring about good.

REACH OUT TO OTHERS FOR HELP

Relating to your doctors:

Are you sticking with your treatment plan and seeing your doctors on a regular basis? They evaluate how you are doing, tracking symptoms or other side effects. They monitor things like weight, blood sugar, blood pressure, and blood levels. Being honest with them is very important. Tell them what has been working, what *hasn't* been working, or what keeps your agreement from working. Were you resisting help from other people? Did you ask for help and no one was

> *I truly believe that for every person life can begin again and again . . .*
> DR. ABRAHAM SCHMITT
> *An autobiography of a dyslexic*

available? Were there people involved that you felt were counter-productive? What can be changed so things run smoothly? Don't hide anything! Lay everything out on the table.

Make sure your doctors' numbers are within reach and easy to read. You may fear calling them if you aren't sure how to explain what is happening. You may have had bad experiences on the phone or simply feel foolish for bothering them. But it is better to be safe than sorry! Try to express your concern in a clear way, and include details, even if you think they aren't important. Your doctor will probably stick with the emergency at hand, asking you to wait to discuss general things until an office visit.

Understanding medication and its place in our healing is important. Some of us despise this reminder of our frailty, while others think it's miraculous! I have come to appreciate the stable platform medication puts under my feet. I have learned to stick with the doses even when I feel well, so I can stay well. If you wonder if it's doing anything, check with those who live with you! They have seen you at your worst and may be able to see the changes better than you can. Feeling their support keeps us encouraged when we sense disapproval from people who do not understand why we need medication. We also need their full support before we try a different treatment plan. After all, who will pick us up if it fails?

When using medication, we need to be workable and stick with the dosage amounts. Adjusting or skipping dosages on our own can throw us into a relapse—something none of us want! Even a tiny shift in schedule can be a threat. Practical things like post-it notes on the bathroom mirror, pill boxes in the cereal cupboard, or alarms on cell phones can help us stay in a safe groove.

Some people use vitamins and minerals alongside their medication. Be up front with your doctors about those things! Tell him exactly what you are using—yes, even those garlic pills—and let him know you will consult him before you introduce anything else. Doing this establishes confidence and prevents you from taking something that is counterproductive. If your doctor does not accept what you are using, then you will need to come his way or consider finding another doctor. Doing your own thing is dangerous. No matter what route you take, you ultimately need to trust someone in order to follow through. Be honest with yourself about who you are willing to trust and why. Do they really merit that trust?

Natural supplements *can* interfere with the productivity of a medication. Some are very potent and it is possible to overdose on vitamins! If you choose to use supplements, find a doctor who is not only well studied, but willing to work with medical doctors. There are too many all natural routes that do not work with science and have not been proven. It is no secret that Plain People fall prey to these cure-alls. Even though vitamins, minerals, and hormones may help prevent certain physical problems, they can also rob us of time and money. If you have found medication to be ineffective but were helped by supplements, you will still need to stick by your doctor's side, being up front about everything you use! Be sure your doctor is as professional as he claims to be by researching the authenticity of the products he promotes. You may save yourself a lot of grief.

Relating to other people:

We need other people! The 'boxes' we hide inside when we feel insecure make us feel safe, but they also cripple and stifle our friendships. Supportive friends keep us from withdrawing into a world of our own making. Supportive arms reach into our 'boxes' and pull us out with their insight and sense of humor. We often find others who struggle like we do! We learn we are not alone.

Our illness has the ability to cloud our minds. We don't like to acknowledge this because that means we can't always trust our own intuition. We tend to become suspicious, fearful, and reactionary, cutting off faithful friends and lashing out at those who are helping us the most. We may even pursue a line of thought, only to realize that we were riding on the hype of an emotion. It becomes hard to sort if an internal nudge is God's spirit or the trick of an ill mind. One way to prevent faulty conclusions is by allowing faithful friends to help us analyze our condition. It is not a good time to latch on to people we barely know!

If we find we can't decipher the issues, we need to 'hand the reins' over to someone else. We may fear we will never get them back . . . that others will take over our life completely! We should make sure we are surrounded by people who know what healthy relationships are—people who have related well to us in the past. Wise helpers will encourage us to pick up again as we are able!

A stitch in time saves nine.
UNKNOWN

REDUCE RELAPSES BY IDENTIFYING WARNING SIGNS!

Are you tuned in to your own 'red flags'? Self-awareness is difficult for some of us. The intensity of our illness may change, impacted by medication changes, seasons, stresses, and various circumstances. Our symptoms may be altogether missing, gentle, or severe. Red flags include a change in eating habits, sleeping problems, an inability to concentrate, irritability, feeling suspicious about people we formerly trusted, spending excessive money, or avoiding social life.

Symptoms vary from person to person, so we need to focus on identifying our *own*. Others can help us with this. Some of these are exaggerated expression, hyperactivity, bossiness or aggression, reckless driving, over-spending, easily becoming upset over minor things, 'a certain look in the eyes', religious hang-ups or delusions, or repetitive behavior. Learn to see these things as 'the train you don't want to get on'. However, in spite of our best efforts we may still find ourselves on the train! Train jumping takes quick thinking, but with practice we can learn how to land on our own two feet without losing our balance. Some of us become immobile and helpless while the train picks up speed; others become exhilarated and giddy with anticipation. The PROBLEM is—once the train starts moving too fast, we can't get off anymore.

When the flags start waving, quick action may prevent things from getting worse. Here are some simple things to do:

1. *Tune in to the changes that are taking place.*
2. *Make sure your thought patterns are balanced, and lower stress levels.*
3. *Talk to someone.*
4. *Have your doctor's and other emergency numbers handy.*
5. *If you sense something is wrong, call him for advice or make an appointment.*

We are not always aware of the changes that take place during a relapse. Instead, we may think the people around us are changing. Because of this, we tend to hold them at arm's length when we should be considering their input. They are often able to identify our symptoms better than we can! Even though we resent such a detailed scrutiny of our life, doing this helps everyone involved get a sense of direction, including us.

BALANCE THINGS OUT!

Tuning in to your feelings and balancing the negatives with the positives helps you stay in charge of your feelings. Pepper the things you don't enjoy with things you do enjoy! If you dread getting up, reward yourself with a cup of hot chocolate and take a short, brisk walk . . . just the sight of a pink sunrise may energize you. Make your plans possible—tedious lists and household clutter are notorious for killing inspiration! Do you dread going to bed? Wash or change the sheets, and use an attractive bedspread. Clean the bathroom *before* taking a bath. Light a candle and try reading something inspirational *after* the dishes are done. Ending the undesirable with something pleasant encourages you, even if you feel you can't—really can't—do it.

To weep and sigh because I'm blind, I cannot and I won't.
FANNIE CROSBY

Staying as mobile and distracted as possible will help divert the pain. Don't become frustrated with your own set of problems; some people work at a normal pace, others can't even follow a simple recipe. If this happens, hopefully your friends initiate doing things together! Make sure you get plenty of fresh air; take walks, ride bike, or hoe in the garden. Spending time in a greenhouse or garden where there is plenty of light work and sunshine is very therapeutic.

ESTABLISH DAILY ROUTINES.

With our love of predictability, it really shouldn't be hard to stick to a fixed schedule. But it is! There are several reasons why. Some of us feel so alive it seems like a waste of time to sleep. Others wish they could fall asleep and can't. Persistent thoughts roll around in their minds. Morning comes way too soon! Then there are those of us who want to sleep all the time. We go to bed early and sleep in late. Sleep shuts out our horrible feelings.

Following our feelings pushes things south fast! Making up for sleep loss by sleeping all day just complicates the problem of getting to bed on time. It is better to get up and go to bed at a normal time, taking catnaps throughout the day if necessary. If our thoughts spin like a hamster on a wheel, it is helpful to take a regular amount of time to unwind before we retire. Find relaxing things to do that help your body and mind to slow down, such as taking a bath or drinking tea. Do not allow yourself computer/electronic time after supper! These things help us fall asleep sooner, get a solid night of rest, and hear the alarm in the morning. If our schedules shift, we should find a new norm as soon as possible. Predictable living creates a framework that encourages our highest potential.

CHANGE NEGATIVE SELF-TALK

The 'dark, heavy feeling' of depression smothers our life, persistently pushing negative thoughts into our minds. Instead of despising these messages, can we slow down and listen to what they are saying? Linking them to the disturbances that set them in motion (like a critical remark or maybe the relapse of an illness) helps us know what to do next. This type of inward focus is healthy. It helps us piece an answer so we can relax and enjoy life again.

How do we sort between a reactive depression (which is linked to daily circumstances or happenings that trigger negative feelings) and the relapse of an illness? Reactive depression is usually short-lived and can be alleviated by a change of circumstances, focus, or simply sharing with others. We tend to super-focus on certain things which keeps us from seeing the whole picture. Hearing someone else's perspective balances our thinking, infusing our minds with encouraging and realistic messages. Many people enjoy writing a journal. Write the condemning thoughts down, and try reversing them on paper. Write poetry, even if it is full of moaning and groaning. Doing something positive is better than sleeping or eating all the time!

- I don't enjoy doing anything.
- I wish I were dead.
- I have nothing to live for. I can't even be a mom to my own children.
- I'm a grand flop.
- people think I am so stupid.
- I will always be this way.

On the other hand, an illness is pervasive, meaning it is very intense, ongoing, and marked by irrational or unexplainable behavior. When this is the case, medication is an effective and healthy way to silence negative self-talk by taking care of the bothersome symptoms! We tend to view this kind of help as a sign of inner weakness instead of inner strength. We think trying harder is the answer. Looking at our struggles honestly helps reality sink in and pushes us towards the next step. Outside of a miracle, medication may be the only thing that can break the grip of our negative reality.

There is a luxury in self-reproach. When we blame ourselves, we feel no one else has a right to blame us.
OSCAR WILDE

DO THE RIGHT THING IN SPITE OF YOUR FEELINGS

Feelings trick us repeatedly; in our vulnerability, our minds fill up with thousands of thoughts. During a depression they tell us: *You'll never make it. You may as well give up.* During a mania, we may feel invincible. *I really have it made. I can do anything!* Simply recognizing what we are feeling helps us counteract these feelings with truth. It is miserable to be doing the right thing and feeling horrible about it, but in time the good feelings return, along with the assurance that we did the right thing.

Stable feelings do protect us from hurtful people and circumstances! Ignoring our gut feelings shuts them down or distorts what is actually happening. If children sense something is wrong but adults cover or deny, they are being taught to ignore their intuition. "Dad didn't want to break your tooth. If someone asks you about it, just tell them you fell off your bike. This is just how dad is and we've got to learn to live with it." Responding like this normalizes crazy behavior and teaches children to shut down. "It didn't hurt. Dad didn't mean it. It's not much of anything. I won't cry over this." Quieting ourselves in this way eventually freezes our emotions. We decide the best thing to do is not feel.

Deciding whether to tune in to or ignore gut feelings is not easy because our illness can distort them. Gut feelings may warn us of having an accident five minutes down the road. They may remind us to turn the iron off eight times before we leave the house. They may insist a friend is betraying us when they are helping us! In time we learn to go against those feelings. Sorting between the effects of an illness and healthy danger signals is something our doctors or therapists can help us with.

The just-smile-your-way-out-of-your-depression band aid is especially frustrating—it is so false and unhealthy to walk around smiling when you feel grotesque inside. We want to stay connected to the genuine parts of ourselves, and we do this by owning up to how we actually feel. Sometimes we do the opposite of what we feel like doing, but we also need to be sure we are not simply laughing when we need to cry, working harder when we need to rest, or doing more for others when we need to be taking care of ourselves.

> *"There was a time when I wanted to mount up with wings as eagles; and if I couldn't do that, at least run and not be weary; Today, Lord, I trust in You for my help, and I'm willing to just walk, if need be, but let me go forward in Thy name. Amen."*
> UNKNOWN

Doing something positive every day, no matter how insignificant it may be, wards off the victim mode. Even simple things like trimming our nails, making the bed, or wiping the kitchen sink fight feelings of helplessness and uselessness. All that is required of us is our best at the present. Feeling guilty for our unproductive times gets us nowhere. Just like therapy, every time we stretch a little more, we gain a little ground. We need to be content with little, maybe even tiny, steps.

COPING WITH COMMON PITFALLS

1. Try to manage your money wisely!

Some of us are especially vulnerable in this area, so beware if you are shopping at your favorite store and all of a sudden you find bargains everywhere. You may want to check yourself if you are buying lots of things not only for yourself but your dad and mom, your uncles and aunts, your neighbors, and your friends. Creative plans that make you feel rich and powerful are dangerous. What *will* you do with five boxes of chicken if you only have one small freezer? Do you find yourself thinking that 500 dollars is equivalent to fifty? Call your husband or a good friend before you pursue a new idea, or maybe even wait a couple hours or days to think it over. The wait can be maddening and makes us feel like we are losing out on some very glorious opportunities. We may even spiritualize our present urge, thinking it must be something the Lord wants us to do.

If you find yourself handing out money too freely, be willing to hand over the checkbook and credit cards. Stay away from your favorite stores and shelf the catalogs for a while. Suspect yourself if you simply HAVE to go to the greenhouse right now, no matter what anyone else says or is doing. Make it hard for yourself to get ahold of large sums of money in a short period of time and thank God if you are a backwards farm wife who doesn't know anything about withdrawing money from the bank or shopping on the internet.

2. Drive carefully.

Elevated mood states or exaggerated emotional responses can be dangerous on the road. Being easily distracted or simply not thinking about our driving habits endangers lives. Does a revving motor make us feel threatened or excited? Do we see fists shaking at us in the rear view mirror? Acting on the surge of an emotion may send us flying down the road at dangerous speeds. Or we may speed because we feel so good—the day is worth living—and we want to get a lot done! But what if you find yourself upside down in a ditch? Sometimes even such brutal realities fail to get through; we pick ourselves up and think about the cat with nine lives. We may even smile into the policeman's face and demand to see his badge. "Do you really have the right to give me a ticket? Who gave you the authority to tell me what to do, anyway?! Maybe you're just bored and need some excitement!" While this may indicate a bipolar mania, others will instantly class it as insolence and the consequences could be humiliating at best!

3. Wait to make big decisions when you sense things are not quite right.

When things are finally too good to be true, flowing too smoothly, and difficult things are making a lot of sense, slow down and check yourself. Suspect suddenly wanting to be the owner of an orphanage, a sudden desire to move, or deciding that the school system is rotten and you'll home-school. Allow somebody to help you think your great ideas through, ironing out the practical and common sense side of things. Give yourself time; don't act upon your ideas immediately.

> *Make haste slowly.*
> UNKNOWN

If you feel easily irritated, like everyone is against you, you are probably also rejecting everyone's suggestions and ideas. Your right to your own ideas or independence may feel threatened, making you insecure. Make it a point to lay down your guns and listen carefully to what others are trying to tell you. Be ready to consider what they are saying. Allow them to guide your thinking.

4. Avoid situations that make it difficult for you to be discreet.

"Oh, it isn't a sexual attraction! I just love everybody right now. What's wrong with that?" Mania, a part of bipolar illness, tends to make us feel giddy over everything, including the opposite sex. We may feel younger, more alive, more eager for attention, and intoxicated without even realizing. If you are unstable, spend as much time as possible with people you both know and trust—someone who will 'head you off' if you lose proper reserve. They should be agreed to take you home if you are acting giddy or impulsive, or are making other people feel uncomfortable by your actions. Every cultural group has their lines of discretion; crossing these established lines may indicate that you are manic.

2. *How do I sort between feeling and fact?*

The feeling right now is that you are terribly frustrating. The fact is that you are trying to help me. The feeling tells me I can't trust you, the fact is that you have proven yourself trustworthy in the past. The feeling tells me that life will never be good again; the fact is that God promises that "all things work together for good to them that love Him." The feeling tells me to give up; the fact tells me it is worth keeping on no matter what.

> *I don't know why we are here, but I'm pretty sure that it is not in order to enjoy ourselves.*
> LUDWIG WITTGENSTEIN

Facts are first because they are based on truth. They are irreversible, steady friends that provide a solid network for our beliefs. Feelings are secondary; they shift and change, but they do put color into life. A life lived without emotion is like a wall without decorations. It looks like no one's at home. Extreme emotion tempts us to shut down, but being unable to feel at all is worse than the intense struggle that comes along with feeling. Strong feelings make our needs obvious, but they also give us the capacity to bless others in special ways. Do we sometimes beg God to change our feelings when He actually wants to use them?

Our illness can cause us to lose touch with reality; feelings take over and guide our perceptions of the present. Reality as we see it may not have any resemblance to actual reality. Facts are lost in the dust of our confused minds and truth becomes distorted. That is why we desperately need the help of other people. If we live by the feeling of the moment, we *will* bob up and down. Remember: feelings are slippery, shiny, and changeable. Facts are rough and dull, but as reliable as the sun coming up in the morning and going down at night.

3. How do I relate to strong feelings of anger and the resulting guilt?

> *"Why do I get angry with people, especially the ones I love? I know I shouldn't but it just boils out of me! If I repress it, it just gets worse. What can I do about it?"*

This is a true dilemma—to hurt the people we love the most! Nothing alienates us from others as quickly as uncontrolled anger; the aftermath of an outrage leaves us limp with guilt and the fear that these dear people will leave us. We may shrug off feeling responsible for our outbursts because we have no idea how to change. Who wants to be apologizing all the time?! We get weary of explaining how we feel and why—it leaves us feeling like we are telling peaches how it feels to be a lemon. It aggravates us when others imply that our struggle has a clear cut solution—Just quit it! Be sweet like we are and don't get angry!

HOW CAN WE WORK EFFECTIVELY WITH OUR ANGER?

1. Understand that even though anger is a negative emotion, it is not evil; it has a healthy place in your life.

Feelings of joy and sorrow are very interrelated; joy isn't any more saintly than sorrow or anger. God made all of our emotions, and an inability to express any certain one of them is a sign that something is wrong.

> *You cannot shake hands with a clenched fist.*
> MOHANDAS GANDHI

Not understanding this can lock us into helpless feelings of frustration and guilt. If we believe that anger is bad, we will feel guilty every time we get angry. We will get angry at ourselves for getting angry. Well-meaning people often handle these struggles in ways that only aggravate and intensify them.

2. Learn to recognize the root of your emotion and make that the focus.

"What is causing me to feel this way? Is my anger a cover-up for the anxiety I feel about losing my job? Am I frustrated because I just don't feel well and am tired of the struggle?" Understanding the cause of our anger helps us to think logically about the *real reasons* we are upset, rather than blame-shifting. It also keeps us from falling into a cycle of self-afflicting thought patterns!

Anger is usually a secondary emotion. We often use anger as a blanket statement for other feelings that may be harder for us to identify or express, like frustration or helplessness. Are we afraid, sad, or hurting? The more aware we are of these feelings and the reasons behind them, the more understanding and compassionate we can be with ourselves and with others. It is easier to feel our anger instead of our pain. As a result, the people we are relating to see "an angry person" because that is the emotion we are showing. If our symptoms intensify to the point we are unable to rein them in, we need to notify our doctor!

3. *Express your feelings in an appropriate way to someone who cares about you. Feel free to be completely honest with God about your feelings!*

This may surprise you, but God knows all about your problems anyway! Like a ringing buzzer, our feelings alert us of them. Anger and frustration can motivate us to positive change, but we want to be careful its cause is pure and that we are expressing it in healthy ways. Anger may be connected to past hurts, but it may also be the result of overactive responses to minor offenses in the present. It is much easier to lash out than to identify, communicate, and find a solution.

Choosing to express our anger or frustration in an acceptable way keeps us from feeling like pawns of emotions and circumstances. We can decide *how* to respond to our challenges! We don't need to slam doors, wave fly swatters, or punch holes in the walls.

4. Never tolerate violence in yourself or others!

Parents who don't control their own anger are not equipped to teach their children how to do it. Teaching them to handle their anger appropriately at a young age is a powerful tool! Not only does it avert many problems, it helps them to know how to use anger in a positive way. They can learn to recognize what their anger is teaching them. They must understand that violent actions require attention; when that line is crossed, there are unique consequences.

Strong feelings of anger are very frightening! It is easier to learn to deal with irrational fears and sadness than with irrational anger. We are often so focused on our own emotion we are oblivious to the hurt we are causing. If we are unable to acknowledge that we are upset, others will need to do this for us. If our helpers set limits, we need to be willing to cooperate. We may not agree with what they are saying about us. If it seems they are accusing us of things that we know nothing about, we need to go for help. A good doctor or friend should be able to help us do the sorting.

It may be hard to identify or explain a problem, making us more vulnerable to unexplainable explosions. Two children went to an eye specialist, because of a problem with their eyesight. As the doctor questioned them, one child hung his head and said very little. The other one held her head erect, met the doctor's eyes, and explained the problem in perfect detail. The doctor understood exactly what she was describing. Testing revealed that both needed bifocals for a time. This illustrates how some people face a specific problem for years without being able to put a finger on it, much less express it.

5. What about guilt?

There are things that should make us feel guilty, like hurting others or speeding on the highway. These things are based on facts or reality. False guilt tends to focus on insignificant details such as how you kneel or how long you pray, or washing your hands just right. It also tends to feed our imaginations. We may subconsciously feel guilty without even knowing why! Communicating our feelings of guilt to others and getting their feedback helps us find a balance. I struggled this way as a young girl, but found a measure of rest in my mom's advice. If she told me something was insignificant, I trusted her.

4. Why must I learn to appreciate guidelines and follow through honorably?

Some of us struggle with a dislike for the structure, discipline, or rules of other people. We don't mind our own boxes, but we don't like to be stuck into somebody else's box. Any interruption to our train of thought spells catastrophe. Our determination to stick with our way of keeping life coherent makes us resent the boxed feeling of others' guidance. Their input often makes us feel out-of-control, a feeling we have come to hate!

While this makes sense to us, we can be some of the most unpredictable, frustrating, changeable creatures. We vote to throw away all the alarm clocks, timers, date books, rulers, or measuring cups in the country. We tend to resent anything that holds us accountable to what we said yesterday or spells out what we have to do tomorrow. We like to do art and music our own way . . . the books confuse us. We try to skip appointments because of the urgent need of the moment. We resent getting to bed on time because we're learning all about the newest method of trapping coons, and then threaten to smash the alarm when it does its job in the morning. This is very trying to people who love logic and common sense!

The brain within its groove
Runs evenly and true;
But let a splinter swerve,
'Twas easier for you
To put the water back
When floods have slit the hills
And scooped a turnpike for themselves,
And blotted out the mills!
EMILY DICKINSON

Our specific aversions may rise from the way our minds work in grooves, or we may simply have a dislike for discipline period. But the truth is, discipline can be positive! We can and need to learn to be workable, instead of living out order in our own way. Even though we think we have the ability to discern a need and follow it through, we end up frustrating others who are meeting other critical needs. We plow right over something important or miss a crisis happening right underneath our noses! We need to consider the way others look at time and how their expectations of time meet ours, so the results are satisfactory for everyone involved. Order, a change of focus, accountability, stable friends and predictable living can help us be consistent and productive.

5. What are some helps for communicating effectively?

Learning to communicate in a respectful, sensible way can be challenging! Strong feelings burst out in ways that harm more than clarify. Sporadic ideas leave people in the dust. What we think and what we say doesn't always match. We need to communicate our needs in a 'language' that people can understand.

We also need to *listen* to what people are telling us! It is easy to let our thoughts run like a wild colt in a pasture, jumping fences. We may need to bring our attention back to the present situation again and again. If we do manage this, we need to be careful we aren't distracted by the pimple on their nose or the lines in their cheeks. It leaves us making a wild guess at the present topic.

Feeling 'fogged in' or experiencing a lot of confusion and pain makes it difficult to express

---

THE LOST THOUGHT

I felt a cleaving in my mind
As if my brain had split;
I tried to match it seam by seam,
But could not make them fit.

The thought behind I strove to join
Unto the thought before,
But sequence ravelled out of reach
Like balls upon a floor.

-EMILY DICKINSON

COMMUNICATION:
When any two people communicate there is:
What you WANTED *to say,*
What you MEANT *to say,*
What you SAID,
What you THINK *you said,*
What the other person HEARD *you say,*
What the other person THINKS *you said,*
What the other person FEELS *about what you said,*
What the other person SAYS *about what you said,*
What YOU *think the other person said about what you said.*
Is it any wonder misunderstandings happen!

UNKNOWN

---

ourselves. It is easier to just hit or scream! We may not share at all for fear we will say things we never meant to say. Most of us have needed to apologize for times like this, because others are affected by what we said, not by what we meant to say.

Proper communication depends on our ability to connect dots and put thoughts into words. How can an inconsistent mind produce consistent words and actions? This is very frustrating, for us as well as for those who are trying to help us. Sometimes it seems like we have a language of our own—one that others simply don't connect with! We process our thoughts from unusual angles. This tries the patience of other people.

We all need to be willing to stretch our thinkers!

6. How responsible are we?

This is truly a million dollar question! It is tempting to tuck all our flaws and failures under the umbrella of our illness. By doing this, we allow our illness to pin us down. We become stagnant, lazy, and irresponsible, victimized by our circumstances.

My dad, whose vision was impaired by a stroke, called me one day. He told me how inspired he was by Fannie Crosby—a blind woman, who wrote, "To weep and sigh because I'm blind, I cannot and I won't." He lived out this commitment; even though his poor vision made it impossible to do certain types of work, he still kept his hands busy. If he wasn't outdoors pulling weeds, he was inside the house stripping wire. His persevering attitude reminded me that even though I am not responsible for my illness, as long as my mind functions, I am responsible for learning how to deal with it!

A mind illness does have the ability to change a person in many ways. It often leaves us asking, "Who am I?" People who are normally very gentle and good-natured may become violent and aggressive when ill. The terror and frustration they feel, or the illness itself, causes logical reasoning to go out the back door. A normally energetic, active person may become immobile and lethargic—in both cases the illness cloaks who they really are. The *truest* part of people is what they are like when they are well.

I cannot do everything, but still I can do something. I will not refuse to do the something I can do.
HELEN KELLER

As Christians, we take personal responsibility seriously; we realize how we live out God's will has eternal implications! Our choices and attitudes will take us a certain direction. Instead of trying to figure out how responsible we are, can we focus on doing our best from day to day? We need to deliberately focus on truth, being open to the help and viewpoint of others who care. If we do lose our ability to reason, we can rest assured that God will tenderly lift us up in His arms! When we are His, our souls are secure no matter what happens to our minds. We are not responsible for what we cannot help!

With mental illness, there is a fine line between accepting our disabilities or saying, "God made me this way, so I'm going to be this way. There is no reason to even try to change!" But God wants to make us a better person through it. We scream and kick on the inside at the very idea. "**This** meant to make us a better person?" That is where we need to look inside ourselves and make the decision between wanting to go through the painful process of letting God make us into a better person, or giving in to the miseries of hopelessness. Life does seem hopeless at times, but that still doesn't change the fact that we do have choices to make during these times—to choose to keep on trying. This may be scary, especially if it means letting someone get a glimpse of how we feel inside so they can help us.

-*'Brenda'*

COCOON

I'm trying so hard.
I hope I'm getting somewhere.
I think I am.
But I can't see myself.
So I ask others.
They say, "Yes, but keep trying. Push harder!"
So I am trying.
I really am.
I work so hard.
Sometimes I wonder if I can keep going.
Then I feel the fresh morning air kissing my wet wings.
Please don't pull me.
Let me burst forth in my own time.
With wings bright and untouched.
Meanwhile—
I work.
The world is so dark,
But through a chink
I see a speck of dazzling sunlight.

I know I'm coming.

-Maria B.

Change is the essence of life. Be willing to surrender what you are, for what you could become.

LIFE'S ROAD

The road I trudge is all uphill,
With jagged stones and prickly weeds,
And over there, a dirt path leads
To shaded meadows, calm and still.
My road is rough.
My lot is tough.
Lord, it's enough!

My road I travel all alone,
Just like a ship upon the sea,
With clouds and waves for company
As winds of strife around me moan.
My road is rough.
My lot is tough.
Lord, it's enough!

But then I think of how my Lord,
Who marked my road with bleeding feet,
Would summon others down this street
To help them would be a reward!
My road is rough.
My lot is tough.
God's grace, enough!

-*'Shawn Yoder'*

WHAT IS FAITH?

Faith is the eye by which we look to Jesus.

A dim-sighted eye is still an eye;

A weeping eye is still an eye.

Faith is the hand with which we lay hold of Jesus.

A trembling hand is still a hand.

And he is a believer whose heart within him trembles
when he touches the hem on the Savior's garment,
that he may be healed.

Faith is the tongue by which we taste how good the Lord is.

A feverish tongue is nevertheless a tongue.

And even then we may believe,

when we are without the smallest portion of comfort;

For our faith is founded not upon feelings, but upon the
promises of God.

Faith is the foot by which we go to Jesus.

A lame foot is still a foot.

He who comes slowly, nevertheless comes.

-George Muller

LIVING A VIBRANT LIFE

I would lie on my bed for ages
Looking out on the dusty street . . .
Where whispers, nor leaves, nor waters
Nor anything cool and sweet;
At my heart this ghastly fainting
And this burning in my blood—
If only I knew Thou wast with me,
Wast with me and making me good.

UNKNOWN

Can our spirits survive the crippling grip of mental illness? We believe the verse "All things work together for good", but this type of problem challenges that belief. Can positive things emerge from something like this?

When our daughter was born with MSUD, a rare genetic disease, we experienced many unexpected changes. The farewell song we sent as a testimony to our friends in Central America says ". . . and we'll never be the same, for we've seen faithful love face to face, and Jesus is His name." We accepted the fact that things would never be the same and recognized God's Hand in it all. In spite of this, my illness brought its own drama to the valley we were traveling. It felt like a betrayal on His part, but in time we realized our *response* to this added trial was the real test. Clinging to God even though we feel let down, transforms us; however, sometimes a positive transformation is long in coming!

Hope is not a way out,
it is a way through.
UNKNOWN

Like a tsunami, our suffering has the potential to wash important parts of us away. It is capable of destroying everything precious to us! Bobbing on the surface of the floodwaters, we often feel alone and forsaken, engulfed in the vulnerabilities of our nature. We face many important decisions—do we acknowledge our troubles or run away from them? Do we think things have to make sense? How do we relate to people who beamingly comment how wonderful life is?! Can we keep on hoping for better days? Can we accept the 'snail's progress'? The gradual wear and tear of daily living has a way of chewing away on our sanity and resolve, putting pressure on our tempers, and sometimes aggravating painful memories. We get tired of crying spells and long to be normal, sane, and stable.

Finding meaning in our suffering becomes the cry of our soul. Mental Illness cripples us emotionally, but it does not need to destroy our souls. The soul grows larger thru suffering, and is capable of experiencing tremendous amounts of both joy and despair. Even though we struggle to hold onto God in our weakened state He still carries us. He sees our true desire even though our illness hampers our ability to choose our thoughts and actions. It takes faith to believe that light always follows darkness—if not here, then in eternity.

Loss is an inevitable part of life and its irreversible results are devastating. It is easy to feel our type of loss transcends all losses, but can we say it exceeds the loss of millions of other losses that exist? Eventually we face the fact that life is not fair. While we are born with negatives into more negatives, life is not a punishment for who we happen to be! Faith sees a Creator behind all these unique patterns and designs. It believes He is still capable of painting a 'masterpiece' with each one of our lives.

Our losses have a way of shaping who we become. Wrong thought patterns have the ability to keep us stuck, like a scratched CD. We may tell ourselves no one else has had it as difficult as we do; we may even find a perverse comfort in remembering how unfair life has been. We may blame everybody from our 'incompetent parents'—to our nosy doctors—to our younger brother who snores too loud. We may blame the food we ate or didn't eat for breakfast, the kind of shoes we're wearing, the bad coffee, the dead car battery, our boring life, or our hormones . . . anything that brings some sense or clarity to the problem. We may even get a perverse satisfaction of making others suffer because we had to. Somehow we don't think about the amount of pain we are bringing to others by our sore attitudes. After all, don't we have a right to feel good?

> *What the future holds, I cannot know, but I have found sweet violets under snow.*
> COREY BORING

Other losses often accompany our personal loss of mental health. Perhaps mental illness shaped our childhood homes, leaving us with emotional scars and a poor set of tools with which to face life. In frustration, we lash out in anger, grabbing those who have hurt us by the throat, even though we know allowing our anger to bubble out of control and multiply is asking for trouble. Reaching out to hurt others not only leads to inward death, but spreads our pain. While we learn to face and deal with our own hurts, we become aware that we unwittingly inflict snippets of the same kind of hurt upon our own children! When we make peace with the things we are angry about, we acknowledge our own human frailties and prevent further damage.

Anger can be a positive force, opening the door to the forgiveness process. It is a sign that we are alive emotionally. It enables us to identify the ways in which life was different for us, the important things we missed, and what should not have been. It wakes us up to the way things should be. It not only helps us to see life realistically, but brings about positive change. It prompts us to ask questions—"In what ways do I want to be like my parents? In what ways do I want to be different? What are my relationships like? Do I know what it means to trust? What are our goals as a couple? Are we able to connect in a meaningful way with our own children? How can we maintain emotional health as a family?"

Facing hard questions that seem to have no answers is unsettling. Someone said "It feels like God is reaching down, slapping me around, and then laughing at me". We like to be able to explain things; the randomness tends to shatter our faith. It makes us feel like aliens in a world where everyone else seems to be living safely inside their little glass balls. It is easy to become angry or terrified, controlling everything around us to avoid more hurt. We may even become obsessed with the future in an attempt to foresee what may be closing in upon us. Uncertainty haunts us.

Where was God? I thought He didn't care or He wouldn't have allowed this to happen. It made me distrust Him; this found me stumbling along through life, searching and not finding. I thank God He sent loving friends to help me through. It took months, but now I can look back and say, "God is good."
'BRENDA'

Only God's mercy can help us take one step at a time without losing our balance, running from fears, or screaming out in rage.

A lot of our questions stem back to wondering if God is as good as He claims to be. If God is weak and cruel, then He isn't God. If He isn't God, then who is God? If there is no God, then why live? Sarcasm and cynicism take over in a wink, and our reasoning becomes laced with mockery. This pulls us toward a careless, tired existence that digs down into the depth of our souls and dislodges all we've ever believed or been taught. We stare around at the motley mound of concepts and wonder if we'll ever believe anything again. But we always return to the fact there has to be a God, and thankfully a God that we can't begin to understand or explain. If He could be explained by human minds, He wouldn't be God, right?!

In Romans Paul wrote that nothing can separate us from the love of God that is in Christ Jesus our Lord. It doesn't matter how earthshaking or destabilizing something is, it will not put a wedge between us and God. Our poor feeble minds insert wedges when we cannot grasp an eternal, perfect love. "His love has no limit, His grace has no measure, His power, no boundaries known unto men; for out of His infinite riches in Jesus, He giveth and giveth and giveth again."

Letting go of our questions and living beyond them takes time and healing. Eventually we realize we are on a journey that is changing us; we can't escape it, figure it out, or outwit it. Succumbing to the encroaching darkness is not an option. When we despair, we lose hope. Hope helps us creep forward, even though we have no idea where we are going. Some steps are clear and simple; others take shape *after* we've taken a step outward into the feared abyss! It is natural to fight and fear pain, but doing this in the wrong way intensifies it and prolongs the healing process. We need to learn to fight the right direction! While we fight certain damaging effects of our illness, *we must not fight* the grief that comes by acknowledging our loss and the changes it has brought into our lives.

Our own beliefs or the beliefs of those around us, have the potential to accelerate and intensify our suffering. These beliefs do have a direct impact on our souls, pushing us forward toward healing or downward into more pain and confusion. For this reason, it is important to be surrounded by people who know us and cushion us with healthy relationships. They help us process our struggles in a healthy way. By mirroring God to us, they help us 'see' the Master we 'can't see.' Feeling condemned by God and others obscures the Light.

Life's paradox is reflected in these words:

> *"Light after darkness, gain after loss, strength after weakness, crown after cross, sweet after bitter, sun after rain, joy after misery, peace after pain"*. . . ending with *"after long anguish, rapturous bliss; right was the pathway leading to this."*

I loved this song as a girl! Not only does it picture the bleakness of life, it brings out the way it makes up for itself. The flip side always comes to greet us when the pangs of pain have done their work. I learned to expect and embrace these refreshing pockets that surfaced when I least expected them. They comforted me and gave me strength in preparation for the next patch of fog.

> *Faith is willingness to trust God when the pieces don't fit, and well as willingness to trust when life moves along smooth, as it will. It is not so important to know why God permitted the suffering, as it is to accept the tension and anguish it has created and transform it. Suffering must become creative.*
> KATIE F WIEBE

Another one of my defenses during a faith attack is remembering the times I experienced God's presence in a real way. Going back to these times anchors me. It reminds me that God proved and is continuing to prove He cares. One such experience was an unbearably hot, coastal day. Of course, missionaries weren't supposed to get depressed, but I was, and Frank thought maybe a change of scenery would help. He took us to town for lunch. In town we were stopped by a young native fellow. He handed us a bagful of brand-new medicines. How strange! Why did he do that? The following week we found out; we all took turns being sick and ended up using quite a bit of that medicine! God impressed me with this message: "Before you call, I will answer. . . . I know your needs better than you do, and I will have what you need at hand and in time."

Facing the loss of mental health gives us the opportunity to choose to love God despite our pain. When we choose to trust Him in the middle of pain, we are grasping in some small way the amount of love He has for us. We are free to choose to believe that He is Love, He is good, and He knows what He is allowing. We are also free to doubt. God sees this choice as a beautiful thing. That is what love is all about.

Our souls thrive on love. Our illness blinds us to the evidence of God's love and, of course, we resent this! We need others to help us hang on in faith so we don't experience soul loss. In time, as healing takes place, we can learn to throw out our arms and love life more than we ever did before. We learn to live the moment with joy, instead of dreading what may be around the next bend.

Sometimes we get the feeling we have nothing to offer others. That is far from the truth! Keep your ear to the ground for people whose mental sufferings have produced priceless gems that we still enjoy today!

In my little kitchen in Guatemala, I posted the song God Moves in a Mysterious Way. For a long time, it poured forth its messages of hope. Only later did I learn it was written by *William Cowper*, a prolific poem and hymn writer who spent some time in a psychiatric hospital. Various times, he unsuccessfully attempted to take his own life. He wrote this song in 1773

Joy and Woe are woven fine
A clothing for the Soul divine;
Under every grief and pine
Runs a joy with silken twine.
WILLIAM BLAKE

---

shortly before descending into a depressive suicidal state. He expresses the way suffering hides us from God's face and the faith that God knows what He is doing. His friend and pastor, John Newton, saved him from suicide more than once; together they produced hymns that have been a source of comfort for many people.

Emily Dickinson lived many years in isolation, scarcely leaving home or having visitors. Only ten poems were published in her lifetime—ten poems that were submitted by friends without her permission. After she died, her sister discovered over 1,700 other poems in a dresser drawer.

If I can keep one heart from breaking,
I shall not live in vain;
If I can ease one life the aching,
Or cool the pain,
Or help one fainting robin
Unto his nest again,
I shall not live in vain.
EMILY DICKINSON

Christina Rossetti suffered a nervous breakdown when she was fourteen years old and continued to suffer severe bouts of depression. Her first poems appeared publicly in the Athenaeum when she was only eighteen. She wrote the song In the Bleak Midwinter, a very descriptive song referring to moaning winds, an earth hard as iron and water like a stone, ending with—"What can I give Him poor as I am, if I were a shepherd I would bring Him a lamb, if I were a wise man I would do my part, yet what can I give him? I'll give him my heart!"

Charles Dickens, another author, brought his characters to life so clearly because he imagined them so clearly. His empathy for hollow-eyed, desperate people of the slums of London comes from his difficult experiences as a child and the deep depressions he suffered. In his story about Oliver Twist, he takes you by the hand through the mud and filth of the darkest slums. He described his characters as flocking around his table in the quiet hours, each one of them demanding his personal attention . . . the miserly Ebenezer Scrooge of *A Christmas Carol*, the slippery Uriah Heep of *David Copperfield* and the tough Madame Defarge of *A Tale of Two Cities*, bent over her knitting, pretending to never see anything.

John Bunyan was the author of the famous *Pilgrim's Progress, Holy War,* and *Grace Abounding.* He grew up in a poor, humble home near Bedford, England. His father was a mender of pots and pans, and his childhood was full of wild and reckless living. Even as a young boy he had disturbing dreams and melancholies that he tried to drown out with mischievous behavior. He married a prudent, virtuous girl at nineteen years of age and began showing interest in reading the Bible and attending the national church to learn more about Christian living. In time, his persistent search for truth ended in triumph. In 1658, his wife died and he married again. His children needed a mother and one of them had been born blind. Because of his persistent preaching in a time when dissenters were in danger, he was arrested and he spent the next twelve years in a filthy dungeon writing the *Pilgrim's Progress* and much poetry.

Charles Haddon Spurgeon was a 19th century preacher in London, who kept on preaching in spite of his struggle with anxiety and depression all his life. His sermons gave many inspirational insights into his life experience:

> *"If you are feeling wretched now, remember- a few more rolling suns, at most, will land thee on fair Canaan's coast. Thy head may be crowned with thorny troubles now, but it shall wear a starry crown ere long; thy hand may be filled with cares—it shall sweep the strings of the harp of heaven soon. Thy garments may be soiled with dust now—they shall be white by and by. Wait a little longer . . . let us go on boldly. Even though the night be dark, the morning comes. . . ."*

Samuel Morse started out as an artist and ended up transforming the world with the telegraph. When he was thirty-four years of age, his wife died followed by his mother and then his father. These losses took him into depression. When Morse eventually did become wealthy because of his inventions, he gave much of it away. Some of it went to poor artists. Morse always stressed that man was only an instrument . . . the chief honor went to God.

When I observed how these people related to their suffering, I began to see my own suffering in a new way. Our experiences CAN give us the opportunity to breathe inspiration into the lives of other people! Together we can enjoy the beautiful thing of individuality, piece the incoherent, relax in the bizarre, and laugh in the face of intimidating trouble. Seeing that life is worth living in spite of all our pain infuses us with hope. It gives birth to inspiration, creating beauty and peace from the seeming rubble of our lives. We realize that just because loss seems to be so random, it does not mean that it is. Like a puzzle piece, it fits into the whole picture, which we may not see until eternity.

Scrawled on the wall of a mental institution by a patient:

Could we with ink the ocean fill,
And were the skies of parchment made;
Were every stalk on earth a quill,
And every man a scribe by trade:
To write the love of God above
Would drain the ocean dry,
Nor could the scroll contain the whole
Though stretched from sky to sky . . .

Years ago, Emily Dickinson penned—the mere sense of living is joy enough!

An aftermath holds a beauty all its own. The quiet inner shock gives way to humble expressions of praise at the wonder of simply being alive.

WE FIND YOU, LORD

We find you, Lord,
When eyesight fails
When hands give out
And dark prevails.
When senses sigh
And thoughts derail
And distant dreams
Fade in the gale.
When trembling limbs
Sink to their knees
And drooping lips
Form silent pleas.
When ears tune out
The surging seas
And hearts stand still
While pressures squeeze.

We find you, Lord,
When we look up
And see beyond
The present cup.

-Anita
2017

LOOKING THROUGH THEIR WINDOWS

My Grace is Sufficient . . .

By Joanna Graber

I don't know when it started or if there is something I could have done to prevent my fierce struggles, but now that I have received help, I can better evaluate those years. Oh, I *didn't* like to class myself as a 'depression case', but whatever it was, it was REAL! It's been a journey, and my utmost desire is to do what God has called me to daily, and do it joyfully.

When I looked at others, I saw many radiant faces. How could they do it so effortlessly? Why did I have to struggle to survive emotionally and mentally and for the inspiration to face life? It made me grouchy just thinking of getting out of bed. I met with God regularly, but had a hard time connecting with Him and His promises. It was hard to connect with people. What are you supposed to say when someone asks you "How are you?" An honest answer meant a negative answer. I wanted to inspire others, but I had no inspiration to give.

How do you continually fight negative thoughts about every area of your life? I'd tell my husband, "I want to, want to. . . ." But how? I was easily frustrated with the fast pace of life and all its pressures. I wished to function normally and spontaneously like others did. I had difficulty thinking clearly and fast enough to teach and train my children. (I still struggle with that, thanks to my slower nature and indecisive brain, but it's more doable, thanks to God's healing and grace.) I fought tears and had some major crying spells, finding relief in crying out to God alone and even writing my heart to Him. I longed to be filled with more faith and praise to my Maker, instead of struggling with 'rebellious' thoughts.

A friend suggested I see a doctor and try an anti-depressant. I saw the huge difference it made in her life, but I still worried about it becoming a crutch. I wanted to depend on God. We felt led to try it with the assurance that I could wean off when I wanted and that there were minor side effects. Well- glory to God- that was a turning point in my life! Medication and natural products both filled a place throughout the years. I was already on a journey with God, but the beautiful thing was once my mind/brain started receiving healing, I could connect with God so much better. His promises, and the Bible as a whole, were no longer dry, empty words. I connected with them, understood, and saw growth. I valued the gift of salvation and I felt more secure and at peace. My prayers went further than the ceiling. I enjoyed church life. It was easier to wear a genuine smile, to participate in ladies' Sunday school, to relate to people, even to have a testimony for the community. It was easier to honor and respect my husband.

The future is not nearly as scary, because I can connect with God. No doubt, I still face daily challenges, and I'm sure there are faith-shakers and faith-builders ahead for me. But God's power is real for me and for you! I also benefited from several good books—*Help Yourself to a Healthier Mind*, Leroy Dugan and *31 days of Praise*, Ruth Myers—as well as the positive encouragement, understanding and listening ear, faithful love, and prayers of my Mom! She gets a golden ribbon.

Your story may be different than mine, and you may find different helpers, but there is hope for you, too! It's God's will for us to enjoy His rich blessings. Sometimes I feel tempted to worry about future trials that may lay me low, again, but my desire is to keep trusting God. He says "I will never leave thee nor forsake thee. My grace is sufficient for thee. Be still and know that I am God." Thank you, Jesus, that I can connect with these promises . . . you are REAL, merciful, and gracious!

Winter can take us to dark places

By Dorcas Smucker
An article taken with permission from
The Register-Guard, *Eugene, Oregon, Dec. 14, 2014*

My first winter in Oregon, I was so tired of the cloudy days. "I used to drive home from work and try to count how many shades of gray were in the sky," I told my daughter on the way home from church last Sunday. "Were there fifty of them?" she joked, referencing the title of the best-selling book. Neither of us has read the book, but we are familiar with winter's varieties of gray and the creeping heaviness of seasonal affective disorder that comes with this time of the year.

This will be my 25th Oregon winter, so I know the pattern. The sunny days of late summer stretch on and on, well into September and sometimes on into October. I pull carrots, go camping, and inspire the family to help me can 50 quarts of applesauce. We try to wash windows but give up when the farmer to the north plows his field and covers the clean window with dust. I ride my bike in the evening and smile into the glorious setting sun.

But then the clouds move in and so does the dark cloud of depression. The rain falls and so do my spirits. Suddenly I sleep a lot more, crave cinnamon rolls, and stop caring about the last of the squash going to waste in the garden. I find excuses to stay at home again. I can't decide on a menu for Thanksgiving dinner but obsess for days about the nasty woman who stepped right in front of my car and then yelled at me in the WinCo parking lot as I was slowly driving away. Oh, she was evil, blaming me for her own inattention, and why couldn't I think of a withering reply? I no longer care about the dirty windows. Lastly, my energy disappears and making my bed in the morning and recycling the newspaper are like wading thru knee-deep peanut butter.

I am able to laugh at myself now because I immediately recognize the symptoms and I know this malady has a name: seasonal affective disorder. Thankfully, it also has a solution—-for me, a careful mixture of vitamin D, nutrition, herbal supplements, taking walks, and connecting with people.

Many of us in the Northwest deal with SAD, I've learned, our symptoms ranging from mild to debilitating. At a midwinter writer's group meeting at my friend Jessica's years ago, the subject of winter depression came up. We all dealt with it, to some degree. Jessica said, "When the sun came out accidentally yesterday, I just had this surge of energy." We all nodded. It has happened to each of us. Jessica said, "Wait. Did I just say the sun came out accidentally?" We laughed. What an apt description of an Oregon winter!

SAD wasn't so funny the first winters that we lived in Oregon, especially when it took over reality to such a degree that I was in full-blown depression. Unfortunately, the deeper one sinks into any mental illness, the harder it is to recognize the problem and ask for help. A friend had the courage to say the words, "You are depressed. You need help."

There's a strange power in that seemingly simple step of verbalizing the truth. Especially for someone with a long family history not only of mental illness, but also of hiding it in silence, our private anguish has to crank up a long and difficult auger before it finally spills out of our mouths as complete words.

"Something is wrong."

"I have a problem."

"I need help."

Having an observant, compassionate friend who articulates it for you can be a godsend, catching you before you fall further or crash completely. Saying it in words enables you to reach out for skilled help, find out that the darkness has a name, and discover hope. This isn't normal. Life can be attractive again.

Recently, in preparation for a speech, I visited the Lane County Office of the National Alliance on Mental Illness. Staffed mostly by volunteers, NAMI offers classes, information, referrals, and—most of all—support. "I wish I would have known about you years ago, "I said, thinking of all the floundering I could have avoided. My hostess nodded, affirming that it's a long route from recognizing the problem to getting help. The important thing, she emphasized, is knowing that others have survived the same issues, and they will help you overcome as well. Recovery is possible.

My first step in fighting SAD was to buy a big white electrical apparatus with the ambitious label of "Happy- Lite", which I placed on my desk and tried to stare at every morning. It worked to some degree, but I found it terribly hard to consistently sit in one spot for half an hour a day. Plus, it invited too many adolescent jokes. One irritated word from me about the dog getting hair all over my skirt again, and a child would snicker, "Mom, did you forget to sit in front of your Happy-Lite this morning?"

One winter I tried prescription antidepressants but hated the side effects, especially the sense of placidity, as though I had no emotion at all. Eventually, I found the combination that works for me. At last, I have weapons at hand when the autumn cloud moves in. It's hard to describe my gratitude for this, the relief, the sense of finally being in control.

Thanksgiving dinner is now an enjoyable challenge. Buying Christmas presents is a huge job, but not overwhelming. I have the mental clarity to pray for the inattentive woman stepping in front of the car and give thanks that she wasn't hurt. "She probably has SAD, poor thing," I think.

The pain of winters past becomes a gift: I not only recognize signs of depression quickly enough in myself to ward it off, but I also see symptoms in others long before they have the ability to say the words for themselves. "This is what I see," I tell them quietly. "I am worried about you, and this is what I suggest." So far, no one has resented my intrusion.

"I hadn't expected the profound relief of someone noticing," one of them told me. "It means I'm not invisible . . . that my pain is not falling on blind eyes all around me."

Winter will likely always have an edge of subtle dread. But now it also has a beauty of its own—a foggy feather across the Coburg Hills, a sun-edged gap in the southwestern sky, bare oak branches black against four distinct shades of gray; and a darkness finding words, past sadness redeemed in new compassion, a heavy listlessness replaced with gentle strength and light.

Acceptance

By 'Miriam'

Accepting my mental illness was a journey. My personal journey includes Bipolar Disorder which has black times of depression along with rosy tinted hypomania; if not caught in time, it blossoms into true mania which is frightening. This includes little need of sleep, rashness of thought, impulsive actions, and more.

Depression came slowly the first time in my teens . . . suddenly life came to a grinding halt. I was unable to eat, sleep, or function. Some of the contributing stresses were my friends going to Bible school and beginning courtship, and a lack of schedule at home. The doctors did numerous tests. Somehow in my distorted thinking, I thought it would be wrong as a Christian to be depressed and did not want to admit it to a non-Christian doctor. Finally, the third time I saw my own family doctor, I hesitantly admitted that I was depressed. A look of relief crossed his face as he reached for a prescription pad. He immediately started me on an anti-depressant. The next weeks continued to be rocky, but I slowly began to feel better. In a half a year I was feeling well and the doctor slowly weaned me off my medication.

But the next autumn or early winter I began to feel depressed again and had a virus similar to mono. (With symptoms of nausea and fatigue) I was basically in bed for several weeks. The support of friends and starting medication before the depression became as severe decreased the severity and recovery time this time around. The following year, a different challenge emerged. Suddenly I had more energy, a decreased need for sleep, and exuberance I didn't have before; at the same time I could quickly become critical if my ideas were opposed. I knew something was wrong, so I booked an appointment with my family doctor. I knew it wasn't depression, but it was frightening to not know what was happening. He requested a second appointment with my parents and me, and that appointment included numerous bewildering questions. He diagnosed me with Cyclothymic Personality Disorder, which means that a person has cycles of mild depression and hypomania. He promptly started me on lithium and prescribed a short-term medication to manage my elevated mood. My increased energy came to a halt, but the lithium helped to give more long term stability to my moods.

I would inwardly rebel when I needed to make a routine visit to my doctor. Perhaps it was a beautiful summer day or maybe I didn't want to go and admit that I am once again struggling with depression and might need my dosage adjusted. Even taking my medication faithfully when I am feeling well can be a challenge. When I realize that my doctor simply wants to help me and am ready give up my pride and the desire to *manage life by myself,* things go much better.

My experience with deep despair occurred many years after my initial diagnosis of bipolar disorder. One beautiful summer, things suddenly worsened and even though I knew the signs and symptoms of depression, I suddenly slid into despair. Contributing factors were family stresses, a difficult work situation, and betrayal by a trusted friend, along with the compound grief of losing several family members (by death). The question of where to turn for help was frightening. If I went to my family doctor and shared my struggle with feeling the futility of living, what would he do? Would he hospitalize me in the hospital where I was currently working? Would he call my managers, or put me on a stress leave? Would I lose my job? What if I shared it with my support group? Would it scare them? Would they hover over me or would they tell my family (who was contributing heavily to the stressors causing the depression)? Was it better to suffer in silence? Would my coworkers see my difficulty in eating my lunch, and recognize the symptoms at work? (They were knowledgeable of the symptoms of depression.) I did not want to lose my job and knew from a previous episode that deep, prolonged depression was not an experience I wanted to repeat.

By God's grace, my story has a happy ending. Finally, I gathered the courage to share my struggle with one of the people in my support group. She allowed me to verbalize my feelings and share why I felt the way I did. She helped me pray through my struggle with despair, and forgive those who had wronged me. She offered support by giving several cell phone numbers so I could reach them anytime I needed to. She did not keep it a secret, but immediately shared it with the other couple in my support group as well.

What really woke me up was when the second friend came to visit me within a day or two. She picked up a delicious meal at a restaurant and sat beside me while I ate it. Eating was difficult and nigh to impossible when alone. She said, "Miriam, I could never forgive myself if something happened to you." I'm not sure if that is a correct statement to make to a depressed person, but it woke me up as nothing else did. Suddenly the realization hit me that even though I don't care what happens anymore, my friend loves me deeply. I loved her and did not want to cause her grief. Now there was purpose in life, I needed to live and get better because I loved her.

My friend offered to accompany me to the doctor's appointment. She said, "I'll get a babysitter for my children and go with you. I want you to tell the doctor how you are feeling." She followed through on her promise, but I went alone by my own choice. She prayed for me, and called after the appointment to verify if I told him the truth.

I did not have the rapport with the nurse that I did with my own doctor and was very quiet when she took me into the room. My usual practice was to share my progress with her, but not that day. Finally she said, "You'll tell the doctor how you are feeling?" and I agreed. My doctor thankfully did not react, but it took great courage to share my condition with him because of the possible consequences. My doctor realized I was feeling down, but I needed to tell him three times that I felt as if life was no longer worth living, before he understood what I really meant. Then he gave me his full attention, support and time; he adjusted my medication, and had me come back for follow up in a short time.

While continuing to meet with my support group, life gradually became brighter. When I was working an evening shift, the one family came to my place; they mowed my lawn, trimmed my yard, and weeded my garden. In despair, the necessity of selling my property hovered in my mind, because I did not have the physical and emotional energy to look after it. Both families called frequently and invited me over for meals. It was almost as if they were saying, "We know you can do it, but we are here to help until you can." God brought healing for the hurts, pain, despair, betrayal, and granted new emotional and physical strength.

That was twenty years ago, but Bipolar Disorder is still part of my life today. It is not easy to accept my limitations which means frequent doctor's visits, never missing a night of sleep, no unnecessary stress, and working with the strain it can bring to interpersonal relationships. If I feel my mood changing, I immediately book an appointment with my doctor. Even though he is very busy, he has an understanding with his receptionist that whenever I call in with a change of moods, he will see me that day or the next. I have been blessed to have the same doctor all these years. I feel having a doctor you can trust is important. After some years on lithium, due to side effects, he referred me to a psychiatrist. The psychiatrist weaned me off the lithium and started me on a newer anticonvulsant with fewer side effects. After a few visits, I was under the expert care of my family doctor again.

Accepting my limitations is challenging because my job is a profession that includes working all hours of the day and night. I have needed to request exemption from the night shift and this causes conflict with my coworkers at times. I need to accept that never again will I knowingly miss a night's sleep because of the risk of causing a re-occurrence of a manic or depressive period. If I notice I am becoming manic, I need to limit my social activity and be sure I get enough of sleep and time alone with God. When feeling hypomanic, I need to remove myself from situations and people before I make rash statements. And frequently, I have to go back and apologize for speaking quickly, rashly, or interrupting conversations.

The level of health I experience now I owe in part to the expert care and quick diagnosis of my family doctor, but most of all to God, my heavenly Father. I was blessed to have a season of counseling with a Christian counselor and his wife to work through hurts in my past, and choose forgiveness. This has contributed greatly to the emotional health I experience today. Life still includes valleys—one was losing three family members in seven months, a mother, uncle and a grandparent; but God has been faithful and I have never been as ill as the first few years of my illness.

A verse in Romans 9:20 is a challenge, "Nay, but, O man, who art thou that repliest against God? Shall the thing formed say to him that formed it, why has thou made me thus?" I have found as I accept my illness and the way God created me, it gives me an inner peace and joy which in turn results in better emotional health. I had an anointing service some years ago, and although I still have this disorder, I feel God has blessed me with more stability in my moods than some people. I was blessed with supportive parents and several couples in my church have acted as a support group for me over the years. There are people who faithfully check up on me when I am depressed, assist me when I am unable to keep up with my physical work, include me in their family life, and offer to accompany me to a doctor's appointment when I am afraid to tell him how truly depressed I am.

Bipolar illness is a gift I would not have chosen, but it has helped me change and grow and made me more compassionate of others with mental illness. I want my life to honor God, with the gift He has given me.

Overcoming OCD

By 'Shawn Yoder'

Pen and paper can scarcely do justice to the fountain of feelings and torrent of emotions that flood my mind as I recall my journey with OCD. OCD stands for Obsessive-Compulsive Disorder which evidences itself in "recurrent obsessions and/or compulsions that are severe enough to be time-consuming or to cause marked distress or significant impairment in a person's daily routine." [1] Obsessions are "persistent ideas, thoughts, impulses, or images that are experienced as intrusive and inappropriate and cause marked anxiety or distress." We all experience anxiety and worries about various things in our daily lives, but the person with OCD feels helpless to arrest, inhibit, and dismiss these fears. He often reacts to these

[1] Definitions given in this article are from the American Psychiatric Association's *Diagnosis and Statistical Manual of Mental Disorders.*

worries (which are many times very unrealistic) with compulsions, which are "repetitive behaviors or mental acts, the goal of which is to prevent or reduce anxiety or distress."

For example, a person who is obsessed with contamination might respond with compulsions like washing his hands every 20 minutes, with a certain amount of soap, in a certain way. Or the person who is obsessed with checking over things might unlock and relock the door 10 times till he can convince himself that the door is locked! Someone who is obsessed with the fear of sinning or blaspheming God may pray quite frequently, using the same words in the same sequence. Or perhaps they will "resay" the prayer at the family dinner table because they hadn't concentrated 100% on every word that was said. And, of course, they must keep their eyes closed the second time as well, or God *might* not accept it. And on and on the anxious thoughts go. The normal person might ask, "Why all the bother? Can't they just dismiss it?" The fact is, to the OCDer, performing his time-consuming compulsions is much less stressful to him for the time-being than the agony of trying to rid himself of the obsessive thought! It gives him a sense of peace for the next few minutes (or moments, depending on how far advanced the illness is). As you can see, OCD is a very cruel taskmaster who demands more and more until the victim crashes emotionally or some concerned family member intervenes. It's like a closed circuit in your brain where the troubling thought keeps firing again and again. And again. After a while you get so weary of resisting it that you succumb with a certain compulsion. And while some of these examples may seem unreal and far-fetched, as many as 3% of the United States populace alone struggle with these types of thoughts to a major degree![2]

My struggle with OCD showed up unexpectedly during my second or third year in school. As is common with OCD strugglers, I was always rather perfectionistic and people-pleasing by nature. My parents watched in alarm as their formerly happy and obedient son developed time-consuming rituals and compulsions that overrided all other authorities in my life (describing those compulsions could in itself be a book!) In their well-meaning ignorance, they spent hours reassuring me and coaxing me to move on. Soon they became my brain's governor, constantly reassuring me and telling me that what I had done in this certain situation or scenario was alright. For a number of years we limped along this way. Interestingly enough, I often improved significantly during the summer months, possibly due to my outdoor activities which gave me lots of sunshine (Vitamin D). So each year, my parents sent me to school with high hopes only to find OCD returning with a vengeance. As you can guess, eventually even summers didn't bring relief and no longer was I content with my parent's reassurances.

Somewhere along the line, I learned that there is a name for what I was dealing with. While my parents had identified my illness as OCD from the start, it took a while for me as a young child to grasp that my weird thoughts and behavior stemmed from an illness that wasn't all that uncommon. As I read articles and books on OCD, I was continually amazed at how these authors laid out word for word exactly what I was experiencing. How comforting to know I was not alone! One of the books, *The Thought That Counts*, written by Jared Kant, laid out the common areas that OCD rears its ugly head. I especially connected with this, since in my experience I have personally struggled in most of these areas to a major degree. I would recommend this book to anyone who is interested.

Now, for the million-dollar question! What can be done to treat and prevent this illness? The good news is that it can be overcome to a manageable level. The bad news is that there is no easy cure. What works for one person does not always work for another. We might as well face the facts. As family members and friends of an OCD struggler, be prepared to give support for the long haul. Sometimes you may come exasperatingly close to your wit's end. But remember: "If God brings you to it, He can bring you through it." Don't give up!

Of course, the sooner the illness is detected and arrested, the less entrenched the compulsions and habits are. In my own experience, we waited much too long to go for medication for my OCD. Don't get me wrong; I still favor natural remedies over the medical field whenever possible. But mental illness is no common cold or headache! For my OCD the medication Prozac (fluoxetine) was, and still is, a God-send. Prozac belongs to a family of medicines known as Selective Serotonin Reuptake Inhibitors or SSRIs. Serotonin is a neuro-transmitter that many scientists believe plays a large part in OCD. SSRIs increase the concentration and activity of serotonin in the brain. Some other medications in this family that have proved helpful to some are Celexa, Lexapro, Luvox, Paxil, and Zoloft. Clomipramine (Anafranil) is an older medicine that has also proved effective. However, it is not a first choice treatment because of its negative side effects. And again, finding the right medication and the right dosage of it may take weeks, months, or even years. Personally, I hit my lowest spell during our search for and trial of various medicines.

Of course, medication in itself is not a miracle cure. It's just a tool that God provides to make it easier for the sick person to exercise his own will power. While there definitely are biological and emotional roots for OCD, we can't ignore the spiritual side of our person. With God's help, we will need to personally overcome the obsessive thoughts in the battlefield of the mind. And counseling has also proved to be very helpful along with medicine. Cognitive-behavioral therapists often use the exposure and response prevention (EX/RP) method in which the obsessive-compulsive patient is purposely exposed to the very things that trigger his compulsions but prevented from responding with his normal rituals. The longer and oftener this can be practiced, the less compelling the anxious thoughts become. One caution with counseling though;

be careful to find a Christian, Scriptural mentor and not just a modern psychologist!

During my OCD odyssey, one of the things that discouraged me most was the people that said things like, "Just tell yourself you must think right. You aren't dealing with your will." Oh! Dear friends, I would never wish OCD on anyone, but just one hour of it would drastically change your perspective! Of course you must think right, but it's not as simple as "just telling yourself." We've already tried to do that thousands of times. You see, we don't like our issues any better than you do, and yet we feel so helpless. I know I'm treading on touchy ground here. But I must. Mental illness is not just a spiritual or will problem! Would you tell a person with a broken leg to just walk on it and it will get better? Of course not! You can see his leg's broken; and if only you could see the "broken brain" of a mentally ill person. . . . If only!

Now I realize that there's a difference between the leg and the brain. The difference being that the brain is intricately involved in governing our will, thoughts, and actions. OCD can express itself through the same channels that a rebellious will can; namely, our thoughts and actions. But consider this. Why would a rebellious child or teenager disobey by using five pumps of soap instead of one, or repeatedly check over school work assignments when he was told it's good enough the first time? That's not mere rebellion; that's mental illness.

But, to the normal person, this idea is hard to grasp. Especially so if this compulsive "disobedience" drags on for five, six, or even ten years while you spend lots of money and time on counseling and trying different medications. And yet, when you finally find the right dose of the right thing and experience the "day and night, black and white" difference it can make, you will understand that mental illness is more than just a spiritual problem. Don't give up on your ill loved one; I don't know where I would be today if people had given up on me.

In closing, if there's any help I can give to others regarding OCD, I want to do what I can. To contact me personally, send a letter with your address and phone number to Anita Martin, Att. Masthof Press (p.303).

I wish each one the spirit
"of power, and of love, and of a sound mind."
(2 Timothy 1:7)

The Train I don't want to get on . . .

By a young girl

I really enjoyed school when I was young, but at times my OCD bothered me. It especially slowed me down in my Math. We were supposed to check the addition and subtraction problems to make sure the answers coincided with each other. I checked and rechecked to be absolutely sure the numbers agreed. Sometimes if I didn't say something exactly the way it was, then I worried I lied. I would tell my Mom or ask if I should apologize to someone else. She would tell me not to worry about it.

When I asked God for forgiveness for the times I failed, I just asked again and again until I *felt* like I was forgiven. I didn't like to be caught in that cycle, but I was powerless to do anything about it.

In my early teenage years, I often apologized to my family because I felt I had to. I was a maid for my aunt and I apologized for mistakes I made. My aunt was understanding and told me not to worry about things. I also told Mom what I worried about and with her help and encouragement, I managed to keep my head above the water; but the year when I was 15, going on 16, things suddenly started getting worse. Whenever an impure thought entered my mind, I felt wicked. I felt like I had to tell Mom to make things right, but since I was too embarrassed, I tried to forget about it. But that didn't work. I felt awful. My brain was telling me I must tell Mom or I'm sinful. So, after a few days of this, I would finally gave in and write a note, briefly stating my thoughts.

I felt some relief, but a cloud still seemed to be hanging over me. Very soon another thought came, and once again I struggled with telling Mom or not . . . since I wanted relief, I'd give in again. It was an endless cycle. I worried about something, told Mom, and soon I was worried about something else.

Week after week went by. I felt impure and sinful with all these thoughts sticking in my mind. Mom was very understanding and patient, and did all she could to help me. Often I would try to ignore my thoughts and go on; for a little while it would be better, but soon I would be back in the same old rut again.

After a few months of this, we went to the family doctor to get medication to help calm my nerves. She started me on something, but it didn't seem to make things better. I had my Learner's Permit and was trying to get my hours of driving in. I was having some violent thoughts, and when I was driving the van with my family in, the thought would sometimes haunt me. . . . What if I'd swerve off the road? It made me fearful and anxious because I didn't want the thought, but it just stuck in my mind.

One day, that day will always be etched in my mind, we went to the family doctor and told her how I was feeling. She said she cannot help me and that I should see a psychiatrist. She had Mom and I sign our names, saying that I may not drive for seven weeks, unless I had permission from a doctor. That day I felt hopeless. Was my mind really that sick that I needed to see a psychiatrist and not be allowed to drive? What would my friends think of me? I almost completely lost my desire to live. Suicidal thoughts entered my mind, making me feel guilty and helpless.

A few days later we went to an appointment with Dr. Gregg Orr at the Green Pastures Outpatient Clinic. I also saw one of the counselors there. I felt so wicked and rather emotional. Mom and Daddy did most of the talking for me. The doctor said he recommends I live at the house on the Green Pasture grounds so he can start me on medication and watch to see if it's the right kind.

I was stunned! I hadn't realized how sick I really was. It took a little while to get used to the idea, but I actually felt relieved and hopeful that help was on the way. One week later I packed up and headed for Green Pastures. Nobody knew how long I would stay. I really didn't feel too bad those first few days. Of course, everything was new and strange, but the obsessive thoughts didn't seem quite as frightening. There were other residents there, and it was comforting to know that I wasn't the only one struggling.

My doctor said it would be good if I kept a diary every day of how I felt. I liked that idea, because I find it easier to write my thoughts down on paper than to talk. I took it along to my appointments so my doctor and counselor could see how my days were going.

It didn't take long to learn to know the other residents, since we were with each other all day. There were a few other young girls there who I made friends with. In the mornings and evenings, the house parents and a mentor went with the residents on a walk. We all had lots of fun together, whether it was eating, singing, working, playing, or talking. There was always a mentor there to keep us occupied. They not only joined in with our fun, but were always ready to lend a listening ear and encourage us.

I saw my counselor three or four times a week. I depended on this time to tell her my worries and struggles. I wasn't always easy to open up, but by telling her how I felt, she helped me view things by the facts and not my mixed-up feelings. She gave me practical advice when I had struggles interacting with other people. She didn't seem surprised when I told her my struggles; instead she helped me appreciate who I was.

We had two group therapies a day on weekdays. A counselor was in charge of them. In the morning group, we shared a little how we're feeling and discussed things. In the afternoon group, one of the counselors had a topic, and we took notes. They taught us many valuable things such as healthy coping skills, accepting ourselves, recovery goals, moods and thoughts, self-talk, etc.

Hope began to rise in my heart. I was beginning to understand that it wasn't really my fault that the thoughts stuck in my mind. My counselor explained how OCD operates. I am missing certain chemicals in my brain which affects my brain circulation. Instead of the brain messages going back and forth in a straight and direct way, they get all tangled and twisted, losing some things along the way; therefore the message is not accurate when the brain receives it. The message is not true, even though it feels like it is. The best way to handle it is to ignore it. Medication helps to get this straightened out so that these untrue messages don't happen. We need the help of others to be able to understand what a correct message is and what a sick message is until we are better again.

I really appreciated Dr. Greg Orr. He pointed me to hope, and commended me for how far I had come, even though I had many things to work on. He helped me understand that I am not inferior to other people. I did a few tests, and the results showed that I had significant anxiety symptoms and also significant depression symptoms. It was recommended that I have counseling to help me manage the OCD symptoms.

After four weeks of living at Green Pastures, my doctors decided that I had improved enough to be able to go home. I was rather apprehensive about leaving all my close friends and the sheltered life I had come to know, but I also felt I needed to move on with my life. So I said my many Good-byes, and went home in a much better state of mind than I had come.

It took a while to make the adjustment. It was nice to be home, but I missed my friends at Green Pastures and felt sad that I wasn't a part of their big family anymore. After a few days I found myself getting back into the home routine, and it was so much better than before. My mind was clear and I was at peace and could enjoy life. Of course, there still were things to work on, but I try to remember the important part is 'letting the train go past' as my doctor put it. When obsessive thoughts go through your mind, let the train go past—don't jump on it, even though it feels like you should. I liked that example. It helped me to understand what I was working with. I feel so awed and thankful when I stop and realize how much I've improved, when it seemed impossible to me.

This is my story, although words can't describe the depths of anxiety and guilt I felt. I hope my story will be an encouragement to you, that there is hope! Don't give up, regardless of where you are or what you are struggling with. With God, nothing is impossible.

My Experience with Bipolar Two

By Lorraine Weaver

The first symptoms of my illness emerged after our first child was born- a beautiful, little daughter. As the days, weeks, and months passed, I began to struggle with anxious, fearful thoughts. . . . terrible things that could happen to my baby . . . things I said when I was growing up . . . how strange people must think I am. I fought them off as well as I could and eventually they passed.

Our first son came . . . what joy! How rich we felt! But I lay awake staring out at the dark night, watching the moon creep across the sky. "Why do I lay awake so much?" I wondered. Nothing came to mind, nothing bothered me, but the baby would soon be awake for another feeding. I wished I could get some sleep! During the day, I had times of boundless energy where I accomplished three day's work in one day . . . we were happy and in a lot of ways life was good.

During my third pregnancy, my emotional state was not good. My nerves were terrible and I felt frustrated over little things. Again, I had a lot of energy, but I was not sleeping well. I began to get panicky feelings; how I hated them! It made me feel like I was dying!

"Lorraine," my midwife said kindly. "You have symptoms of depression. It will only get worse after the baby is here. You really need to start an anti-depressant." What! I am not that bad! In my mind I pictured sad, haggard-looking people—puffy-faced and spaced-out from their medication. "That's not going to be me!" I thought. "I will be fine." I could get ahold of myself. I might be a little imbalanced, but depressed? No! I am not depressed!

But my midwife went on. "Your family will suffer. . . when mom is not doing well everyone is affected." I had to agree with that.

Another little girl arrived and we were so excited and happy. Some difficult adjustments came, and I found myself dragging thru my days, finding it a challenge to keep after the little ones. I knew God was good to me, but I didn't feel that way. I prayed that God would take control of my feelings and make them more stable. Some days I struggled with depression and accusing thoughts; other days I felt good, inspired to sew and sew for my girls, even though they really didn't need more dresses.

Acting normal after church wasn't easy. I tried to fool others by slipping into the nursery and hiding there with my little girl. Sometimes I wished for the faith I used to have. I was sure people could tell I am not the carefree Lorraine that I used to be. Who was I? I didn't even know myself?!

With each weed I pulled, I wished I could jerk a thought out of my mind and throw it away. Where was my energy this summer? Was I just lazy? And these headaches! It was a rough week with little sleep. I took a sleeping pill, but it didn't help much. Exhausted, I plodded to the house and fell onto the sofa. I tried to rest, but my mind raced, my heart raced, and even though I was so tired, sleep wouldn't come. I prayed for tears because I couldn't cry even though I wanted to. The phone rang and in spite of the chirpy hello on the other end, I couldn't think of anything to say. I felt like I had an empty hole. . . . I knew God can fill any void; why didn't He take care of this?

"Lord, I know you love me. Help me to feel that love. Lord, build me up emotionally so I don't feel like I am going to pieces, to not hurt so quickly over what others may think, not to always assume I'm wrong. I don't want medication. Please help me to sleep at night and may I have tears so I can cry? Here's my hand—keep me from letting go."

Busy canning season arrived. My mind filled with more delusions. I woke up in the night and couldn't get rid of a story in my mind. I finally got the courage to call the lady and ask her if there was anything to it, and she reassured me there wasn't. She seemed very concerned that I wasn't sleeping and asked me to stop thinking the story over and call her anytime I want. How comforting she was! As I hung up the phone the world looked so much better and for a few days that terrible condemnation was gone.

I sank into my recliner and remarked to my husband, "I sure feel good about all I accomplished today. I weeded the strawberry patch, went to the store, mowed the whole lawn, and picked up corn in the field. With what I did last week that makes a pickup load!" "Yes, it sounds like you got a lot done," he replied, "But you really should pace yourself and not over do it." Oh, but I felt so good these last days! My headaches weren't even bothering me. Things were going to be o.k!

The saliva test I took to check for hormone trouble came back clear. I could have cried. My doctor seemed to think it might be hormones, but he also asked me if I ever heard of bipolar illness. Oh, I could quake at the name! Please, let it only be a hormone thing. I started using progesterone cream.

I woke up early in the morning and couldn't stop my mind. It went from one thing to the next. Why couldn't I sleep? I struggled to decide if things were true, confessing them over and over again. I was so thankful for friends who cared for me and prayed for me. But I wished I was normal again.

Once again, my midwife told me that I should be taking an anti-depressant. I spent some time stewing over this medication thing. One of my friends told me she doesn't think it is right to take medication. Another friend gave me the book called *Telling Yourself the Truth.* It was very encouraging at the time . . . just what I needed with all the lies I tell myself! I wanted to buy several copies. I also heard a message on Christian Emotions and he said if we are depressed we should look at what we are thinking about. Going into depression is a process and it will take time to get out of it. But it was hard to sort thru all this when my mind was telling me things are way worse than they are, and so much isn't true, **where do I start?**

Leaning over the kitchen sink, one hand in sudsy water, I flipped the pages on the inspiration calendar, silently crying for a ray of hope to get me thru the day. If only Jesus would burst thru the clouds and take us all home! I found myself just longing to leave. I no longer cared about anything. I wished I could just sit in a chair and stare into space, but I knew I need to force my foggy brain to focus on something and keep going. Slowly I began realizing that I need help and that maybe that help is medication!

Just going to the doctor brought a sense of relief. Maybe there WAS hope. He started me on a medication, warning me to watch if I get worse. He wasn't sure of his diagnosis. I minded the negative side effects—nausea, dry mouth, and feeling sweaty. I backed off to half the dose the first month. But I treasured the positive effects! My mind felt clearer and I was able to be calm with my children. I even felt motivated to wave my hand at my husband as he drove by on the tractor. And guess what? I FELT like waving! I recovered the wonderful gift of being in touch with normal emotions, including the ability to cry.

My sleep gradually improved over the next month; it felt so good to work and plan my days again! It was so relaxing and in the evening I was blessed with a normal tiredness. *Thank you, God, for this gift!* Yes, I had some bad days, but what is one day?

After the birth of one of our children, I distinctly noticed mood swings; approximately 4 days low, and then normal for about that many days. The doctor called this a form of bipolar. He added a small dose of Seroquel to my Zoloft and it worked great for me!

A sick mind blows things way out of proportion . . . we believe ANYTHING! I learned to work with this in various ways. When I called someone I wrote things they said down so I could come back to it later on and not feel foolish. Things like, "I am glad you called, don't keep thinking it over, I love you, call again, and I understand," were comforting words to me. Sometimes writing my thoughts down and looking at them later helped me see how unrealistic they were. It was a good reminder how warped my thinking could get. This helped me realize I am not what I FEEL I am.

Several years later I tried cutting my medication back. It worked okay over the summer . . . I argued back to my thoughts, knowing where they would take me. I thought maybe I had the answer! But as summer gave way to fall, and I struggled through a miscarriage, my depression and thoughts once again spiraled out of control. I returned to my normal dose, admitting that I had not 'attained' after all.

Now I wonder why I waited two years after the midwife told me to get help before I did it. But then I remembered how I still question by times why I need medication, and I realized I needed those years to see my need and learn lessons God had for me. I went thru a period of feeling let down because I really believed God would see me thru and I wouldn't need medication. I needed to learn to trust again and turn my burdens over to Him. I needed to accept He does care and will make a way, even though it wasn't the way I wanted.

Looking over my journey, I thank God for it. It was a steppingstone in maturing me in my spiritual and personal life. One of the greatest blessings was that I learned to have a caring and compassionate heart for other hurting people. I never want to lose that! I am grateful that I am able to live a normal, healthy life and I want to give it back to God in service for Him.

In Health or in Sickness

By a mother

Our married life began with many good, sunny years. There were children to bless our hearts and home. Life was so good to us. Jim was my 'shining knight', snatching me from a home with some unhappy secrets. Sure, people knew my dad was *odd,* but no outsider could understand what tension we lived under with a father whose uncontrolled temper ruled our home. Fear, not love, dominated our lives. Without a loving, gentle mother, I could not imagine how we would have survived.

Jim was an almost-perfect husband and a wonderful Dad. Our children were enjoying a carefree childhood. I determined they would never know what I and my siblings had experienced. That was completely in the past. I felt secure in the love that surrounded me as Jim continued to treat me as the girl he had married. Adjustments came as the older children reached their teen years, and the youngest was a toddler. But life was good, even with 'new normals'.

Then the unforeseen happened. My normal days were abruptly changed—changed drastically. It couldn't be otherwise when my nighttime hours became sleepless nightmares. My mind was invaded with haunting memories. Endless, wordless prayers were mixed with those memories. Some nights my mind relaxed, but then my heart would begin thumping, making sleep impossible. By morning I was drenched in sweat. Something was wrong-totally wrong.

A visit with our family doctor offered some help and hope. The doctor wasn't sure of the cause of the symptoms so she chose to have my thyroid tested. She thought maybe stress brought on a period of depression . . . maybe an early stage of hormone changes. "Let's give you a prescription of an older anti-depressant that should help you sleep at night. A newer type would be better for long term which I'll prescribe for you also." She sounded reassuring despite her inability to know the underlying cause.

AH, it was such a relief when I could sleep again! It was wonderful to feel like taking care of the family. The ability to go to church and listen to a sermon with a clear, restful mind was such a blessing. I could talk freely with my friends again, with no annoying fog hanging over me. The clouds had departed and I was soaring high!

Two years later, I felt a slow relapse. It was the same old story. Fears and guilt trips came more frequently while sleep began to elude me. This time my mental torture was more difficult. I pictured myself in the psychiatric ward of some hospital, completely disoriented. My children knew something was wrong with me. I was not myself, frequently retreating to my bedroom. Close friends were becoming aware of my struggles. Some dropped in with meals, and some found other ways to care.

Jim did not treat me as a hopeless case, yet he often felt helpless as he spent hours, day or night, listening to me. Memories of the past became enormous burdens of guilt. If only I would have been more committed to God, I could have done better in showing respect to my parents, especially my father. I knew I had been proud that Jim had chosen me. Had our friendship become more precious than my relationship with God? Were the romantic feelings we had before marriage totally pure? I was sure my mothering was full of failures. One of the fears that terrorized me was the fear that I might be at fault if one of my children rejected God. I could not stand the thought of a child born to me going to hell. That fear would sometimes overwhelm me to the point of uncontrollable weeping. Jim did his very best to show me how much he cared. He tried to reassure me that I was not a failure; that our children did have a good mother.

My greatest comfort was the thought of going to be with Jesus. I trusted my faith would cover all my personal failures. "Even so come, Lord Jesus . . . come now," my heart would beg. Planning for my funeral became a compelling escape from my torturing fears. I wanted lots of singing. I chose my favorites and had as many as twenty songs on my list. I used to be afraid Jim would die, leaving me and the children behind. Now I *knew* I would be first! The joy of release from this affliction was so comforting to contemplate. Bizarre as it sounds, I actually wondered who would become a mother to our children. She would be a better mother, of that I was convinced.

Jim knew we needed to see the doctor again. Unfortunately, he was out of town and they scheduled my appointment two weeks into the future. In desperation, I tried some natural sleep aid, with no results. So I requested help thru another doctor. What he prescribed did give me a few hours of sleep each night, but it wasn't nature's real, refreshing sleep.

The doctor was not sure how to handle this second spell of deep depression. Another thyroid test was as useless as the first one. She offered some adjustment to my prescription and wished us "better days ahead." Gradually the storm within quieted. Being able to relax and sleep through the night hours was a relief beyond measure. I felt release from all those past sins which had marched relentlessly across the computer screen of my mind. I had thoroughly repented and I was free! Surely God is gracious and won't let this happen again.

In retrospect, I felt another freedom taking place. I now felt empathy for my father. Never before had I understood the countless times he would spend days in bed or on a couch in the living room. During those times it was unpredictable whether he would join the family at mealtimes or not. It was just one of those hidden secrets of our family.

Although we were convinced these spells of depression were directly related to my hormone changes, we began to understand that the type of depression I experienced had a genetic source. This realization shed light on the lives of some of my siblings. I chose to become open about my mental health issues, but realized others within my family felt differently. I was very thankful for my husband and children who accepted my weakness, and for a circle of caring friends.

There were more valleys for me to pass through again. Thankfully, I never had such long stretches of sleepless nights. A month without restful sleep is miserable beyond description. When I started into sleepless nights again a few years later, I told Jim I needed help *now.* I knew that I was physically less able to cope with more deep depression. This time my family doctor urged me to contact a GYN, who had testing done to determine my hormone levels. The test confirmed I should once again begin treatment to help balance my hormones. With time, I noticed the benefits of that treatment.

We were also recommended to a well-known psychiatrist, who was very kind. He was puzzled by some of the things this "good woman", as he called me, was going through. He was sure that an old-time medication used for psychotic needs would be the answer. I reacted to the medication with an annoying rash. The next medication he offered made me feel totally restless, and I began pacing the floor. Yet another medication made me feel sick on the stomach.

At the end of three months, it was evident that nothing the psychiatrist offered worked. We decided to go back to the family doctor, who prescribed a different antidepressant, very recently made available at an affordable cost. My mental health improved but controlling my emotions continued to be a struggle. I cried when I didn't want to, and laughed too much at other times. Sometimes I gave quick, ridiculous comments in family conversations that I later regretted.

The very worst was the wear and tear on our marriage relationship, something that I hate to admit. I knew Jim sometimes wondered what was happening to the girl he married. I made comments to him that were unkind and critical. Other times my questions made *no* sense to him, so he chose to ignore them. What had he done to deserve this? I knew that I needed God's wisdom and grace . . . this was becoming a spiritual battle and I knew that medication wasn't my only need. Without God we would be shipwrecked!

I also experienced days when my concentration was very foggy, even though I seemed to be sleeping well. A friend introduced me to another doctor who admitted she had experienced depression caused by a thyroid problem. Because of that, she had studied more extensively into antidepressant medication. She looked at my prescription and told me, "What you are taking is good. I think what you need is another medication that will hopefully help you out of that foggy concentration which you have described to me."

I was excited and hopeful. And I was not disappointed! This knowledgeable doctor was a wonderful blessing . . . like an angel sent from God. Not only did I feel blessed, but so did the family! I was so grateful that some of the hurts in our marriage relationship had healed. Yet we needed to reckon with the fact that medical aid was not a total cure. It seemed like each spring and fall the change of the seasons affected my ability to cope with life.

I have not gotten beyond my need for medication, nor do I know if I ever will! If this truly is a genetic disorder, I may need that help for the rest of my life. People with diabetes, heart problems, and other body malfunctions depend on what helps them to function and enjoy life . . . this isn't any different. I compare my experience with an old car when its timing chain has slipped. Without help from someone who can fix the problem, that old car will never run again.

I share my experience because I know a journey through years of tears is a difficult one. The right medication isn't always found immediately. One doctor says that in mental disorders they try to choose a medication that deals with the symptoms, which is a trial and error method; whereas other physical problems can be treated after the *cause* of the symptoms has been found. Thank God, friend, for what He can do for you through medical knowledge, whether you choose what seems like a more natural way, or if like me, you choose from the medical profession.

I want to share one of my favorite verses:

My heart is fixed, O God, my heart is fixed;
I will sing and give praise.
PSALM 57:7.

A Path toward Healing

By a mother

"Mom, are you having a breakdown?" I could hear the anxiety in my fourteen year old daughter's voice as she questioned me from time to time. I looked into her worried eyes. "I think I'll be o.k." I tried to reassure her and myself at the same time. But I could feel myself slipping. It was hard to cope with simple stresses. I could feel the questions in the air as we silently ate supper together. I was not hungry, but I tried to keep going thru the motions. I knew I should keep eating.

It was November, 2013. My last three breakdowns, from 1996-2001 had been severe. I was first hospitalized in 1996, after our oldest child was diagnosed with cancer. I had not been feeling well for months, and the shock and trauma of her diagnosis put me over the edge. I was in Phil haven for a while until my husband signed me out, and the next year our precious daughter died. Over time, we continued to doctor with prescribed medications and slowly, slowly my condition improved. I broke down after the births of our last three children, but eventually I felt well again. What a joy to be able to function normally and care for my family!

After enjoying good mental health for many years, the doctor gradually weaned me off all my medications except for one—Abilify. And I still felt well! Gradually the desire grew within me to see if I was healed enough to go off medication altogether. But my doctor cautioned against it, considering how ill I had once been.

We heard of a new product, called Empower Plus that seemed to be helping many people. With my husband's blessing, I decided to try it. Over a 6 month period, I slowly decreased and weaned off the Abilify, while increasing accordingly on the EmpowerPlus. October 16th I took my last small dose. Still things seemed to be going o.k! But by the end of October, I began not sleeping well, and could feel myself losing control of my thoughts. I felt tense and could hardly handle simple stresses. For a day or two I also felt really light—like I was walking on clouds. Others said I was hyper. We realized what was happening and I started taking Abilify again, also calling my doctor for an appointment. It took three weeks until I was pulled back out of the fog. By sharing this, I do not want to discourage others who are using this product. For some people it works very well! I want to encourage you to use what works for you.

As I looked back at that difficult time of my life, various memories stand out:

One Saturday, while I felt like I couldn't even cope with being around my family, I went on a walk by myself in the woods. It was on the well-worn path that my husband and son often used to bring in our supply of firewood. It was refreshing to stand beside the stream and gaze at the bubbling little water falls. My heart felt strangely comforted and blessed before I headed back to the house again. Sometimes my husband walked the path with me. And even when we didn't say much, it felt good just to do something like that together.

My mother came all the way from Ohio to spend a couple days with me. It made my daughters' load lighter and was such a blessing! She even painted my kitchen door, giving it a fresh, white coat. One evening when my husband, son, and I returned from a walk, we heard singing. I listened from the sofa to my daughters' and mother's sweet, comforting singing.

"With my eyes fixed on Jesus, I can face another day . . . all your anxiety, all your care, bring to the mercy seat, leave it there, never a burden He cannot bear, never a friend like Jesus!" Tears trickled down my cheeks as my thirsty heart drank in the words.

"Would you like to do a puzzle?" Mom asked me the next day. She was planning to leave for home after lunch. Eagerly I began fitting in pieces. Each piece had a meaning in my mind.

Soon tears began to flow. Life was such a puzzle, and I couldn't keep doing the puzzle either. Mom sat down by me, and did it while I watched. The day before while we went shopping, everything had spiritual implications that condemned her and I. And now, today, I watched her drive out the lane and felt badly, seeing her vehicle loaded with supplies and thinking how it pointed to a dark, hopeless end. My thoughts were churning deep inside. It was very hard to express them, and I felt badly when I did. When people tried to assure me of Heaven, I felt like they were just saying that to make me feel good . . . they didn't really mean it.

I was home alone for a short while, feeling depressed and confused. I heard the phone ringing and eagerly reached for it. It was Sister Mae, checking up on me, concerned with how things were going. "*May I come over and cut out a dress on your kitchen table?*" she asked. I was very glad to have her come! With cheerful words and smiles she made herself at home, busying herself with laying out the fabric and pattern pieces. As I sat and listened to her kind words, I wondered, listlessly, when or if I would ever be able to cut out another dress.

Later, she walked around our pond with me, singing a song for me. As she prepared to leave, I falteringly asked her to make a list for me:

Turn a singing tape on.
Look at pretty pictures in books or calendars
Do the wash.
Call a friend.
Put dry dishes away.
Rest.
God is making a way for you. Your friends and family love you.

"Does it suit for us to come today?" my daughter asked an aunt on the phone. Faintly, I could hear the cheery reply as she welcomed us to come. My daughters keenly felt the responsibility of everything, and going away helped them to cope as well. Slowly I put on my shoes and coat and followed my faithful daughter to the van. Life had become a blur. I could barely keep track of the days and felt out of touch with reality. It had been years since I was this low.

On our way there, I thought everyone knew my thoughts, including the other cars on the road. They all knew I was headed for hell and were showing me how to calmly face it, by steadily driving onward. The condemning thoughts raced deep within my mind and made me wish for death. The end would come sooner or later, and it would not be pleasant. The years I had felt good seemed like a faraway dream. My crazy thoughts raced on- out of control- as we raced down the interstate. The reason the large semi-truck stayed ahead of us for a while was because he, too, knew I was going to hell and was showing me how to face it. The cars passing us knew all about me and my helpless, hopeless condition—or so I thought. They all knew this sick creature was zooming down the highway in the passenger seat of the van. Somehow I thought I was controlling them and they me, onward-forward to no future or hope in this life or the next.

We arrived safely at my Aunt's house. She came out to greet us with a big welcome. Opening the van door for me to get out, I made no move to get out. "I'm sorry we don't have a wheelchair," she said with her infectious chuckle. Of course, I soon got out. Feeling awkward and so unlike myself, I stood in her kitchen, watching her scurry around baking. She was making sticky buns. My daughter offered me a chair and my condemning thoughts raced on. *I was too sticky with people, which is why I was still here. I really should die. Aunt Sheila knew that, too, that is why she is baking sticky buns.* Even what she served for lunch condemned me.

Later in the afternoon, I falteringly asked "What should I do?" Cheerily my aunt replied, "Well, you could help to icing these whoopee pies!" So I tried, but I could hardly do it. Even that was condemning. I just felt unable. My cousin saw the tears in my eyes and came and took me in her arms. "Just cry," she said. "It's good to cry." I did a little. Sometimes tears came and sometimes they didn't.

It was hard to go to church. Everyone knew what I was thinking and somehow, even my preacher knew, planning his messages according. Sometimes I felt like he was reading my mind, and I felt humiliated and exposed. It was hard to meet people after the service. I didn't know if I should greet my sisters or not. How could I . . . when I wasn't a Christian and they knew it??

"God made each person in a special way—even the snowflakes, not one is the same," a sister's kind voice spoke to my troubled heart at the end of another service. I nodded, somehow feeling she understood my struggle. When our church hosted special meetings, my husband kindly stayed home with me. One afternoon service I asked to go, but he gently reminded me that it would be hard for our children to see me, like I was presently, in front of so many people. Then I was glad to stay home instead. We listened in, over the phone, but even then the message spelled only condemnation for our family. Was there any hope for us? It felt better to just go on another long walk.

I was at a friend's house feeling mixed up and depressed. The phone rang. It was another friend calling to encourage me. "God is holding you near, even when you can't feel it," she spoke soothingly. I tried to tell her that I felt like I was destined for hell. "That is how you may feel right now, but God is still holding you near as His precious little lamb," she assured me. She sent this to me in the mail:

> *It is TOO much to make sense of everything right now.*
>
> *It is enough to let go and let God carry you during this time. Let others support you.*
>
> *And then, when the time is right, as God places stepping stones in your path that you can recognize, to step on them, as He gives you strength to take the step.*

These papers meant so much to me during my time of illness, and still do even now that I am well again!

One day we went to a friend's house for lunch. I felt unable to communicate, but did enjoy the walk we took together. Later, as we sat side by side on the porch swing, she read me some writings of another friend who experienced breakdown. I marveled at how the writer could express her feelings so well, and could keenly relate to many of the things she wrote about. It gave me a tiny ray of HOPE. Others have walked this path, too; they felt this way and got better!

I spent an afternoon with my cousin. I usually loved going to her house, but I was tired of being around people. When I can't communicate my thoughts well, I feel like a burden. "You may rest, you look tired," she said kindly. I reclined on the sofa while she and my daughter slipped away to another room to talk. Sleep would not come, and my thoughts continued racing. Finally, I got up and went to find them. They put on a singing CD that meant a lot to me in the past. "There will be a light; there will be a way" . . . the words of the song floated by, registering in my foggy mind. But my mind told me the Light was hell. Sometimes music is comforting, but not right now.

"Shall we pray before you leave?" she asked me. We knelt while she earnestly asked God for healing and strength to go on. My heart warmed as I listened to her pray, and I felt strengthened to go on . . . taking one step at a time, even when all was dark.

One morning I awoke, struggling in helpless despair. How could I face this day? If only I could stay here, where the covers- at least- were soft! Suddenly the phone beside my bed rang. Lately, I hadn't even felt like answering it, but now I picked it up. My aunt said, *"This too shall pass. You are depressed again right now. But I know you will get better."*

Slowly I climbed out of bed and dressed. Even deciding which pair of socks to put on had a spiritual meaning and threw me into indecision. Which pair would help me more today?? Then I remembered my husband's words—these things do not have spiritual meaning. I tried to believe him. I grabbed a pair and went to face another day, feeling condemned at my choice of socks. I felt there was no hope for me or my family. I was even starting to feel it was better if I didn't read the Bible or pray anymore. I was so far from God it must blaspheme Him when I do. I could no longer believe that His promises were for me. Everything I read, when I opened the Bible, pointed to judgment, condemnation, and the hell ahead. Time was one big blur in my foggy, struggling mind. Tears flowed down my cheeks as I tried to eat a little breakfast. The children quietly kept to themselves. I knew they were suffering, too, yet they only showed kindness to me.

. . . One morning I woke early and found my husband awake also. I began sharing my thoughts with him. The more I talked- the more I realized with great joy and delight- that my mind was clearer! The confusion was gone, along with the condemnation. I felt like a normal person again! The depression had lifted and I was coming out of a long, dark tunnel. I could see light ahead and I could feel it bringing hope, and life, and healing to my tortured heart and mind.

Eager to start the day, I got up and opened my Bible. I read the precious promises and knew it was for me, too! I could already look back and see God's love and guiding hand thru the storm. He had done this thru the folks he sent . . . the ways they cared and supported and prayed. The calls, and meals, and visits were from God, through His people. I prayed God's blessing on each of my family and friends. I felt eager to start this brand new day! My family looked on in surprise and wonder to see me making pancakes for breakfast! God had granted healing, giving me the privilege to serve them again.

. . . I still marvel how God brought me through it all. For me, medication made a big difference and I am so thankful for the options and answers there are! I long to be an encouragement to others . . . I felt carried through my experiences by the help and prayers of others, even though I felt so alone and abandoned. I know God was always there, bearing me up, especially in the eye of the storm when all my props seemed to give way spiritually, emotionally, and mentally. My prayer is that He would also be with you, and that His throbbing heart of love will be revealed to you in whatever you are facing.

Does Jesus care? O YES, He cares!

My Battle with Bipolar Illness

By 'Keith Shirk'

In August of 2005, I started my own auto repair shop, following a very stressful time at my last place of employment. This venture began rather slowly. I puttered along low-key, which suited my normal laid-back style. I worked by myself, operating the front office as well as doing all the actual car repairs. However, I began to push myself harder and harder, developing a grandiose goal of a big, prosperous business.

In November of 2006, I made a reckless decision to buy into an exorbitantly expensive shop management program. I told my wife repeatedly that this is something we have to do now to make our business successful. We couldn't afford not to! I got no further input or advice. I did not take the time to consider or compare. In about 24 hours several credit cards were maxed and plans were made to go to Los Angeles for training. While jumping into such an expensive purchase was uncharacteristic, I argued that it would surely pay off. Besides, I felt important traveling to CA on a business trip.

I became increasingly driven. I hired two employees, changing from an easygoing life-style to one full of abundant energy. It seemed the harder I pushed, the less sleep I needed, which meant getting only a few hours of sleep many nights. I couldn't slow my mind down. I was easily distracted in my work and communications. I would promise to place orders then forget about them.

I decided we needed a new house and quickly went into much deeper debt to pay top dollar for a parcel of land. I looked at house plans and contacted a contractor, but before long I dropped that project. Then I decided it was no longer good enough to rent a shop building, I needed to buy my own place. After an obsessive search, I found one, paying top dollar for it. Of course, it took money to repair and remodel this place, so I maxed out the rest of my credit cards, then took out a home equity line of credit and spent that to the limit, too.

While I was friendly and sociable before, I began to talk or joke with almost anyone. I would embarrass my wife by my lack of reserve, joking with the nurses when accompanying her on a doctor visit. I lacked boundaries where my school responsibilities called for evening schoolteacher visits. I needed a secretary at the shop, so I hired a young woman against my wife's wishes. I promised to set boundaries, but I never followed through. Many times, my wife was brought to tears as she noted the change in me. She stated that I was not the man she had married. We argued about the time I spent away from home, and the fact that I did nothing anymore for the family. I could see nothing wrong, it was just me.

By mid-2008 I began having unexplained physical symptoms, and my mood slipped downward. My wife became quite concerned and wanted me to see a doctor, but I refused to acknowledge that anything was wrong. My Dad had open-heart surgery in 2009, and the day before the operation, I impulsively decided to go to him, leaving my family behind. I drove sixteen hours there, and after several days with very little sleep, I drove all the way home by myself through the night.

Soon after my return, my depression deepened. I had uncontrollable crying spells and lost my appetite. My boundless energy plummeted and fatigue took over. Finally, I agreed to go to a doctor. He said my heart palpitations and depression were stress induced. The medicine he gave did not help my depression and I began to lose the will to live. Various methods of ending my life passed through my mind. Sometimes when I was waking up, I saw images like a whirlwind or a big, black ball hovering overhead. My wife took me on a drive or just held my hand. I was in a big black hole where her love and care just could not reach. I was under 24-hour supervision, and my wife removed anything I could hurt myself with while my doctor desperately searched for a psychiatrist who had an opening. Then, with no explanation, my mood lifted a little, and I ate for the first time in three days.

The first psychiatrist I saw diagnosed me with Major Depressive Disorder with psychosis. She strongly recommended hospitalization and considered committing me involuntarily, but finally left me go when we agreed to seek admission to Green Pasture Rest Home, adjacent to the Phil Haven Hospital in PA. I stayed there for three and a half weeks, attending group therapy, individual therapy, and receiving medication. After hearing about the recent months, the medical staff there felt my diagnosis should be Bipolar Disorder. When I was discharged, I seemed to be on the road to recovery.

However, I continued to dip into sad, angry moods. I also had extraordinarily good days. In late 2009, my psychiatrist hospitalized me because of suicidal depression. She also recommended a therapist to help me work through life issues. A month or two later, my doctor did a complete medication overhaul, adding lithium. I sputtered along for a few months, and was hospitalized again when I began to experience hallucinations and paranoia. I was discharged after four days with the addition of an anti psychotic. At a follow-up visit to her office, my psychiatrist confirmed a diagnosis of Bipolar Disorder. She mentioned that an antidepressant doesn't work for some bipolar patients, but didn't want to take me off of mine now. She did not offer any more help, instead she made me feel that if I tried harder, I would feel better!

I was not able to work at all over this time. Sometimes I had a slight bit of motivation, but usually I was down with irritability, anger, and no motivation. I wanted to be left alone. I didn't like to be around anyone except my wife. I begged for her presence continually, even though I snapped at her or didn't talk at all, just like I did to the rest. I struggled with obsessions of various types.

With no real answers in sight, plans were made to return to Green Pasture. It was about exactly a year after my last slump. I stayed for six weeks this time and was evaluated by a different doctor. We had reflected a lot on the past year, so we were able to share with the doctor. He quickly recognized the manic phase of a Bipolar 1 illness that started my journey, and promptly changed my medication to treat it. Finally, I had an explanation for why I had so many mood swings, even while majorly depressed, and why I'd just seem to snap out of it sometimes. The whole picture became clearer now that we had a doctor that understood! By the end of that stay, the depression had definitely lifted to a degree.

In retrospect, that stay at Green Pasture and the accompanying med change seem to have been a turning point! However, there continued to be a rise and fall in moods, though not quite as high or low as before. There was an overall downward slope, so in 2011, we contacted Green Pasture to see if any more could be offered. My doctor was retiring, and a new one was taking over. The new doctor thought I should find a local doctor to provide ongoing treatment. We strongly preferred staying with a doctor who understood our way of life and told him we would do whatever it takes to see him. He agreed, but recommended a full medication overhaul. I returned to Green Pasture for the third time, spending three weeks there. My medications were changed to Seroquel and Lamictal. That change has proven to be the one that "worked."

It took more than seven years of struggle to put my life back together again. There were frequent doctor and therapist visits and struggles to understand and cope with the emotional, relational, and financial wreckage. Normal human passions are accentuated with a mood disorder! Spiritual moorings are shaken that need to be regained. Obsessions, impulsivity, and guilt need to be worked through. And difficult circumstances continued, such as the death of a nephew, the loss of an employee, my wife's difficult pregnancy. These all greatly challenged my mental health. I tried to focus on the bright spots, and do what others have done, trust in God with firm resolve.

I still struggle with irritability, especially when I have high energy levels. Some days, I can let things run off my back. Other days, the irritation, frustration, and lack of patience is overwhelming. It seems to worsen when I am making progress or at least trying to make progress. If my schedule gets tight unexpectedly, my thoughts race and get muddled. I over react, and say things I need to apologize for. I try to focus on getting my sleep. A little down time always helps, but it is so hard to come by! I have to force myself to be aware of my actions and feelings, and CALM DOWN. If I snap at my wife, it upsets her, and in turn upsets me more. Talk about a vicious cycle!

I also struggle with distractibility. It has always been difficult for me to focus, which is extremely frustrating. Many times while I'm at my job working on something, I have a thought coming out of left field. It distracts me. I immediately gravitate to the new thing and as a result, I end up bouncing back and forth. I may eventually complete my project, but it takes a considerable amount of willpower to do so.

Change is difficult for me. I tend to stay stuck in a comfort zone, not willing to take the risk of improving things. I fear the unknown, and even if others feel the potential benefits far outweigh the risks, I still hesitate and dither. I fail to make a move until everyone else is exasperated. Anxiety has also been a problem, especially with low mood. It's been worse in the past year or so, with a few panic attacks where my heart pounds and my stomach knots up. I feel a lot of head pressure and get light headed. It happens in social situations, like church, and I've had to go out and sit in the van.

Our marriage has endured severe stress over the course of my illness. I am trying to learn what works for my wife and what her needs are, instead of dumping my struggles, complaints, and mood swings on her. Continually being 'needy' and leaning on her for moral support drains her emotionally. I read this somewhere: "Just because someone is a friend, a family member, or a partner, it does not follow that he or she is the best person to turn to when you need help with mood swings. No matter how much someone cares for you, if you constantly assault them with your needs, they will get overwhelmed." I truly believe that her care and support is the reason I am still here, and at my lowest it may have been the last barrier that kept me from taking my life. I know she still cares deeply, but she has her limits, too. We all turn to those who are the closest when we need help, but it seems like I have more struggles than normal, and it works better for both of us if I have someone else to help me sort through things. I am very grateful for my therapist who has proven to be trustworthy and tremendously helpful over the past nine years. A good therapist is trained for this very thing. He can hear your needs and give help without getting overwhelmed.

On the other hand, I'm also realizing that communication with my wife is important if we are to understand each other. I find this extremely challenging. I want to keep the communication lines open without dumping all my burdens on her; at the same time I want to keep from closing up because I'm afraid of burdening her.

I still find myself scrutinizing my value as a human being, especially as a husband and father. The question of whether I am worthy of life and love is something I still struggle with in the dips and elevations of mood.

I try to accept the fact that some days I feel good and some days I don't. Some days my thoughts are clear; other days they are jumbled, with a lack of focus. Some days I lack motivation or find it extremely difficult to do certain things. I try to capitalize on the days I do have energy and clarity, realizing that tomorrow I just might not be able to! I try to WILL to do things on bad days, tiny things that feel impossible, instead of waiting till I have the motivation. A tiny accomplishment does feel good and just maybe I'll be able to do another. Maybe I can build enough momentum for the next thing.

Sticking with routine stabilizes me, getting up and going to bed at the same time, leaving for work at the same time, and having quiet time for paperwork or research before the shop opens. Weekends, especially Saturdays, are often challenging for this very reason--it feels less structured. Sundays have a definite schedule, but I often struggle to keep my mind focused because it is so different from the weekday routine. The same thing is true if I take off part of a workday for any reason. Taking trips are also extremely challenging! Nothing is the same. I try to organize, keep some kind of structure or schedule, get sleep, and every other 'normal' thing I can think of to survive. I try to allow more time to meet deadlines, get to unfamiliar places on time, and keep the schedule as manageable as possible.

I look back at the last ten years, and strongly feel that events and stress triggered the illness that I was genetically susceptible to. Mental illness is prolific in my mother's side of the family; depression, bipolar, anxiety, and suicide are all there. I do not link my illness to specific childhood difficulties, although some memories seem out of the ordinary. The most prominent one is anger outbursts that I could not control, that seemed to cycle through my life. I did not understand why this was, but years later, after the upward spiral followed by the crash, I began reflecting and wondering. I am certain that the intense, unrelenting stress from my last employment, and starting my own business eventually triggered my illness.

I have tried to learn as much as I can about the illness, and I still do a lot of reading. I accept that I have a chronic condition that demands lifelong management, and that relapse is likely if I go off my medication. I just hope I can stay committed every day, even though it is very discouraging. It is such a slow grind upward toward balanced thinking, but what else is there to do but go on?!

When I don't feel well, whether it's a dip in mood or an elevated mood, I have become "master of the mask". This is what I call my public face, when I go about my day. Very caring people might assume that I am 'cured' or 'normal' if I'm going to work on a daily basis and meeting my responsibilities. But I have mastered the good face (to everyone but my wife) which hides most of the daily struggle I have with my illness.

Isn't there a certain amount of pressure, either personal or part of our upbringing, which makes us want to hide our true feelings? This is especially true when trying to cope with a mental illness. People find it difficult to relate to this type of ongoing struggle. Is this because of the stigma that lingers over mental illness and the misunderstandings that surround it? Or is it because people don't know enough about mental illness? I don't want to be blaming people; I'm just saying it contributes to the daily struggle.

I have had more advantages and opportunities to get better than many. I am not cured or living life without further impairment, and am almost certain I never will be. But, praise God, I have been brought to the highest level of functioning in years!

If I can be of any help to others who may be struggling with bipolar illness, I am willing to do that. Contact me personally by sending a letter with your phone number and address to Anita Martin, Att. Masthof Press, (p.303.)

REFERENCES

MENTAL ILLNESS IN GENERAL

Holding Out Hope .... *Dr. Tony Byler*

When Someone You Love has a Mental Illness .... *Rebecca Woolis*

Extraordinary Grace .... *Gary D. Chapman*

It's So Much Work to be Your Friend
(for children) .... *Richard Lavoie*

Why do Christians Shoot Their Wounded? ..... *Dwight Carlson*

Nothing to Hide .... *Interviews by Jean J. Beard and Peggy Gillespie*

DEPRESSION

I Have Chosen You (Post-partum) .... *Rachel Troyer*

Dark Clouds, Silver Linings .... *Dr. Archibald D. Hart*

Slaying the Giant .... *French O'Shields*

Depression or Bipolar Disorder .... *Dwight Evans and Linda* Andrews

Darkness Visible .... *William Styron*

Audio—the Types, Causes, and Biology of
Depression .... *Dr. Joel Yeager*

SCHIZOPHRENIA

Welcome Silence .... *Carol North*

Schizophrenia.............................. *Rachel Gur and Ann Johnson*

I Never Promised You a Rose Garden .... Joanne Greenberg
pen name Hannah Green

Elaine's Thorn in the Flesh .... *Kathryn Martin*

MANIC DEPRESSION OR BIPOLAR ILLNESS

The Bipolar Child...*Demitri Papolos*

A Promise of Hope.....................................*Autumn Stringham*

An Unquiet Mind .... *Kay Redfield Jamison*

Darkness is My Only Companion.... *Kathryn Greene-McCreight*

The Bipolar Survival Guide....................... *David J. Miklowitz*

Mood Swings .... *Paul Meier,*
Stephen Arterburn,
and Frank Minirth

The Bipolar Handbook... *Wes Burgess*

A Brilliant Madness..*Patty Duke*

Win the Battle.. *Bob Olson*

Riding the Roller Coaster...................................Marja Bergen

OTHER ILLNESSES

The Thought That Counts
(Obsessive Compulsive Disorder) .... *Jared Kant*
Attention Deficit Disorder .... *Thomas W. Phelan Ph. D.*

Brilliant Idiot (Dyslexia) .... *Dr. Abraham Schmitt*

Stop Walking on Eggshells
(Borderline Personality Disorder) .... *Paul Mason*

I Hate you, Don't Leave Me (BPD) .... *Hal Straus*
and Jerold Jay Kreisman

CONTACT INFORMATION:

Help for Suicide Survivors .... *Ann Shank Wenger*
call—717-273-5622

Philhaven/Green Pasture in Lebanon Pennsylvania
.... 717-989-8661

Oaklawn/Rest Haven in Goshen Indiana 574-535-0759

Woodside/Springhaven in Mt. Eaton, Ohio 330-359-5400

Readers wishing to contact the author can send letters or e-mails to her through Masthof Press:

Anita Martin
Attn: Masthof Press
219 Mill Road
Morgantown, PA 19543

orders@masthof.com

We thank Thee, Lord, we bow before Thy sacred throne, to praise Thee for Thy love so kind and true . . . for Thou hast heard our voice, when we call on Thee Thine answer speaks with courage to inspire our souls . . . although we must walk through trouble, Thou wilt protect us and Thy right hand will guide us . . . O Eternal Lord, intervene in our behalf, Thy great goodness never fails . . . we thank Thee, Lord; we bow before Thy sacred throne to praise Thee for Thy love so true—we thank Thee, Lord.

Choral Hymn
From Psalm 138
Hazel S. Tkach